TRUTH IN VIRTU

The analytic/synthetic distinction looks simple. It is a distinction between two different kinds of sentence. Synthetic sentences are true in part because of the way the world is, and in part because of what they mean. Analytic sentences—like all bachelors are unmarried and triangles have three sides—are different. They are true in virtue of meaning, so no matter what the world is like, as long as the sentence means what it does, it will be true.

This distinction seems powerful because analytic sentences seem to be knowable in a special way. One can know that all bachelors are unmarried, for example, just by thinking about what it means. But many twentieth-century philosophers, with Quine in the lead, argued that there were no analytic sentences, that the idea of analyticity didn't even make sense, and that the analytic/synthetic distinction was therefore an illusion. Others couldn't see how there could fail to be a distinction, however ingenious the arguments of Quine and his supporters.

But since the heyday of the debate, things have changed in the philosophy of language. Tools have been refined, confusions cleared up, and most significantly, many philosophers now accept a view of language—semantic externalism—on which it is possible to see how the distinction could fail. One might be tempted to think that ultimately the distinction has fallen for reasons other than those proposed in the original debate.

In *Truth in Virtue of Meaning*, Gillian Russell argues that it hasn't. Using the tools of contemporary philosophy of language, she outlines a view of analytic sentences which is compatible with semantic externalism and defends that view against the old Quinean arguments. She then goes on to draw out the surprising epistemological consequences of her approach.

Gillian Russell is Associate Professor of Philosophy at Washington University in St Louis.

Truth in Virtue of Meaning

GILLIAN RUSSELL

OXFORD
UNIVERSITY PRESS

OXFORD

UNIVERSITY PRESS

Great Clarendon Street, Oxford OX2 6DP

Oxford University Press is a department of the University of Oxford.
It furthers the University's objective of excellence in research, scholarship,
and education by publishing worldwide in

Oxford New York

Auckland Cape Town Dar es Salaam Hong Kong Karachi
Kuala Lumpur Madrid Melbourne Mexico City Nairobi
New Delhi Shanghai Taipei Toronto

With offices in

Argentina Austria Brazil Chile Czech Republic France Greece
Guatemala Hungary Italy Japan Poland Portugal Singapore
South Korea Switzerland Thailand Turkey Ukraine Vietnam

Oxford is a registered trade mark of Oxford University Press
in the UK and in certain other countries

Published in the United States
by Oxford University Press Inc., New York

© Gillian Russell 2008

The moral rights of the author have been asserted
Database right Oxford University Press (maker)

First published 2008
First published in paperback 2011

British Library Cataloguing in Publication Data
Data available

Library of Congress Cataloging in Publication Data
Data available

Typeset by Laserwords Private Limited, Chennai, India
Printed in the United Kingdom by
Lightning Source UK Ltd., Milton Keynes

ISBN 978-0-19-923219-2 (Hbk.)
ISBN 978-0-19-969473-0 (Pbk.)

For my teachers

Contents

II. A DEFENSE

III. WORK FOR EPISTEMOLOGISTS

Preface

Sometimes it seems as if the debate over the analytic/synthetic distinction didn't get resolved, so much as left behind. At its zenith, the tussle was between the Carnapians and the Quineans. For those in the Carnapian camp, the distinction was a consequence of some apparently obvious facts about language; it seemed amazing that the Quineans couldn't see that. For Quine and his followers, the disappearance of the distinction was a consequence of the drive to import scientific rigour into philosophy; some things that had seemed fine—or even obvious—to the naked eyes of Kant, Bolzano and even Frege, dissolved under the microscope of precision; the world, at base, wasn't quite as it seemed, and among the mere illusions were the "obvious facts" supposed to support the analytic/synthetic distinction. Of course, this is too simple a sketch, but I think it will do for the preface.

The view of language that makes the existence of analytic sentences seem inevitable is a very intuitive one: expressions (both sentences and subsentential expressions like words), have *meanings* and an expression's meaning plays three roles; (i) it is what a speaker has to grasp or know in order to count as understanding the expression; (ii) it determines what objects in the world the expression applies to (less colloquially: it determines a function from possible worlds to extensions); (iii) it is what the expression says or what it contributes to *what is said* (a proposition) by a sentence which contains it.

That's all but, with this picture in the background, the analytic/synthetic distinction emerges very naturally. Suppose we stipulate that a new word *tove* is to mean the same as a word already in our language, say, *cluster*. Given the assumptions above, the sentence *all toves are clusters* seems to have some special properties. First, *tove* and *cluster*, having the same meaning, must pick out the same objects in the world, by (ii), which, given the meanings of the rest of the expressions in the sentence, is enough to guarantee its truth—we might call it *true in virtue of meaning*. Now by (iii) the sentence's meaning is the proposition it expresses. Since that is such that it cannot be false, the sentence expresses a necessary proposition. Finally, since its truth follows from the meanings of the expressions it contains, and by (i) a competent speaker has to know those meanings, we might expect a competent speaker to be in a position to work out that the sentence is true, even if he has no particular experience of the world. Sentences with these three properties—truth in virtue of meaning, necessity and something like a priority—seem special, and it isn't unnatural to mark that specialness by calling them *analytic*. The Quinean camp raised a lot of problems for this picture of analyticity but in the meantime, the "obvious" picture of meaning that supported it started to slip for relatively independent reasons. In three astonishingly influential pieces of philosophical writing, Putnam (1985[1973]) argued that meaning couldn't be *both* what a speaker grasped *and* what determined extension, Kaplan (1989b) argued that what determines extension (character) and what got contributed to what a sentence said (content) came apart in the cases of indexicals and demonstratives, and Kripke (1980) argued that what determined the extension of a name or natural kind term need not be known in order for a speaker to understand the expression, nor was it what was contributed to the proposition expressed by a sentence containing one. Each was suggesting that the roles attributed to a single thing—the expression's *meaning*—in the picture above, can be played by distinct things.

If that is right, then the expression *meaning* requires some disambiguation, and in this book I use the following terminology for that purpose:

- **character**: what a speaker must know in order to understand an expression
- **content**: what an expression contributes to the proposition semantically expressed by a sentence containing it
- **reference determiner**: a condition which an object must meet in order to be the referent of, or fall in the extension of, an expression

With this terminology it is still possible to express the old view, on which character, content and reference determiner are all names for the same thing, but it is harder to pass that view off as inevitable, since it is easier to express views that run counter to it. Given that the old view provided intuitive support for the traditional conception of analyticity, perhaps it is unsurprising that Putnam, Kaplan and Kripke each produced examples of sentences that aren't easily classified as either analytic or synthetic on the old conception: Putnam can be construed as arguing that the putatively analytic *all cats are animals* is true in virtue of meaning if it means what we think it means, but (since we don't know for sure that it means that) it is not a priori and not necessarily true, and hence not analytic. Kaplan's *I am here now* seems analytic, but it is not necessary, and *Hesperus is Phosphorus* seems true in virtue of meaning in some sense (and so not synthetic), but not a priori (and so not analytic). With the obviousness of the picture supporting the distinction gone, and the extension of the distinction newly unclear, the analytic/synthetic distinction might seem to be based on substantial—and questionable—assumptions after all. One might even be tempted to think that it was an artifact of a view of language that we have left behind.

My aim with this book is to tempt you with something else. As I like to think of it, our old view of analyticity was based on a naive theory of meaning, and some Quinean challenges to it were basically right. *But our new theories of meaning will support a new picture of analyticity*, one which—being based on a better theory of meaning—admits of a more robust defence.

To this end, the first part of the book develops an account of analyticity that is intended to sit better with the kind of view that one might loosely call an externalist and contextualist approach to language. It is also designed to take account of a number of developments and improvements that have taken place since the heyday of the original Quine–Carnap debate: I try to be more careful about things like the objects of analyticity, about distinguishing between analyticity, necessity and a priority, and one of my main goals from the beginning was to explain how *I am here now*—a contingent sentence—could be analytic, while *Hesperus is Phosphorus*—a sentence that might be thought to be necessary and true in virtue of meaning—was not.

Though this was my main aim, I hope that by the end it seems plausible that an account of analyticity—an account of truth in virtue of meaning—will always be parasitic on a theory of meaning: given different accounts of the meaning of a sentence, we may get different answers to the question of whether the sentence is analytic. Though I will tend to use simple versions of some currently well-known pictures to illustrate my view, there's no reason why the same account of analyticity couldn't be adopted for use with opposing views, and the plausibility (or lack of it) of the results would bear on the plausibility of both that theory of meaning and my account of truth in virtue of meaning.

I am grateful to the Killam Trust and the University of Alberta for the postdoctoral fellowship which allowed me to to write much of this book.

g. k. r.

Acknowledgements

In the summer of 2002, Greg Restall gave an informal talk for Melbourne University post-graduate students on the topic of *what he wished he had known before he entered the academy*. Greg's main point: he wished he had understood how *social* an activity philosophy was. This would probably have been unwelcome news to me when I started work on this topic in 2001, but seven years on, I have a 'thank you' list that would make an Oscar winner balk, and which includes people from Princeton, where I did my Ph.D., from my time as a postdoctoral researcher at the University of Alberta in Canada, from Washington University in St. Louis, where I am currently an assistant professor, and from the philosophical community in Australia, where I have tended to spend all my northern summers—not to mention the audiences all over the world who have commented on and objected to presentations of this material. And that's just the philosophers.

Thank you to Scott Soames, my Ph.D. advisor. I spent hours and hours and hours in his office, going over my work, and sometimes discussing the rest of my life as well. Many students owe big ideas or philosophical pictures to their advisors—the Lewis approach to metaphysics, for example, or a certain approach to explanation. I not only owe things like my picture of natural kind terms to Scott, but he is also the reason I know how to use corner quotes, and the reason why it no longer reads "find quotes to support this point" in a footnote in Chapter 5. Part teacher, part skeptic, part advocate, part example, part copy-editor and part counsellor—a mixture to be emulated, I think.

Other faculty at Princeton who provided me with helpful discussion on early versions of this and related material include Paul Benacerraf, John Burgess, Gil Harman, Delia Graff, Mark Greenberg, Mark Johnston, David Lewis, Béatrice Longuenesse, Jim Pryor and Gideon Rosen. No doubt if I'd listened better I'd have avoided more mistakes.

Of the people who were graduate students with me Cian Dorr, Ant Eagle, Mike Fara, Benj Hellie, Zena Hitz, Vera Koffman, Chris Mole, Jessica Moss, Mike Nelson, Mark Schroeder, Kieran Setiya and Nick Smith all deserve a special mention. Thanks to Barry Lam, the disillusioned Princeton Blogger, and Mike McGlone, for talking me out of a bad idea on the way back from the 2003 Yale Philosophy of Language Conference. Thanks to Casey O'Callaghan and Simon Keller, who taught me that one doesn't grow up, but simply ceases to regard everyone else as grown-up, and thanks to my mentor, Jeff Speaks, philosopher of language, sometime *bon vivant* and now proud father. Jeff was my buddy before Gil invented the Buddy System, and he'll always be a grown-up to me. Thank you to my housemates: Ant, Colin, Eliza, Lizzie and the inimitable Nate. Thanks to Chris Chappell, an amateur philosopher who knew why *I am here now* was true, and who knows not to ask me whether Kripke is "as good as Derrida" when I've been drinking.

Thank you to Ann Getson, who endured my personality flaws with the bemusement you might expect from the graduate secretary of Princeton's Philosophy Department.

In the spring of 2000 I sent an unsolicited email to Graham Priest and asked how he would feel about having a random British graduate student hanging around his department for the northern summer. To his credit, Graham thought this was a great idea and so I got on a plane and went. This began what is now a seven or eight-year association with the Australasian philosophy scene. I have been a visiting student in the philosophy departments at the University of Queensland, and Melbourne and Monash Universities, and this book owes a debt to many, many Australasian and Australophile philosophers with whom I've interacted, especially Craig Barrie, Matt Carter, Alan Hazen (who first introduced me to Gentzen), Lloyd Humberstone, (hope the LaTeX is working out, Lloyd), Andre Gallois, Daniel Nolan, Leonie and Ramy Omar, Charles Pigden, Graham Priest, Greg Restall, Su Rogerson (she and Bolly took me in again and again), Michael Smith, Lenka Ucnik and Ashley Woodward. Thank you to Gerald Keaney and Rob Sparrow, poets, punks, martial artists and revolutionaries, who taught me the value of environments in which it is ok to get things wrong, and who made me want to get everything right.

From Canada: thanks to the inimitable Adam Morton, to Bernie Linsky and Elizabeth Millar, Bruce Hunter, Cressida Hayes, David Kahane, Amy Schmitter, Rob Wilson, Ali Kazmi, Richard Zach, Elizabeth Brake, Mark Migotti, Nicole Wyatt, and to Angela, Elizabeth, Marianne and Grace, Octavian, George and everyone else who embarrassed themselves at Suburbs, and of course to Al and Orion.

From St. Louis: thank you to all my colleagues: I *love* my job here and I'm grateful both for all the occasions on which you've given me help and support, and also for the times when you've left me to go it alone.

I would also like to thank John Hawthorne, David Braun and Frank Artzenius for helpful comments on presentations of earlier versions of this material. Thank you also to two anonymous readers from Oxford University Press.

I owe thanks to Margaret Lo and Ping Foong of the Princeton branch of the JKA, for keeping me sane in grad school, to Tammy and Steve from Edmonton and Kenji Yoshimi and Bill Heron of the University of Alberta Aikikai for keeping me sane as a postdoc. Thanks to John Doris. And thank you Dave Lowry and the rest of my SMR seniors in St. Louis, and to the karateka most responsible for the bruises I have to hide or explain: Joe Swisher, Sharath Cholleti, Emily Miner, Pete Coxeter, Robin Chisnell, Dan Modaff, Dan Stein, David Speetzen, Bill Bridenbaugh, Chris Teter and anyone from TKRI who I've left out.

And finally some particularly personal thank yous: thank you to my father, John Russell, who had to endure transatlantic phone conversations in which he was quizzed about whether *cats are animals* could be false. Thanks to Iain, my younger brother, and to my mum, Elaine Russell, who let me move to a different continent with (hardly) a whimper.

I think it will be clear to the cognoscenti that I owe a large debt to the work of two philosophers I've never met: David Kaplan and Saul Kripke (in fact, I've seen them both in real life, but I didn't have the guts to talk to them.) There is also a very real debt to V. W. O. Quine, who, on closer inspection, turned out to be more interesting and more right than I expected.

Bob and Josh and Anais: what can I say? I'm grateful to you, but maybe more grateful *for* you. Stay warm!

Introduction

TRUTH IN VIRTUE OF MEANING

According to one standard story told to introduce the analytic/synthetic distinction, many sentences are true in part because of the way the world is, and in part because of what they mean. The sentence *snow is white*, for example, is true in part because snow is white—the world is a certain way—and in part because of what *snow is white* means; if it had meant what the sentence *snow is red* means instead, then it would have been false. Such sentences are synthetic.

Analytic sentences—putative examples of which include *all bachelors are unmarried* and *copper is copper*—are meant to be different; their meaning alone suffices for their truth, so that no matter what the world is like, they *must* be true. Consistently with this story, *analytic* is sometimes taken to be roughly synonymous with *true in virtue of meaning* and to imply *necessary truth*.

But sometimes *analytic* is understood to imply more. The standard story continues: anything with the special property of being true in virtue of meaning will also have special epistemic properties, such as being a priori, or at least being knowable by anyone who understands it. Given the philosophical interest in these epistemic properties, some have chosen to see the epistemological import as essential to the concept of analyticity, in the sense that no property which fails to entail the relevant epistemic properties can count as analyticity (Quine 1965[1954]: 110; Harman 1999*b*: 127). One recent writer goes even further. In the most well-known contemporary *defence* of analyticity, Paul Boghossian distinguishes truth in virtue of meaning from the epistemic properties it is meant to deliver and concedes that Quine's attacks on the former were *entirely successful*:

[Defending truth in virtue of meaning] is, I believe, a futile project. In general, I have no idea what would constitute a better answer to the question: what is responsible for generating the truth of a given class of statements? than something bland like 'the world' or 'the facts.' (Boghossian 1997: 336)

Boghossian then founds his own account of analyticity on the idea that we can jettison the idea of truth in virtue of meaning from our account of analyticity completely.

Though I agree that the epistemological properties of analytic sentences are important, I aim to persuade you not to make Boghossian's concession—that is, not to give up on truth in virtue of meaning. A central thesis of this book is that the idea of truth in virtue of meaning can be made sense of in a way that underwrites a conception of analyticity.

Here in the introduction I will suggest some reasons for being interested in the analytic/synthetic distinction, present a brief history of the distinction and get some important (but perhaps tedious) preliminaries out of the way in preparation for Chapter one.

MOTIVATIONS

There are really three sets of reasons for being interested in analyticity. The first arise from considerations of intellectual dissatisfaction with the current state of the debate: given the controversy, it would be satisfying to settle the issues of whether the distinction makes sense and whether there are any sentences that are analytic.

The second kind of reason is perhaps just one of elegance. Following analytic philosophy's rediscovery of the distinctions between the concepts of necessity, a priority and analyticity (Kripke 1980), metaphysicians and epistemologists seem to have tasks laid out: it is the metaphysician's job to clarify the expression *could not have been otherwise* and give a theory of necessity (if such a thing exists), and the epistemologist's job to clarify *knowable independently of experience* and give a theory of a priority (if such a thing exists.) Similarly, philosophers of language have a task of their own: clarify the expression *true in virtue of meaning* and give a theory of analyticity (if such a thing exists.)[1] For some of us, that is reason enough.

But there is a third, more pragmatic, reason to care about analyticity. According to legend, analytic truths have special epistemological powers:

---

[1] Indeed, this is a helpful way to think about this book: I take *true in virtue of meaning* as a gloss on *analyticity* and see my task as being that of clarifying and defending truth in virtue of meaning.

they are a priori, or knowable by anyone who understands them. Such legendary epistemological features make truth in virtue of meaning of interest outside of the philosophy of language. The promise of analyticity is the promise of a new path to knowledge—one free of any associations with a mysterious faculty of intuition—which could be of use in any area that is struggling for an epistemology, most immediately in the philosophy of mathematics and logic, but perhaps also in the philosophy of science and in value theory.

HISTORICAL BACKGROUND

This is not really a historical book, and I couldn't claim to be a proper historian of philosophy, but it *is* a book with a thesis about analyticity, and I suspect that some appreciation for the history of the analytic/synthetic distinction will make this thesis more compelling, and to that end I present some historical background here in the Introduction.

Kant and before

Though philosophers often write as though the analytic/synthetic distinction were Kant's invention, there were precursors in Leibniz's account of necessary truths (1968[1714]: §33), in Arnauld's Port Royal *Logic* (1964/1662: 320), and in the writings of the British Empiricists.[11] Locke's *Essay Concerning Human Understanding*, in particular, contains a long discussion of what he calls *trifling propositions* (1993[1690]: Book IV, chapter VIII). He identifies two kinds of trifling proposition, identity propositions, such as:

(1) A centaur is a centaur.

(2) What is a soul, is a soul.

(3) A fetiche is a fetiche.

---

[11] In their introduction to a 1964 edition of the Port Royal Logic, Dickoff and James write "The *Logic* can be read as prefiguring the grand themes of the English Empiricists and the continental Rationalists—the origin of ideas, the relation of ideas in analytic and synthetic judgements, the question whether relations of ideas reflect relations between things, and the degree of certainty of the knowledge we possess." (Dickoff & James 1964: xlviii)

and those within which "*a part of the complex* idea *is predicated of the name of the whole*: a part of the definition of the word defined." Locke's examples of the latter include:

(4) Every man is an animal.

(5) All gold is fusible.

(6) Gold is yellow.

This second type of trifling proposition also includes all propositions within which "the *genus* is predicated of the *species*, or more comprehensive of less comprehensive terms." (1993[1690]: 350, Book IV, chapter VIII). Locke argues that all these propositions are "true and self-evident" and yet that they "bring no increase to our knowledge."

It is but like a monkey shifting his oyster from one hand to the other: and had he had but words, might no doubt have said, 'Oyster in right hand is *subject*, and oyster in left hand is *predicate*'; and so might have made a self-evident proposition of oyster, i.e. *Oyster is oyster*, and yet, with all this, not have been one whit the wiser or more knowing . . .'. (Locke 1993[1690]: IV, VIII, §3)

Yet it is with Kant that most philosophers associate early definitions of analyticity.[III] Kant characterised analytic judgements in three *different* ways; first, as judgements in which what is said by the predicate is nothing more than what was already thought in the subject:

Analytic judgements say nothing in the predicate except what was actually thought already in the concept of the subject, though not so clearly nor with the same consciousness. (Kant 2004: 16 §2)[IV]

Second, as judgements in which the relation between the subject and the predicate concepts is identity:

[III] The *word analysis* has a much longer history, however, and dates back to ancient Greek geometry. Michael Beaney writes: "The prefix *ana* means up, and *lusis* means loosing, release or separation, so that *analusis* means loosening up or dissolution. The term was readily extended to the solving or dissolving of a problem, and it was in this sense that it was employed in ancient Greek geometry and philosophy. The method of analysis that was developed in ancient Greek geometry had an influence on both Plato and Aristotle. Also important, however, was the influence of Socrates' concern with definition, in which the roots of modern conceptual analysis can be found." (Beaney Summer 2003)

[IV] In the original: "Analytische Urteile sagen im Prädikate nichts als das, was im Begriffe des Subjekts schon wirklich, obgleich nicht so klar und mit gleichem Bewußsein gedacht war." (Kant 1965*b*: 14, §2)

Propositions whose certainty rests on *identity* of concepts (of the predicate with the notion of the subject) are called *analytic* propositions. (Kant 1992: 606 §36) and third, as judgements in which the predicate is contained in the subject concept:

> Either the predicate B belongs to the subject A, as something that is (covertly) contained in this concept A; or B lies outside the concept A, although it does indeed stand in connection with it. In the one case I entitle the judgements analytic, in the other synthetic. (Kant 1965*a*: A7/B11)ᵛ

These different definitions can, I think, without very much strain, be interpreted as loose characterisations of the same idea. One way for something to be contained in something else is for it to be part of that thing, and in the case of concepts it might be that the predicate concept is contained in the subject concept because it is identical with (a part of) the subject concept.ᵛᴵ Moreover, if we assume that thinking the subject concept requires thinking its parts, the predicate concept will already have been thought in the subject concept if the judgement is analytic. The 'already being thought' formulation adds temporal and psychological connotations, but the essential idea is that a judgement is analytic iff the predicate concept is contained in the subject concept. Kant's examples of analytic judgements include:

(7) All bodies are extended.

(8) Gold is a yellow metal.

Since the predicate concept has already been thought in the subject concept, Kant says that the negation of an analytic judgement is always contradictory (Kant 1965*b*: 15 §2) and this has import for the epistemic and modal status of analytic judgements. I need only consider whether the negation of an analytic judgement such as *gold is a yellow metal* is contradictory in order to come to know that it is true. Thus I

ᵛ In the original: "Entweder das Prädicate B gehört zum Subject A als etwas, was in diesem Begriffe A (versteckter Weise) enthalten ist; oder B liegt ganz außer dem Begriffe A, ob es zwar mit demselben in Verknüpfung steht. Im ersten Fall nenne ich das Urteil analytisch, in dem andern synthetisch." (Kant 1911[1787]: 33)

ᵛᴵ Such a thought is encouraged by Kant's examples of analytic and synthetic propositions in the Jäsche logic, in which he gives (what seem to me to be) representations of the judgements in parentheses, and the predicate concept is indeed represented as being a part of the subject concept: "An example of an *analytic* proposition is, To everything x, to which the concept of a body (a+b) belongs, belongs also *extension* (b). An example of a *synthetic* proposition is, To everything x, to which the concept of body (a+b) belongs, belongs also *attraction* (c)." (Kant 1992: 606, §36)

need no experience beyond what was needed to learn the concepts in order to know that the judgement is true. The modal status of analytic judgements also follows from the fact that their negations are contradictory:

> I have only to extract from it [the analytic judgement], in accordance with the principle of contradiction, the required predicate, and in so doing can become conscious of the necessity of the judgement. (Kant 1965a: B12)

Though Kant disagrees with the empiricists about *which* judgements are analytic, taking the truths of arithmetic and geometry to be synthetic, (indeed, synthetic a priori), his account preserves Locke's idea that analyticity is a matter of a judgement's meaning—the idea or concept its parts express—and that containment relations between the meaning of the subject and the meaning of the predicate are key.

Frege

Kant had also adopted a Lockean conception of the relation between analyticity and logic, according to which the negations of analytic claims are contradictory. With Frege and Carnap—the last important patrons of analyticity before the Quinean backlash—logic would become more central to the definition of analyticity, and the role of Kant and Locke's containment relations between concepts or ideas—deemed too psychological—would be replaced with definitions.

According to popular legend, Frege struck a blow for empiricism by showing that the truths of arithmetic were not synthetic a priori, but instead were empirically-respectable, analytic a priori truths. Frege of Legend accomplished this by showing that they followed from definitions and general logical laws and, although his technical demonstration of this hit a technical problem with Russell's paradox in 1902, three different versions of the legend give three different reasons as to why that is unimportant: (i) because we can reconstruct the proof without reliance on the principle which leads to Russell's paradox (and so arithmetic is analytic after all) (ii) because Frege relied on second-order logic, which is set theory and not logic at all, (so his proof didn't even come close to showing that the truths of arithmetic are analytic) (iii) because there is no such thing as analyticity anyway.

But, as Benacerraf (1981) pointed out, the historical Frege was no empiricist and he criticised and revised Kant's definition of analyticity, making it unclear whether he is really addressing the same question as

Kant. Benacerraf has also argued that the redefinition of *analyticity* has obscured the fact that Frege's real interest was in the technical question of whether or not arithmetic could be proven from the laws of logic and definitions ((MacFarlane 2002) examines this question in detail.)

Frege certainly saw himself as settling an epistemological question:

> I hope in this monograph to have made it probable that arithmetic laws are analytic judgements, and therefore a priori. (Frege 1964: 107, §87)

And he did *mean* to contradict Kant, though perhaps not in the service of empiricism:

> I see a great service in Kant's having distinguished between synthetic and analytic judgements. In terming geometric truths synthetic and a priori, he uncovered their true essence . . . if Kant erred with respect to arithmetic, this does not detract essentially, I think, from his merit. (Frege 1964: 108, §89)

Frege criticised Kant's conception of analyticity on the grounds that it only applied to a restricted set of judgements, those of what he calls 'universal-affirmative form', that the metaphor of containment relations between concepts was too psychological, and that it was not fruitful enough (Rey Fall 2003; Katz 1992). The heart of the last criticism is that Kant's conception of *meaning* is too simplistic. He wrote as if giving the meaning of a predicate is a matter of listing the features, which an object should have if it were to fall under the concept of the predicate. But Frege maintains that sometimes there will be no such list of features using antecedently understood predicates, because fruitful definitions may carve up the world along new lines: "the more fruitful type of definition is a matter of drawing boundary lines that were not previously given at all" (Frege 1980[1884]).

So Frege rejects talk of Kantian concepts and containment relations for talk of definitions and logic and his replacement definition of analyticity remains familiar today:

> The problem [of distinguishing analytic from synthetic truths] becomes, in fact, that of finding the proof of the proposition, and of following it up right back to the primitive truths. If, in carrying out the process, we come only on general logical laws and on definitions, then the truth is an analytic one, bearing in mind that we must take account also of all propositions upon which the admissibility of any of the definitions depends. If, however, is is impossible to give the proof without making use of truths which are not of a general logical nature, but belong to the sphere of some special sciences, then the proposition is a synthetic one. (Frege 1980[1884]: §3)

To put it in the form of the familiar slogan, a truth is analytic if it 'follows from logic and definitions.'

Carnap and Quine

Those logical positivists who made use of analyticity made greater demands on it than Frege did. The positivist movement was characterised by respect for science and mathematics and the rejection of traditional metaphysics as meaningless. It invoked the verificationist theory of meaning, according to which the meaning of a sentence is to be identified with the classes of observations that would confirm it or disconfirm it, to distinguish the meaningful theses of science—those which could be confirmed or disconfirmed by observation—from the meaningless theses of metaphysics, which were thought to be immune from such confirmation or disconfirmation.

The truths of mathematics—such as '2 + 2 = 4'—and of logic—such as '$\forall x(x = x)$'—present a problem for this kind of view, since they appear to make reference to *unobservable* objects, and imply sentences, such as *the number 2 exists* which would fail the verificationist test. As Carnap summed up the problem:

Empiricists are in general rather suspicious with respect to any kind of abstract entities like properties, classes, relations, numbers, propositions, etc. . . . However, within certain scientific contexts it seems hardly possible to avoid them. (Carnap 1958*a*: 205)

Some empiricists, such as Mill, have responded by claiming that the theses of mathematics and logic are empirically testable generalisations, but many positivists rejected this solution on the grounds that it failed to account for the certainty, necessity and a priority of mathematical and logical truths (Ayer 1990[1936]; Carnap 1958*a*; Hempel 1985[1950]). Instead their solution invoked analyticity. They claimed that true sentences of logic and mathematics were analytic, where this was to say that they were true in virtue of meaning. Any sentence which was true in virtue of meaning was thought to be necessary, on the grounds that if its meaning guarantees its truth, then it cannot be false. This positivist doctrine is sometimes referred to as *the linguistic doctrine of necessary truth*. Such statements were also thought to be a priori, because they were true in virtue of something that had to be known about by anyone who understood the statement. This positivist doctrine is sometimes referred to as *the analytic theory of the a priori*.

Carnap was a prominent advocate of using analyticity to account for necessity and a priority of mathematics, semantics and logic, and Quine's early attacks on analyticity are at least in part addressed to Carnap's doctrines.

Carnap's *Logical Syntax of Language* (1934) characterised the notion of analyticity for a formal language L in terms of L-consequence, a syntactically specified notion of logical-consequence, but by the time of the publication of *Meaning and Necessity* (1947), Carnap had adopted a semantic explication of analyticity in the form of L-*truth*, which in turn was defined in terms of state descriptions.[VII] A state description (relative to a language L) is an assignment of truth or falsity to every atomic sentence of the language, *or* its negation, but not both, and to no other sentence. The truth-values of all other sentences are determined by the semantical rules of the system, which might include rules like:

SR1 $\ulcorner \neg S \urcorner$ holds in a given state-description iff S does not hold in it.

SR2 $\ulcorner S_1 \vee S_2 \urcorner$ holds in a given state-system iff either S_1 holds in it or S_2 holds in it. etc. . . .

A sentence S is then L-true in a given language iff S holds in all state-descriptions, and analytic just in case it is L-true. (Carnap 1958*b*: 1–13) At this point Carnap's definition of analyticity looks very like a definition of logical truth.

Carnap explained his informal philosophical views on analyticity in "Empiricism, Semantics and Ontology" (1950), in which he wrote that whenever we begin to talk about a new kind of entity, we have to introduce a *linguistic framework*, which may be either logical or factual. The framework in which we talk about physical objects is factual and in such frameworks questions about the entities are to be answered by empirical investigation. The framework in which we talk about numbers and other mathematical objects, and the framework in which we talk about propositions, are both logical. In a logical framework questions about the entities are answered using logic and by investigating the language of the framework, based on the rules of the framework:

. . . the answers are found, not by empirical investigation, but by logical analysis based on the rules for the new expressions. Therefore the answers are here *analytic, i.e. logically true.* (Carnap 1958*a*: 209, my emphasis)

[VII] Tarski's semantic approach to logical consequence was published in Polish in 1933 and Carnap is not thought to have seen it before publishing *The Logical Syntax of Language*. (Murzi May 2004)

Since the answers can be obtained this way, without empirical investigation, they were also a priori.

The first major attack on analyticity was Quine's "Truth by Convention," (1936) which criticises the idea that the sentences of logic and mathematics are true because of our adopting a particular linguistic framework (1965[1935]). One interesting thing about this article is that for much of it Quine appears to be trying to make the idea he is criticising *work*. He explores various ways the idea that mathematics and logic are true by convention can be understood and states his aim as being to show, not that the idea is bad, but to "question its sense."

By the time of "Meaning Postulates" (1952) it is clear that Carnap has been taking note of Quine's writings and he begins to distinguish, following Quine, truths of logic, such as *Fido is black or Fido is not black*, from a broader class which includes *If Jack is a Bachelor, then he is not married*. This second class, again, following Quine, he calls "analytic", but he states explicitly that he disagrees with Quine about analyticity:

But I do not share Quine's scepticism; he is doubtful whether an explication of analyticity, especially one in semantics, is possible. (Carnap 1958c: 222)

Carnap employs the notion of a *meaning postulate* in his defence of analyticity. Logical truths such as *Fido is black or Fido is not black* are those statements which are consequences of the semantical rules, and analytic truths, such as *If Jack is a bachelor, then he is not married* are those statements which are consequences of the semantical rules *and the meaning postulates*. In the current case Carnap lays down the following as a meaning postulate:

$$P \qquad (\forall x)(Bx \supset \neg Mx)$$

This makes it analytic that everything that is B is not-M.

Quine's "Two Dogmas of Empiricism" came out in *Philosophical Review* in 1951. Its influence has been large, so much so that Creath says:

"W.V.O. Quine's 'Two Dogmas of Empiricism' is perhaps the most famous paper in twentieth-century philosophy." (Creath 2004)

Yet the importance of the paper is sometimes hard for modern readers to appreciate. Harman provides some sociological context:

Quine's paper, "Two Dogmas of Empiricism", questioned whether it was possible to make any useful analytic–synthetic distinction in an acceptably scientific way. Although few philosophers were converted to Quinean scepticism about the distinction at first, there followed an intense exploration of the issue in which numerous attempts to defend the distinction proved ineffective. By the late 1960s, opinions had shifted to the extent that philosophers of an analytic bent came to fear the challenge, "Aren't you assuming the analytic-synthetic distinction?" The change in philosophical climate was not an immediate consequence of the publication of "Two Dogmas of Empiricism". So it is a mistake to suppose that this change can be understood or assessed simply by analysing that important paper taken just by itself. The ensuing discussion was equally important in showing that a certain philosophical line was not sustainable. (Harman 1999*a*: 148)

The major theses of "Two Dogmas" are that analyticity can only be defined in terms of concepts in a particular suspect group, a group which includes meaning (in the sense of *intension*), synonymy, semantical rule and necessity, and that an argument from confirmation holism and verificationism should cause empiricists to reject the analytic/synthetic distinction as a mere dogma.

Carnap responded with "Meaning and Synonymy in Natural Languages" (1955), in which he aimed to show that there *are* ways to verify sentences which attribute intensions to natural language sentences. He describes a method of experimental testing for intensions, which involves describing possible situations and asking speakers whether or not they would apply the word in that situation and argues that the concept is needed to explain and predict the linguistic behaviour of speakers.

Quine's reply comes in 1960 with *Word and Object*. In chapter two he outlines the notion of *stimulus meaning* and shows that this notion is sufficient for the prediction and explanation of linguistic behaviour, even though it falls short of what we would intuitively expect of full-blown intensions. Once again the intuitive notion of meaning or intension seems redundant. Three years later in "Carnap and Logic Truth" Quine again attacked the notion of analyticity, this time in the guise of the 'linguistic doctrine of logical truth,' again arguing that the attractive features of the doctrine are also features of other, more parsimonious doctrines.

After Quine: five recent developments

Quine's distrust of meaning was not new. One sometimes feels that it is only in desperation that his positivist predecessors appealed to meanings to explain necessity and a priority and that, when they did so, they were at pains to try to recast meanings as more empirically respectable objects, such as sets of observations. Carnap, moreover, reports on Tarski's anxiety about presenting his work on the semantic conception of truth at the 1935 Unity of Science conference in Paris:

> He thought that most philosophers, even those working in modern logic, would be not only indifferent, but hostile to the explication of his semantical theory. (Feferman & Feferman 2004: 95)[VIII]

And, amusingly, the programme for the same conference reads:

(1) Scientific philosophy and logical empiricism

(2) Unity of science

(3) *Language and pseudo-problems*

(4) Induction and probability

(5) Logic and experience

(6) Philosophy of mathematics

(7) Logic

(8) History of logic and scientific philosophy. (Feferman & Feferman 2004: 97, my italics)

Even those positivists who took semantic issues seriously, such as Carnap, tended to restrict their work to the study of artificial languages.

One post-Quinean development that has had an impact on views about analyticity has been the upsurge in the scientific study of natural languages, with *meanings* sometimes being taken seriously as postulates of scientific theories. From linguistics, both Noam Chomsky, and later Jerrold Katz, have defended analyticity (Chomsky 1975; Katz 1967, Katz 1974, Katz 1992, Katz 1997).[IX] Katz in particular has argued that a transformational grammar should include a semantic component in order to account for speaker intuitions about the *sense properties* of expressions, which include analyticity (e.g. all women are female), redundancy (e.g. female women), and semantic deviancy (e.g. colorless green ideas). Katz holds that our best theories of these intuitions

---

[VIII] "Although the Vienna Circle was dying out as a discussion group, it had a spectacular rebirth and transformation in the Unity of Science movement. The first Congress at the Sorbonne from 16th the to the 21st September 1935 was attended by 170 participants from more than twenty countries." (Feferman & Feferman 2004: 96)

[IX] Quine's reply to Chomsky is in (Quine 1975), and (Horwich 1992) has commentary on this debate.

postulate senses, in terms of which analyticity can be defined. Katz then, like Carnap before him (Carnap 1955), holds that attributions of meaning and analyticity admit of empirical testing. But just as Quine challenged Carnap's claim that the best theory of language required the postulation of intensions, so Harman (1976), and more recently Margolis and Laurence (2003), have challenged Katz' claim that the best linguistic theory requires the postulation of senses.

Another significant post-Quinean development has been the rehabilitation of metaphysics in contemporary philosophy. Some philosophers have argued that meanings and analyticity should be analysed in terms of things that the Positivists would have rejected as too "metaphysical"; David Lewis (1976), for example, has argued for the existence of possible worlds and used them to analyse semantic concepts in linguistic theory, including the concept of analyticity. And more recently Kit Fine has argued for the existence of essential properties (as distinct from necessary properties) and then used the notion of essence to analyse analyticity (1994; Fine 1995). But in this kind of work the definition of analyticity has often seemed to come as an afterthought—a happy consequence of the work the author is primarily focused on—and the authors rarely provide extensive defenses of their theories of analyticity against Quine's arguments, or worry about the consequences of subsequent developments in the philosophy of language—for example, semantic externalism—for their theory of analyticity.

With the rise of externalism about meaning, analyticity has faced a major new threat. Externalists are not skeptics about meaning, but they hold a view of meanings which has seemed not to fit very well with traditional accounts of truth in virtue of meaning. To speak very loosely, externalism tends to divorce speaker knowledge from things like knowledge of the conditions under which an expression applies to an object, and to suggest that a speaker could be competent with two words which (in some sense) have the same meaning without being able to tell that they have the same meaning. This threatens to divorce any putative conception of truth in virtue of meaning from a priority. Quine's skepticism about meaning might be thought of as the Achilles heel of his views on analyticity; it was so radical that potential sympathisers were put off, and actual detractors could always fall back on the cheap (but effective) "your modus ponens is my modus tollens" defense. Contemporary semantic externalism has the advantage that many philosophers already accept it for independent reasons. If it is incompatible with the analytic/synthetic distinction, then the distinction looks—as a matter of dialectical strength—as if it is in much more trouble.

Moreover, some of the leading lights of the externalist movement have applied their insights to argue that some sentences which were thought to be analytic cannot really be: Putnam (1962b), Kripke (1980) and Donnellan (1962), for example, have all provided examples of sentences which have been thought to express necessary analytic truths but, which they argue can be false (and so, on the traditional story, they can't be analytic after all.) Putnam, for example, argues that *all cats are animals* is not necessary, since if we discovered that cats had all along been robot spies from Mars, we would say that they are not animals. Kripke argues that *gold is yellow* cannot be analytic since if we discovered that its looking yellow was only the result of idiosyncratic effects of the earth's atmosphere, and that taken outside of that it looked blue, we would say that gold was really blue.[x] Millianism about names has also provided us with further problem cases: if, as Millians maintain, a name's only meaning is its referent, then there is a sense in which *Hesperus is Phosphorus* is true in virtue of its meaning. It is true because *Hesperus* and *Phosphorus* have the same meaning, and given that meaning, it couldn't but be true. Yet *Hesperus is Phosphorus* isn't the sort of sentence that would normally have been classified as analytic.

But from my point of view the most exciting development in the area of analyticity since Quine has been the discovery of the contingent analytic truths. Versions of Kaplan's essay "Demonstratives: An Essay on the Semantics, Logic, Metaphysics and Epistemology of Demonstratives and Other Indexicals" began circulating in 1971 (though it wasn't officially published until 1989) and in it, Kaplan presents examples such as:

(1) I am here now

arguing that there is a sense in which the meaning of this sentence guarantees that it expresses a truth, even though the truth it expresses: *that* I am here now, need not have been true; I might not have been here now: I could have gone home at midnight. This development matters because it gives us a new data point—a new phenomenon that a theory of analyticity ought to be able to explain—and hence a new

---

[x] Katz (1997) responded to such examples by revising his account to a view he calls "the new intensionalism." He argues that sense does not determine referent, and that analytic sentences can be *false* with respect to worlds where their referents do not exist.

tool for testing our accounts. I also think it points the way to seeing how analyticity is compatible with semantic externalism.

There has been one recent, serious, well-known attempt by a philosopher to reconcile the traditional doctrine of analyticity with more contemporary philosophy of language. In 1996, Boghossian published a paper entitled "Analyticity Reconsidered" in which he distinguishes two kinds of analyticity, a metaphysical and an epistemological one. On Boghossian's view (1996: 363) a sentence is metaphysically analytic "provided that, in some appropriate sense, it *owes its truth value completely to its meaning,* and not at all to the facts." Whereas a sentence S is epistemologically analytic "*if mere grasp of S's meaning by T suffice[s] for T's being justified in holding S true.*" Boghossian provides extensive defense of epistemological analyticity, but follows Quine in rejecting the metaphysical analyticity—the notion that is often referred to as "truth in virtue of meaning."

THE CONTENTS OF THIS BOOK

Part I: The Positive View

This book has three parts. **Part I** develops the positive account of truth in virtue of meaning. In Chapter 1 I show to understand the *in virtue of* in *truth in virtue of meaning* in a way that takes account of a seminal argument of Quine's to the conclusion that truth in virtue of meaning is either trivial or incoherent. Then in Chapter 2 I suggest that the debate over truth in virtue of meaning has been hampered by widespread tacit acceptance of a folk theory of meaning, which makes a certain—flawed—conception of analyticity look inevitable. The work of Quine and Putnam can be understood as challenging that folk theory and pointing out the flaws in the traditional account of analyticity that it supported. But I argue that a revised approach to meaning will support a revised conception of truth in virtue of meaning as well—one that is immune to, or can comfortably absorb, the old criticisms. Four kinds of meaning—character, content, reference determiner and referent—are distinguished and the work of Kripke and Kaplan is employed in arguing that these roles can be instantiated by distinct things. I argue that truth in virtue of meaning should be disambiguated as truth in virtue of *reference determiner.*

Which sentences one considers to be true in virtue of meaning will depend on one's views about the meanings of individual sentences, which in turn will usually depend upon one's views about the meanings of their parts. Views about the meanings of parts of sentences, such as names, natural kind terms, descriptions and quantifiers, are often controversial. To some extent I aim to explicate truth in virtue of meaning in a way that is independent of particular views about meanings (even though some of my views on this topic will probably be clear.) Yet it is often useful to give examples of a property one is trying to describe, and so at the end of Chapter 2 I assume some views about the reference determiners of various expressions, and show which sentences would count as true in virtue of meaning on those assumptions. Given my assumptions, it turns out that there are contingent analytic truths and, more surprisingly, that there are a posteriori analytic truths.

But a problem remains and in Chapter 3 I argue that this is not a problem unique to my account of analyticity, but rather one which besets many attempts to explicate semantic concepts in modal terms. In the second part of the chapter I describe a more fine-grained metaphysical picture, which will support a stricter kind of truth in virtue of meaning.

This first part of the book also contains an Appendix in which a three-dimensional formal model theory is presented. The theory is an extension of Kaplan's logic of demonstratives (LD) and my hope is that the kind of philosopher who finds formal semantics illuminating will be helped by this work.

Part II: A Defense

"Quine's attack on intuitive semantics is no seamless web", wrote Michael McDermott (2001: 977), and I am inclined to agree and extend this remark to the case against the analytic/synthetic distinction in general. There is no such thing as *the* argument against the distinction, and though it is easy to get the impression that "Two Dogmas of Empiricism" contains the most important arguments, perhaps with the paper's skepticism about meaning supported by the book *Word and Object*, in fact Quine's work contains a wealth of different attacks, many of which can be found in the early paper "Truth by Convention" (1935) and the later "Carnap and Logical Truth" (1954). In addition to Quine's offensive, we have to contend with the rise of the picture of language known as the causal theory of reference, with arguments from externalism and vagueness, and with the minor philosophical industry of providing outlandish counterexamples to putatively analytic claims, which began with Mill, and continues in the work of Putnam and Harman. The three chapters of **Part II** defend my conception of analyticity against a total of fourteen arguments against the distinction: Chapter 4 focuses on the arguments from "Two Dogmas", Chapter 5 addresses a variety of Quinean arguments concerning the nature of definitions and Chapter 6 confronts a mish-mash of other arguments, including arguments from vagueness and content externalism.

Some readers may be disappointed that skepticism about meaning does not receive a more extensive treatment in Part II. One of the reasons for this is—in a sense—methodological: I try to avoid writing about issues when I have nothing interesting to say. In this case it also seems to me that someone else has already shown that the argument from Chapter 2 of *Word and Object* is invalid (Soames 1997; Soames 1998; Soames 1999*a*). But another reason for my lack of engagement with skepticism has its origins in the general way I think about semantics and the study of language. I think of meanings as abstract objects, things which more than one person may think about, and which more than one expression, in more than one language, may express—a bit like numbers and sets. Some have argued that such entities are philosophically disreputable, usually on the grounds that they are ontologically unparsimonious and we don't need them. They suggest that we can make do with ersatzes, such as stimulus meanings, or language-relative meanings, or that we should do away with the notion of meaning altogether. Though I am not convinced by the skeptical arguments, neither can I offer convincing reasons in support of my conviction that propositions, whatever their ultimate metaphysics, exist. But I am not inclined to let such a stalemate hamper work in the philosophy of language any more than I would let disputes over the metaphysics of mathematical objects hamper work in mathematics, or disputes over the metaphysics of the external world hamper work there. Lots of interesting philosophy of language gets done when skeptical worries get bracketed. New developments in logic, psychology and linguistics have combined to present contemporary philosophy of language with new data, and new techniques and theories to employ in explaining that data. If positing abstract objects makes it easier for us to think about language, to discover patterns and compare data, then let's posit them and see where that gets us. There is, I suppose, some irony in such a Quinean defence.

Part III Work for Epistemologists

"If there is no such thing as *a priori* knowledge, then analyticity loses its philosophical interest." (Sober 2000: 260)

The apparent epistemological power of analyticity is a large part of its attraction for philosophers, but does analyticity have to allow a priori justification to be interesting and useful? In Chapter 7 I argue that—with respect to this debate anyway—we should stop worrying about a priority and simply consider whether analytic truths afford any *distinctive* kind of justification, whether that is genuinely a priori, or just a special kind of a posteriori justification. I consider three theories of *analytic justification*, and argue for the third. The last few pages of the book address some of the consequences of the proceeding account for some traditional theses about analyticity—including the prospects for seeing analytic justification as full-blown a priori justification.

The section is ambiguously titled "Work for Epistemologists" because although this is work for *for the sake of* epistemologists, I think there is much more work to be done here, especially in considering particular cases such as the sentences of logic and mathematics, and no doubt in exposing my errors, so that the chapter also represents work which epistemologists might be interested in *doing*.

A FEW PRELIMINARIES

Here I draw attention to a few distinctions and conventions assumed in this book. Readers familiar with contemporary philosophy of language might safely skip to the next section.

There was a time—unfortunately coinciding with the height of the debate over the analytic/synthetic distinction—when many philosophers used the expressions *analytic, necessary, certain, logically true* and *a priori* as if they were synonymous. Following Kripke, I will take them to mean different things. Roughly, a claim is necessary if and only if it could not have been false, and a priori if and only if it can be known independently of experience. I will not be adopting Kripke's stipulative definition of *analytic*, since that would be to beg a lot of the questions with which this book is concerned. None of these notions are as well understood as they might be, and all are controversial, but they are understood well enough to be recognised as conceptually distinct (Casullo 1992) .

I will also make a point of distinguishing the objects of such properties. I take it that necessity and a priority adhere to propositions.[XI] Classic expositions of the role of propositions include (Cartwright 1962) and chapter 1 of (Soames 1999*b*).

Logical truth, on the other hand, I take to be a property of sentences.[XII] Sentences are syntactic items which bear meanings. In particular they bear contents relative to contexts and languages, or characters relative to languages.

It is not always important to distinguish sentences and the propositions they express, but it is important when discussing truth in virtue of meaning. As an illustration of the possible pitfalls, consider the specific thesis of *conventionalism*, which holds that the truth-values of analytic truths are determined by the linguistic conventions which govern certain words. The plausibility of the thesis—and what counts as an argument against it—depends on whether we take it to say that some *sentences* are true by linguistic convention, or that some *propositions* are true by linguistic convention. The claim that the sentence *all bachelors are men* is true by linguistic convention has a certain plausibility. After all, all sentences are true in part because of what they mean, and they mean what they do because of our linguistic conventions. So perhaps some sentences could be true entirely because of our linguistic conventions. On the other hand, to say that the *proposition* that all bachelors are men is made true by the conventions governing the words in the English sentence *all bachelors are unmarried*, is to make an outrageous claim. The words in this sentence can apply to objects outside of the English speaking community. *Bachelor*, in particular, applies to Germans, Iranians and Americans without prejudice. So why would it be the conventions for the English word *bachelor* (as opposed to the German word *Junggeselle*) that are responsible for the fact that all bachelors are men? The proposition that all bachelors are men is true independently of our

---

[XI] In the case of necessity, this is because truth adheres, in the first place, to propositions, and being necessarily true is a mode of being true. In the case of a priority it is because a priori knowledge is a kind of knowledge, and the kinds of things that can be known are the kinds of things that can be believed. Propositions are the objects of belief.

[XII] One reason not to take it to be a property of propositions is that 'a = a' and 'a = b', in which 'a' and 'b' are interpreted as distinct logical names for the same object, express the same proposition. Since one is a logical truth and the other not, they cannot both have inherited this status from the proposition they express.

linguistic conventions, though the sentence *all bachelors are men* might indeed be true in virtue of our linguistic conventions in some sense (Sober 2000).

Both the existence and the nature of propositions is controversial—that we should distinguish talk of them from talk of sentences is much less so.

Given that it is important to distinguish between expressions and their meanings when talking about analyticity, it is also important for an author to distinguish between references to expressions, and references to their meanings. In this I will follow some fairly standard conventions. When I wish to mention a linguistic expression, rather than use it, I will either place the expression in single quotation marks, as in (10), or in italics, as in (11).

(9) Snow is white.

(10) 'Snow' has four letters.

(11) *Snow* rhymes with *grow*.

Italics will also be used for emphasis, and the difference between emphatic use of italics and mention use of italics should hopefully be clear from context. Though this book distinguishes many different kinds of meaning, I have tried to keep the new use/mention conventions to a minimum, and will often refer to meanings by description, for example

(12) The reference determiner of *bachelor* is sensitive to context of evaluation.

(13) The character of *Hesperus* is minimal.

Towards the end of Part I, flanking downwards arrows on either side of an expression are sometimes used to form a name for the expression's reference determiner, as in (14).

(14) $\downarrow$ Bachelor $\downarrow$ is sensitive to context of evaluation.

This can be loosely paraphrased using a description as in (15).

(15) The reference determiner of *bachelor* is sensitive to context of evaluation.

I will also make occasional use of corner quotes. Here is an example which may aid the reader in interpreting sentences which employ this device:

(16) Where α is a description, the denotation of $\ulcorner \text{dthat}[\alpha] \urcorner$ with respect to the context of utterance $\langle a, p, t, w \rangle$ is the denotation of α at time t with respect to the context of evaluation w.

This can be read as in (17).

(17) Where α is a description, the denotation of the expression formed by writing *dthat*[followed by the description, followed by a closing square bracket, with respect to the context of utterance $\langle a, p, t, w \rangle$ is the denotation of α at time t with respect to the context of evaluation w.

The Objects of Analyticity

When we distinguish sentences and propositions, and identify propositions as the bearers of truth, necessity and a priority, and sentences as the bearers of logical truth, the question of the proper objects of analyticity presents itself: what kinds of things can be analytic?

Two main constraints help us to answer this question. The first is that analytic truths are supposed to be true. This narrows our search for the objects of analyticity down to truth-bearers. The second is that analytic truths are supposed to be true *in virtue of meaning*. This point is, I think, naturally interpreted as requiring that it is only things which *have* meanings that are apt to be analytic. Thus it allows that sentences may be analytic, but rules out that *propositions* can be analytic: propositions do not have meanings, rather they *are* the meanings of sentences.[XIII]

Another reason to think that analyticity is a property of sentences comes from examples of contingent analytic sentences containing indexical expressions. Sentences containing indexicals, such as *I*, *here* and *now* may express different propositions with respect to different contexts of utterance. Now consider Kaplan's famous example of a contingent analytic sentence:

(I) I am here now.

There is an interesting and intuitive sense in which the meaning of this sentence guarantees its truth. Anyone who understands the sentence can tell that, regardless of the context in which it is uttered, the sentence will

---

[XIII] Later I will have the opportunity to weaken that claim a little. I think that in the case of a subset of analytic sentences it would be harmless to say that the proposition expressed is analytic.

express a true proposition.[XIV] But the proposition that gets expressed in any particular context need not have been true—it is usually the case that I might have been elsewhere. Moreover, it seems that someone else might have expressed that same proposition using a non-analytic sentence, for example, *she is there now*. Thus it seems that *I am here now* did not inherit its analyticity from the proposition it expresses.

Two more minor points provide additional support for the idea that it is sentences, and not propositions, that are analytic. First, sentences of the form *it is analytic that* . . . do not seem quite proper, especially when compared to sentences of the form *Sentence 1 is analytic*. A priority and necessity, which are properties of propositions, are naturally attributed to propositions in the expressions *it is necessary that* . . . or *it is a priori that* . . . . Secondly, saying that analyticity is a property of sentences preserves its intuitive connection with logical truth, which is also a property of sentences. Suppose that two sentences of the form 'a = a' and 'a = b' express the same proposition, i.e., suppose that 'a' and 'b' are interpreted as distinct logical names for the same object. The first is a logical truth, the second is not, so they cannot both have inherited this status from the proposition. There is an intuitive sense in which analyticity is a naturally occurring version of artificial logical truth, and the selection of sentences as the objects of analyticity is in harmony with this intuition.

Inference and Implication

Following Harman (Harman 1986; Harman & Kulkarni 2006) I distinguish *inference* from *implication*. Modern logic is the study of *implication*—relations of truth-preservation between sets of premises and conclusions. It is not—though it is often falsely described as—the study of the principles of *reasoning* or thinking, nor does it tell us what we should infer, given what we already believe. That is another topic, *inference*, as opposed to implication.

One way to see this is to see that knowledge of one is not sufficient for knowledge of the other. Suppose that S believes the content of the sentences A and B, and comes to realise that they logically imply C.

[XIV] It is true that, for present purposes, I am ignoring cases such as someone leaving a message on their answer machine saying *I'm not here right now*. I consider this to be a simplifying measure for the purposes attempting to discern what is special about sentences like *I am here now*.

Can we conclude that she should believe the content of C? No. Here is a counterexample:

Suppose C is a contradiction. Then she should not accept it. What should she do instead? Perhaps give up belief in one of the premises, but which one? Logic does not answer the question—as we know from prolonged study of paradoxes—because logic only speaks of implication relations, not about belief revision.

Hence these questions about inference and belief revision—about what she should infer given (i) what she already believes and (ii) facts about implication—go beyond what logic will decide. That is not to say that logic is never relevant to reasoning or belief revision, just that it isn't the science of reasoning and belief revision. It's the science of implication relations. This distinction will be especially important when it comes to making sense of Chapter 7.

PART I

THE POSITIVE VIEW

PART ONE (ABSTRACT)

The first part of this book develops a positive account of truth in virtue of meaning. I hold that truth in virtue of meaning makes sense, and can be used to explain analyticity—in fact, I think it *is* analyticity. But the reader may be skeptical of these claims as a result of Quine's seminal argument to the conclusion that truth in virtue of meaning is either incoherent, or applies to *every* sentence—making it useless for explaining analyticity (Quine 1965[1954]). In Chapter 1, I present Quine's argument and provide a way to understand the 'in virtue of' in 'truth in virtue of meaning', which makes it invulnerable to Quine's criticism.

In Chapter 2 I argue that debate over the analytic/synthetic distinction has been hampered by widespread tacit acceptance of a folk theory of language which conflates several different types of meaning. I disambiguate these and argue that truth in virtue of meaning is best disambiguated as truth in virtue of just one of these types of meaning—reference determiner.

But the account still faces a problem, one which arises because of the very general difficulty of defining semantic notions in modal terms. Just as directly referential expressions cannot be distinguished from rigid designators within a modal framework (Kaplan 1989*b*), so analyticity cannot be characterised in a sufficiently fine way if we limit ourselves to modal terms. In Chapter 3 I propose a more metaphysical picture of analyticity. I hold that just as direct reference explains rigidity, so the metaphysical picture of analyticity explains the distinctive modal profile of analytic sentences. Part one also contains an appendix in which I extend Kaplan's formal framework to include some of the ideas introduced in these first three chapters. My hope is that the kind of philosopher who finds formal treatments of semantic notions illuminating will find the appendix useful in pinning down ideas.

1

The 'in virtue of' Relation

1.1 THE TWO-FACTOR ARGUMENT

In "Carnap and Logical Truth," Quine writes:

Another point . . . was that true sentences generally depend for their truth on the traits of their language in addition to the traits of their subject matter; and that logical truths then fit neatly in as the limiting case where the dependence on traits of the subject matter is nil. Consider, however, the logical truth, 'Everything is self-identical', or, '$(x)(x = x)$'. We *can* say that it depends for its truth on traits of the language (specifically on the usage of ' $=$ '), and not on traits of its subject matter; but we can also say, alternatively, that it depends on an obvious trait, viz., self-identity, viz., of everything. (1965[1954]:113)

The idea, I think, is this: Quine agrees that, in general, there are two factors which determine the truth-values of sentences: the world, and language. But he points out that it does not *follow* from this that some sentences have their truth-value determined more by language and less by the world, or vice versa, and so, of course, there is no reason to think that there might be a limiting case on such a (possibly fictional) continuum. Moreover, he asks us to examine a standard example of an analytic truth: *everything is self-identical*. Even in this case there is a state of the world that corresponds to the sentence, and we can think of that state as making the sentence true; everything *is* really self-identical—that's a fact about the world—just as snow is really white, and this is part of the reason why the sentence *everything is self-identical* is true.

The standard story is thus challenged in two places. First, it is pointed out (quite correctly) that the fact that some sentences are true in virtue of both the way the world is and the meaning of the sentence, does not ensure that there are other sentences that are true solely in virtue of meaning. The 'limiting case' idea may be a neat picture, but we do not yet have a reason to believe that the picture is true to life.[1]

This first point should be conceded to Quine. The 'limiting case' idea is pretty, but I cannot think what it would be for one sentence to be 'more' true in virtue of meaning (or the world) than another. There is no argument for the existence of analytic sentences to be had here.

Quine's second challenge is this: not only does the conclusion (that some sentences are true solely in virtue of meaning) not follow from the premises, but it looks as if it is not even true. The standard examples which get presented as sentences that are true in virtue of meaning are not really examples of sentences that are true in virtue of meaning. Take the case of *everything is self-identical*. If we look at the world, we will note that all the things in it really are self identical. It seems that the world makes even this sentence true.

This second point is troubling and deserves a substantial answer. How can an analytic sentence be true in virtue of meaning (except in the trivial way that all sentences are) if even the best examples of analytic sentences seem to be true in part because the world is a certain way?

Boghossian's Version of the Argument

Boghossian rejects truth in virtue of meaning on similar grounds, writing:

I want to register my wholehearted agreement with Quine, that the metaphysical notion [of analyticity] is of dubious explanatory value, and possibly of dubious coherence.

Boghossian sets the objection up as a dilemma. He claims, very reasonably, that it is a truism that for any statement S,

(1.1) S is true iff for some p, S means that p and p.*

He then asks:

. . . how could the fact that S means that p make it the case that S is true? Doesn't it also have to be the case that p?

---

[1] This point also has some useful (and legitimate) rhetorical force for the Quinean: it suggests where the supporter of analyticity may have gone wrong; he was understandably bewitched by this neat but inaccurate picture of what is special about, for example, logical sentences.

* I reproduce Boghossian's text exactly here.

He points out that there is *one* sense in which we might say that a sentence is true in virtue of meaning: it is because of the fact that the sentence means what it does that it says that p and so, given that that p is true, it is because of the sentence's meaning that it is true. Boghossian points out, however, that this is just the sense in which *every* sentence is true in virtue of its meaning, and so it is not a sense of *true in virtue of meaning* that will be useful for understanding analyticity.

According to Boghossian, the only *non-trivial* way a sentence can be true in virtue of meaning is if the fact that the sentence's meaning that p by S, "*makes it the case that p*." He ridicules this idea:

Are we really to suppose that, prior to our stipulating a meaning for the sentence "Either snow is white or it isn't," it wasn't the case that either snow was white or it wasn't? Isn't it overwhelmingly obvious that this claim was true before such an act of meaning, and that it would have been true even if no one had thought about it, or chosen it to be expressed by one of our sentences? (1997)

Sober also dramatises the counter-intuitiveness of this idea. He imagines the outrage of French bachelors when they discover that we think it is the meaning of the English sentence *all bachelors are unmarried* that makes it the case that all bachelors are unmarried:

'Quelle impertinence!' one can hear them exclaim. The fact that bachelors are unmarried is no more dependent on English than it is on French. (Sober 2000: 247)

And so, one way to arrange the objection as a dilemma is as follows: suppose we say that a sentence, such as *all bachelors are unmarried* is true in virtue of meaning. Then we may be saying one of two things. We might be saying that the meaning of the sentence contributes in some way to, though it does not totally determine, the truth of the sentence. But in that case what we are saying is trivial: *every sentence* is true in virtue of meaning in that sense. Alternatively, we might mean that the meaning of the sentence is entirely responsible for its truth-value, but in that case what we are saying is wrong: Quine simply points out that we may as well take the *fact* that all bachelors are unmarried as contributing to the truth-value of *all bachelors are unmarried*, while Boghossian maintains that to make *all bachelors are unmarried* true, the meaning of the sentence would have to make it the case that all bachelors are unmarried. This claim is clearly absurd once understood.

1.2 DISAMBIGUATING 'IN VIRTUE OF'

I wish to deny the disjunctive claim in the dilemma. One may say that a sentence is true in virtue of meaning without meaning either that the meaning contributes to the truth-value in the trivial way in which meaning always contributes to truth-value, or (as Quine suggested) that the world plays no role at all in determining the truth-value, or even (on Boghossian's version) that the meaning makes the proposition expressed by the sentence true. Rather, one may have a *third* determination relation in mind.

It may seem quite unlikely that such a third determination relation between the meaning and the truth-value of a sentence is available, since the two options already presented can appear to divide up the logical space of determination relations exhaustively. On the 'trivial' option, *determines* is interpreted so that the meaning partially—but not wholly—determines the truth-value. On the 'absurd' option, *determines* is interpreted to mean that the meaning wholly determines the truth-value. What remains?

I will proceed first by presenting a sentence which should help to elicit the intuition that there must be a third way. Then I will give a non-linguistic example of this third kind of determination relation, and finally I will present definitions of the distinct kinds of determination relation.

I am here now

We can get an intuitive grip on the idea that there is a third option by considering the sentence *I am here now*. Intuitively, the meanings of the expressions in *I am here now* guarantee that the sentence is true in a way in which the meanings of the words in *snow is white* do not guarantee that *snow is white* is true. This is so even though the meaning of *I am here now* did not *make it the case* that I am here now. (I'm slaving away at the kitchen table this rainy Monday evening because I skipped out on post-talk drinking to finish my book, not because of the meaning of the English word *I*.) So, intuitively, there is a third, non-trivial (since it doesn't apply to all sentences), yet non-absurd (since it applies to at least one sentence), sense in which the truth of a sentence can be determined by its meaning.[2]

---

[2] One thing that might contribute to confusion about what is required for truth in virtue of meaning is the false belief that x *makes it the case that* distributes across

Examples from arithmetic

We can see clear examples of this determination relation I am trying to isolate in arithmetic. Consider the binary multiplication function on the natural numbers:

$$x \times y = z$$

In general, the product of two numbers is determined in part by the value of the first argument, and in part by the value of the second argument. Suppose we decide to multiply two numbers, say 3 and 5:

$$3 \times 5 = ?$$

The value of the function for these arguments is (of course) 15. Why is it 15? The value is 15 in part because the first argument was 3 (if it had been 20 the answer would have been 100 instead) and in part because the second argument was 5 (if it had been 15 the answer would have been 45.) There are, if you will pardon the pun, two factors that determine the value of the function.

Now consider a special case. Set the value of the x-argument to 0 (zero). We could let the y-argument be, well, 5:

$$0 \times 5 = ?$$

But there is a sense in which it just doesn't matter what the second argument is anymore; whatever we set it to the result will be equal to 0. In this special case we can know, just by looking at the first argument, what the value of the multiplication function will be. The first argument was sufficient, in a sense on its own, to determine the result. But let's

conjunction. Though it might seem as if, in order for me to make it the case that G and T, I have to make it the case that G and make it the case that T, in fact I do not, as the following counterexample shows:

Suppose Harman makes it the case that the head of the Frist campus center is fired. Then Harman makes it the case that there is one and only one head of the Frist campus center and that that person is fired. But in order for this to be true, Harman does not need to have made it the case that there is one and only one head of the Frist campus center. (Thanks to the combined forces of Gilbert Harman and Scott Soames for this insight (and the gleeful example.))

Thus x *makes it the case that* does not distribute across conjunction and we are not forced to take the outrageous horn of the Quinean dilemma by the semantics of x *makes it the case that.*

say that we set the second argument to 5 anyway. Then *because we multiplied* 5 *by* 0 is still a perfectly good answer to the question *why was the answer* 0? It is not as if there was no second argument whatsoever.

This simple arithmetical example—two factors determining a product—is analogous to the case of the world and meaning determining a truth-value in a number of ways. In order to set those out clearly, I need a more technical vocabulary than I have been using so far; I do not wish to go on saying confusing things like *in a sense, on its own* and *in a sense, totally determines*. I will present four disambiguations of *determine* first, in an intuitive way, which I think should be sufficient for understanding what follows, and then I will present more careful definitions of the four kinds of determination.

Four intuitive senses of determine

Suppose that, relative to some function, an argument determines a value, but only in conjunction with other things, for example, as 3 determines 15 as the value of 3×5. Then we will say that that factor *partially determines* the value and that the value of the function is 15 *partially in virtue of* the fact that the x-argument is 3.[3]

We will say that the x- and y-arguments *conjointly determine* the value of the multiplication function; once you have fixed these two things, there is, in all cases, only one possible value for the function.

Where the x-argument is 0, we will say that the x-argument *fully determines* the value of the function.

Where the x-argument is 0, we will say that the y-argument *redundantly* determines the value of the function.

Now I will try to define these notions and then we will be able to use them to say just how the meaning of an analytic sentence determines its truth-value.

Defining the four determination relations

We can think of functions as sets of n-tuples. For example, the binary function on the natural numbers is the set of all triples of natural numbers $\langle x, y, z \rangle$ in which the third member is the product of the first two. We can also represent a function from meaning and world to truth-value as a set of triples in which the first member is a meaning,

---

[3] In general I will assume that we can translate back and forth between 'in virtue of' talk and 'determines' talk in the following way: the value of x determines the value of y, if, and only if, the value of y is what it is in virtue of the value of x.

the second a state of the world, and the third a truth-value: $\langle m, w, v \rangle$. I will refer to this as the M-function, and the M-function will get more sophisticated as we go on, but for now, let us say that the M-function takes *a meaning*, which for now we will assume to be a proposition, and a *state of the world* as arguments and yields a truth-value.

Relative to a function, we can define the following four senses of determine:

Definition 1 (partial determination) *An argument place* i *partially determines the result-place* $n + 1$ *with respect to a function* F *just in case there exists a pair of* $n + 1$-*tuples* $\langle x_1, \ldots, x_i, \ldots x_n, y \rangle, \langle x'_1, \ldots, x'_i, \ldots x'_n, y' \rangle \in F$ *such that* $x_1 = x'_1, x_2 = x'_2, \ldots x_i \neq x'_i, \ldots x_n = x'_n$ *and* $y \neq y'$.

For example, the first argument place of the multiplication function partially determines the result-place, since the following two triples are members of the function:

$$\langle 2, 3, 6 \rangle$$
$$\langle 3, 3, 9 \rangle$$

Moreover, the first argument of the M-function—the meaning of the sentence—partially determines the truth-value, since the following triples are members of that function:[4]

$\langle$ the proposition that snow is white, w_a, T$\rangle$
$\langle$ the proposition that snow is black, w_a, F$\rangle$

And so, of course, does the state of the world, as witnessed by the fact that these triples are also in the function:

$\langle$ the proposition that snow is white, w_a, T$\rangle$
$\langle$ the proposition that snow is white, w_b, F$\rangle$

Definition 2 (conjoint determination) *A subsequence of argument places,* $\langle i, \ldots, k \rangle$, *conjointly determines the value of a function* F *just in case there is no pair of* n-*tuples* $\langle x_1, \ldots, x_i, \ldots, x_k, \ldots x_n, y \rangle$,

---

[4] In what follows w_a denotes the actual world, and w_b denotes a possible world in which snow is black.

$\langle x'_1 \ldots, x'_i, \ldots, x'_k, \ldots, x'_n, y' \rangle \in F$ *such that* $\langle x_i, \ldots, x_k \rangle = \langle x'_i, \ldots, x'_k \rangle$ *but* $y \neq y'$

For example, the subsequence consisting of the first and second argument-places conjointly determines the value of the result position for a function if there is no pair of series like this (in which the first two arguments match, but the values differ) in that function:

$$\langle 1, 2, 3, 10 \rangle$$
$$\langle 1, 2, 4, 15 \rangle$$

If we ignore the possibility of vague propositions for the moment, we can say that meaning and the state of the world conjointly determine a truth-value relative to the M-function.

Definition 3 (full determination) *The arguments* $x_i \ldots x_k$ *in argument positions* $i \ldots k$ *fully determine the result* y *with respect to a function* F *just in case for all* $n + 1$*-tuples in* F, *if the values in positions* $i \ldots k$ *are* $x_i \ldots x_k$, *then the last member of the* $n + 1$*-tuple is* y.

For example, the argument 0 in first argument-position of the multiplication function fully-determines the value 0, since there is no n-tuple in the multiplication function such that the first argument is 0 and the value is *not* 0.

Definition 4 (redundant determination) *An argument* x_i *in an* $n + 1$*-tuple* $\langle x_1, \ldots x_i, \ldots x_n, y \rangle$ *redundantly determines the result* y *with respect to a function* F *just in case (i) the argument place* i *partially determines the result-position of* F, *but (ii) there is no* $n + 1$*-tuple* $\langle x'_1, \ldots x'_i, \ldots x'_n, y' \rangle \in F$ *such that* $\langle x_1 = x'_1, x_2 = x'_2 \ldots x_i \neq x'_i \ldots x_n = x'_n$ *and* $y \neq y'$. *(So in this particular n-tuple it is not the case that changing that argument could change the result).*

If the argument in the first argument place of the multiplication function is 0 and the second is 5, then the first argument fully-determines the value of the function to be 0 and the second redundantly determines the same value, since the first argument-place partially determines the value of the multiplication function, but the function contains no triple such that 0 is the first member and the value is not 0.

Let me make two observations about these definitions which I hope will stave off misunderstanding. First, the 'fully-determines' and 'redundantly determines' relations hold between different kinds of objects than the other two determination relations. It is a *particular argument*, say 0, in an argument-place, (like the first place) that fully-determines or redundantly determines a particular result. Partial and conjoint determination, on the other hand, hold between *argument-places*, marking the fact that whatever value you put in that place it will contribute to the value of the result-place.

Second, given these definitions, the fact that a result is fully-determined by some value is not inconsistent with that value also being redundantly determined by another argument. Though 0 in argument-place 1 of the multiplication function fully-determines that the result will be 0, in the n-tuple $\langle 0, 5, 0 \rangle$, 5 still redundantly determines the value.

It seems to me that what the supporter of truth in virtue of meaning should say is that which truth-value a sentence has is conjointly determined by two factors: the meaning of a sentence and the way the world is. For synthetic sentences that value is fully-determined by neither argument. But with an analytic sentence the truth-value is fully-determined by the meaning of the sentence.

These claims do not imply that there is no state of the world corresponding to the sentence, (just as to say that the value of the multiplication function is fully-determined by the x-argument (when the x-argument is 0), is not to claim that there is no y argument); rather the state of the world redundantly determines the truth-value of an analytic sentence.

What the supporter of analyticity should say when Quine and Boghossian demand an account of truth in virtue of meaning which is neither trivial nor incoherent is that analytic sentences are true in virtue of meaning in this sense: their truth is *fully-determined* by the meaning of the sentence.

1.3 COLLAPSE INTO NECESSITY?

This response can seem to run into difficulties concerning the modal profile of analytic sentences. There is reason to think that on this interpretation of *in virtue of*, analytic sentences must be all and only the sentences which express necessary truths. In the rest of this chapter I will explain why this seems to be a consequence of the account, and then give several reasons why this would be a serious problem—if it were really a consequence of it. Then in the next two chapters I will draw some distinctions and use them to refine the account and show that it is *not* a consequence of it. Ultimately I will argue that the undesirable consequence comes from assuming that the *meaning* in *true in virtue of meaning* is a reference to the content of the sentence. However, the *meaning* in *true in virtue of meaning* is *not* referring to content, but to something else.

Here is the objection. In giving the response to Quine and Boghossian I assumed that the meaning of the sentence was a proposition. Someone sensitive to the danger of collapsing analyticity into necessity might express the following worry:

> Which proposition is that? Presumably you mean the proposition semantically expressed by the sentence. But if this is what you mean, then you seem to be committed to the claim that all and only sentences which express necessary truths are true in virtue of meaning. Here is why: necessary truths are just those which will be true no matter what the world is like. So the meaning of a sentence which expresses a necessary truth will fully-determine the value 'true' and so the sentence will be true in virtue of meaning in your sense. Conversely, if a sentence is true in virtue of meaning in your sense then its meaning fully-determines the truth-value *true*, so the sentence will have to be true with respect to each state of the world, that is, what it says will have to be necessary. This idea of a sentence that is true in virtue of meaning is just the idea of a sentence that expresses a necessary truth.

There are three reasons to think that that alleged consequence is undesirable.

Sentences expressing substantive necessities

Some philosophers have thought that all metaphysical modality some-how reduces to language. Others think that there are, or could be, substantive metaphysical modal truths; they think that there can be metaphysically necessary truths even where there is no linguistic expla-nation for this. For example, Bolzano writes:

> Not everything that can be predicated of an object, even with necessity, lies already in the concept of that object. For example, one can predicate of every rectilinear triangle that the sum of its three angles = 180 . . . nevertheless, no one will believe that these properties of the triangle are contained as constituents of this concept. (Coffa 1991: 36)

Another kind of philosopher who will think that there are necessary, yet non-analytic truths is the Lewis-style hyper-realist about possible worlds. Take a sentence like *the morning star is the evening star*. There doesn't seem to be anything about the meaning of these descriptions that guarantees that *the morning star* and *the evening star* will refer to the same object. But suppose you were a hyper-realist. Then if it turned out, surprisingly, that in fact there were only fifteen possible worlds, and in each of these worlds the morning star and the evening star are the same object, then you would (if you somehow learned of this fact through some hardcore metaphysics) say that in every possible world the morning star is the evening star, and hence say that it is necessary that the morning star is the evening star and that the English sentence *the morning star is the evening star* expresses a necessary truth. But even if this were the case, it doesn't seem right to say that such a substantive metaphysical truth is true in virtue of meaning.

It is not only modal realists who allow that there might be substantive modal truths. Most philosophers think that the truths of arithmetic are necessary. But many of those philosophers also think that logicism is false, that is, they reject the idea that the truths of arithmetic are analytic. Such a philosopher will want to say that '2 + 2 = 4' expresses a necessary truth, but reject the claim that it is true in virtue of meaning. That suggests that the expressions *expresses a necessary truth* and *is true in virtue of meaning* are not trivially equivalent.

True identity sentences involving names

A less obvious worry is that I might be misclassifying the sentences whose truth is sometimes said to be *semantically guaranteed*. There *is* a linguistic explanation of why *Hesperus is Phosphorus* is such that, given its meaning, it will be true regardless of the state of the world (ignoring, for simplicity, the worlds where Venus doesn't exist.) The names *Hesperus* and *Phosphorus* are rigid designators of the same object.

Nonetheless I don't want to say that *Hesperus is Phosphorus* is analytic. The obvious reason to be worried is that *Hesperus is Phosphorus* does not seem to be epistemically accessible in the way that analytic sentences are usually taken to be. Analytic sentences are sometimes thought to be such that understanding one is sufficient for being justified in taking it to be true. This is clearly not the case with *Hesperus is Phosphorus*.

However, this is not my main worry. (Ultimately I will be arguing that truth in virtue of meaning is one thing, and that the Positivists thought that it brought a special kind of epistemic status along with it, but that they were only *partly* right about this.)

The worry I have in mind is this one: *Hesperus is Phosphorus*, unlike *Hesperus is Hesperus*, is not a logical truth. But logicians treat analytic sentences and logically true sentences as closely related. Many logicians think of the question of which words to take as logical constants (and hence which sentences of the language to count as logical truths) as a practical question equivalent to the question of how many *analytic* truths one wants to formalise in the logic. Truth-functional logic, in taking say *or* and *not* as logical constants enshrines:

(TF) Snow is white or snow is not white

as a logical truth but leaves:

(Q) Everything is white or not white

as a mere analyticity. First-order predicate logic adds Q to the list of logical truths but leaves:

(L) If it is necessary that snow is white then snow is white

out in the cold. Deontic logics add *it ought to be the case that* and the logic of demonstratives adds indexicals to make sentences like *I am here now* logical truths, but it is thought that, for pragmatic reasons, it is often best to leave some conceptual connections to be formulated explicitly by the users of the logic. The worry about taking *Hesperus is Phosphorus* to be true in virtue of meaning is that it is not on the list of sentences we would ever treat as logical truths.

Contingent analyticities

The third kind of sentence I would be misclassifying if my response to Quine and Boghossian committed me to identifying analytic truths with sentences which express necessary truths is that of contingent analytic sentences, such as *I am here now*. Kaplan holds that *I am here now* is an analytic truth and there does seem to be something to this thought (1989b). What the sentence means somehow guarantees its truth. But the sentence, relative to a context, normally expresses a contingent truth. I am here now, but I need not have been.

These three kinds of sentence—sentences expressing substantive necessities, sentences like *Hesperus is Phosphorus* and analytic sentences expressing contingent truths—make it undesirable to have it as a consequence of one's account of analyticity that analytic sentences are just those expressing necessary truths. Fortunately, that is not a consequence of my account. The suggested argument to the conclusion that it *was* a consequence of the account made two false assumptions. The first was that the meaning which fully-determines the truth-value of the sentence must be the sentence's *content* (as opposed to some other aspect of its meaning) and the second was that the state of the world which redundantly determines the sentence's truth-value was a possible world against which the sentence is evaluated for truth. In the next chapter, I will motivate the rejection of both these assumptions.

2

Meaning

I contend that a pervasive pre-theoretic picture of the way language works—a mistaken picture—has been responsible for the intractability of the debate over the analytic/synthetic distinction. The problem with the picture is that it conflates three different kinds of meaning and in doing so supports an untenable account of the analytic/synthetic distinction. Implicit acceptance of the picture is very natural, but it tends to make the untenable version of the analytic/synthetic distinction look inevitable.

In this chapter I will draw on the work of Kripke and Kaplan to undermine the language myth. Then I will argue that the *meaning* in *truth in virtue of meaning* refers to a particular one of the three kinds of meaning, which the myth conflates and that the refinement of the positive account that this disambiguation allows gives us a version of the analytic/synthetic distinction which is invulnerable to many of the old objections. It will also allow a solution to the problem presented at the end of the last chapter, according to which the idea of an *analytic sentence* collapses into the idea of a *sentence which expresses a necessary truth.*

2.1 THE LANGUAGE MYTH

Here is the heart of the misleading folk picture, and the theory of analyticity which it supports. I expect that the picture will seem familiar to those readers who are members of the folk, and the extension of the picture will be recognisable to many philosophers. Since I need a name for the misleading folk picture, I will call it *the language myth.* Here is what it says:

Expressions (both whole sentences and subsentential expressions like words) have meanings, and meanings play three roles. First, meanings are what speakers know when they understand expressions, since to understand an expression just is to know what it means. For example, to say that my brother understands the word *atavistic* is to say that he knows what it means and to say that my brother understands *wovon man nicht sprechen kann, darüber muss man schweigen* is to say that he knows what *that* means. Second, the meaning of a sentence is what it says, and when a smaller expression is used in a sentence the meaning of the word contributes to the meaning of the sentence as a whole; it is partially responsible for what the sentence says. For example, *dogs are animals* says that dogs are animals, and not that *cats* are animals, in part because the subsentential expression *dogs* means *dogs* and not *cats*. Finally, the meaning of a word determines what objects in the world the word applies to. For example, it is because *cat* means what it does that it applies to cats. It is because *bachelor* means *unmarried male* that it applies to Jeff. Moreover, if it had meant something different—say *unmarried female* then it would not have applied to him. That is the core of the folk picture and it can be summarised in the following three theses:

(1) To understand an expression is to know what it means.

(2) The meaning of an expression in a sentence contributes to what the sentence as a whole says.

(3) Which object(s) an expression applies to is determined by what it means.

Perhaps some incautious pre-theoretics would also accept a fourth thesis:

(4) The meaning of an expression *is* what it applies to.

For example, 'Hesperus' means *Hesperus*, 'dead' means *dead* and (even more incautiously) 'and' means *and*. But they may also discover natural antidotes to this confusion in cases such as 'creature with a heart' and 'creature with a kidney'—in which the expressions apply to the same objects but do not mean the same thing—and so come to believe that 'means' and 'meaning' are ambiguous; in one sense the meaning of an expression is the thing(s) in the world it applies to, but in another sense it is something else, the thing which satisfies theses (1)–(3). Let us, the sophisticated pre-theoretic might say, call the first of these the *extension* and the second the *meaning* of the word.

What is distinctive about the language myth—and what is mistaken about it—is the assumption that theses (1)–(3) are always satisfied by a single thing. That is, that what a speaker must know to count as understanding an expression is the thing that determines its referent, which is what it contributes to the content of any sentence in which it is used.

2.1.1 Analyticity given the Language Myth

There is a theoretical overlay that is a natural addition to this picture: a definition is an identity statement involving two synonymous expressions, for example, *A bachelor is an unmarried man* or *gold is a yellow metal that is resistant to rust*.[1] Suppose someone understands both expressions. Then, by (1) they know that they both mean, say, *M*. This means that the referents of the terms must be determined in exactly the same way and so, if a speaker knows this, then regardless of whether they have checked to see, they can know that the meanings cannot help but apply to the same objects; the identity sentence will express a truth. Since this is known on the basis of understanding the terms, we might call it 'a priori'. The truth expressed by the sentence will also be necessary. For suppose there is a possible world where the identity statement is false, that means that the meanings of the expressions have determined *different* referents—so the expressions are not synonymous, contrary to hypothesis. Such sentences are obviously special, and so to mark their distinctiveness, let's call them *analytic* sentences.

Neither the pre-theoretic picture nor the extended theory involving definition, necessity and a priority, are quite right, though the picture makes the theory almost irresistible. There are many linguistic expressions that do not work the way the theory demands and we can use these to show that *meaning* is really multiply ambiguous. There is no single thing that satisfies all three pre-theoretic 'meaning' principles. There are not just two different things here, but four. Since I contend that *meaning* is multiply ambiguous it will be helpful to introduce some new terms for the different senses of the word.

- **character**: the thing speakers must know (perhaps tacitly) to count as understanding an expression
- **content**: what the word contributes to what a sentence containing it says (the proposition it expresses)

[1] These are only identity statements in an extended sense of that expression, according to which statements of the forms '$\forall x(Fx \rightarrow Gx)$', '$\forall x(Fx \leftrightarrow Gx)$' may express *theoretical identities*, such as *water is H_2O* and *cats are animals*. The expression has been explicitly used in this extended sense in (Soames 2001) and (Kripke 1980), though other authors have called such statements *identity statements* without drawing attention to the fact that they are not of the form '$a = b$', e.g. (unsurprisingly) (Locke 1993[1690]).

- **reference Determiner:** a condition which an object must meet in order to be the referent of, or fall in the extension of, an expression
- **referent/ extension:** the (set of) object(s) to which the term applies. e.g. *horse* correctly applies to all and only horses, *Tim* applies to Tim . . . .

The language myth is rarely explicitly stated and accepted, rather, it is an intuitive picture of how language works that is naturally and easily presupposed. But one result of presupposing such a picture is that certain consequences of it—such as the extension involving analyticity, definitions, a priority and necessity—can appear *obvious*, with the result that the denial of those consequences appears absurd and sophistical. I think many thinkers find themselves in this position with respect to analyticity. Whatever ingenious arguments were adduced against the analytic/synthetic distinction, they would not give the distinction up, because they did not see how there *could* fail to be a distinction. For such philosophers—among whom I count an earlier self—the arguments against the analytic/synthetic distinction did not bring enlightenment, only apparent paradox.

The work of dismantling the language myth has been the work of many twentieth-century philosophers, including Quine, Putnam, Burge, Kripke, Kaplan, Donnellan, Evans, McDowell, Soames and Salmon. (Putnam 1962*a*, 1975; Burge 1991[1979], 1986; Kripke 1980; Kaplan 1989*b*; Evans 1973, 1982; McDowell 1977; Salmon 1982; Salmon & Soames 1988; Soames 1987, (2001). Often that work has consisted of offering alternative pictures of linguistic meaning and for the purposes of debunking the language myth, it is not so important that those pictures are accurate, as that they are seen to be possible ways in which parts of our language *could* work; much of the support for the language myth comes from the thought that its way is really the *only* way. Once alternate models become available, the consequences of the original model no longer seem *obvious*.

Here I will present only two outstanding examples of linguistic pictures that run contrary to the language myth. My hope is that this will give any reader who has absolutely no idea how the language myth could turn out to be false a sense of how alternatives could work. The first is Kripke's approach to names, and the Millian extension of that view, on which the reference determiner of a name is identical to neither its content, nor its character. The second is Kaplan's approach to indexicals, according to which the character and content of indexical expressions come apart.[2]

2.2 KRIPKE AND KAPLAN

2.2.1 Kripke

The positive picture of names presented in *Naming and Necessity* played an important role in exposing the language myth by providing an alternative picture of the way language works, along with extensive criticism of a popular version of the language myth which identified the content, character and reference determiner of a name with the content of a description. Kripke described the alternative as follows:

> Someone, let's say, a baby, is born; his parents call him by a certain name. They talk about him to their friends. Other people meet him. Through various sorts of talk the name is spread from link to link as if by a chain. A speaker who is on the far end of this chain, who has heard about, say, Richard Feynman . . . may be referring to Richard Feynman, even though he can't remember from whom he first heard of Feynman . . . A certain passage of communication reaching ultimately to the man himself does reach the speaker. He is then referring to Feynman even though he can't identify him uniquely. (1980: 91)

So what, on this picture, is the reference determiner for my word *Feynman*? That is, what is the condition that an object must meet in order to count as the referent of a use of the name? One natural answer is that it is the chain linking the use of the expression to the referent, but I am uncomfortable with the idea that the reference determiner for an expression might be different for different speakers. I think the following is a plausible alternative: it is the condition specified by the baptiser (using a description, or by pointing) and used to pick out a referent for the name when it was introduced. What it is to be Feynman, is to be the object that fitted the description when the baptiser said,

---

[2] A note about terminology: my use of *character* differs from Kaplan's, though the similarity is clear. On Kaplan's use, *character* is a part of the meaning which plays *two* roles: that of being what a competent speaker must know, and that of being the condition or rule that determines the referent. The Kripkean discussion of names will make it clear that these two roles may be played by different things. I reserve the term *character* for the thing that the speaker must know to count as competent, and *reference determiner* for the condition or rule that determines the referent.

say, *Let's call the new baby 'Feynman'.*[3] [4] I get to use the word with that
reference determiner—even though I do not know what it is—so long
as, when I first learn the word, I form the intention to use it with the
same meaning (whatever that is) that my interlocutor uses it with. This
is a picture of reference determination for names that does not insist
that in order to be competent with the name a speaker must know how
its referent is determined. It is thus a theory on which character (what
the speaker has to know) and reference determiner are distinct. So it is
a theory on which the language myth is false.

Contemporary Millians believe that the *content* of a name is identical
to its referent. On this extended Kripkean view we can see that the
content of a name and its reference determiner will also be different
entities. The content of *Feynman*, for example, will be the man himself,
whereas the reference determiner will be the condition expressed by the
description (or action, such as pointing) used to introduce the name.

What about the final identity which forms part of the language myth:
content with character? Does a speaker have to know what the content
of a name is in order to count as competent with it? I think the issues for
names are somewhat complicated, but this will not matter for present
purposes, since, in proposing his account of indexicals, Kaplan provided
us with a picture on which content and character come apart.

2.2.2 Kaplan

Crucial to Kaplan's picture is the idea of *direct reference*, which presents
an alternative to the traditional Fregean picture of how language works.
On the Fregean picture words and sentences express a sense. The sense
of a sentence is the thought (proposition) it expresses and that sense is
determined by the senses of the component expressions in the sentence.
Thus sense plays the role of content for the Fregean. But the sense of an
expression also determines its referent. To find out what an expression
refers to, one must first find out what its sense is, and then one can
'take that sense to the world' to see which objects it applies to. Kaplan's
diagram (figure 2.1) representing the key ideas in the Fregean picture
will help make the contrast between it and the direct reference picture
clearer.

---

[3] I suppose it is more plausible to think that they used the name *Richard*, but this
accidental awkwardness of the example could be rectified.

[4] Why not say that the reference determiner for a name is the entire chain leading back
to the baptism? Because then it would be a different reference determiner for everyone.

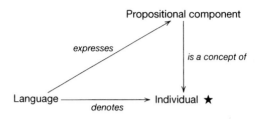

Figure 2.1 Fregean picture.

By contrast, to say that some terms are directly referential is to say that they refer to their referents without the mediation of a Fregean sense. Rather than being determined by content, the referent is determined by some other (possibly pre-semantic—like Kripke's naming-chain) mechanism, and direct reference theorists then identify the content of the expression with the referent.

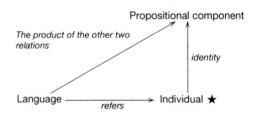

Figure 2.2 Direct reference picture.

Kaplan maintains two central theses about indexicals and demonstratives. The first is that the referent of a pure indexical depends on the context. The second is that indexicals are directly referential. The former states that the referent of an indexical is sensitive to the world in a certain way. The latter implies that the referent of an indexical is *insensitive* to the world in a certain way. In order to understand Kaplan's view it is important to get clear on how these ways differ.

The referent of a use of an indexical like *I* in a sentence such as *I am angry* depends on the state of the world *in which the sentence is uttered*, but not upon the state of the world against which the proposition expressed is evaluated for truth. If Nelson Mandela utters the sentence *I am angry* his word *I* refers to Nelson Mandela. If Archbishop Tutu utters *I am angry* then *I* refers to Tutu instead. This is because there is a rule for determining the referent of *I*: *I* always refers to the agent (the speaker or writer or signer) of the context of utterance.

But suppose I want to think about whether things could have been otherwise. Consider the modal sentence *I might not have been speaking now; Archbishop Tutu might have been speaking instead* as uttered by Mandela. That sentence will be true just in case there is a possible world in which Mandela is not speaking and Tutu is speaking instead. Despite the fact that in the world imagined the agent is Tutu, *I* still refers to the speaker of the context of *utterance*—Mandela. The referent of *I* varies depending on the context of utterance, but once we have fixed that, *I* will refer to the agent of that context of utterance, *regardless of the circumstances of evaluation*.

Not all expressions work this way as we can see by comparing indexicals with descriptions: take a description like *the shortest spy ever*. The referent of the description depends on who has been a spy and how tall the various spies have been, and it will vary given different contexts of evaluation. Relative to a context of evaluation in which the shortest spy ever was Austin, *the shortest spy ever* refers to Austin, but if Mata Hari had been the only spy ever, *the shortest spy ever* would have picked out Mata Hari. But the context in which the sentence is uttered is irrelevant to determining the referent of *the shortest spy ever*.

Content and character

Though Kaplan thinks that indexicals are directly referential, and hence that their referent is not determined by a Fregean sense, he does not claim that the only meaning an indexical has is its referent. Rather, indexicals have descriptive meanings, known by speakers, that semantically determine their referents. It is part of the meaning of *I* for example, that *I* refers to the agent of the context.

It is because indexicals have this descriptive meaning that their referent *can* vary from context of utterance to context of utterance. We can think of this meaning as a function from context of utterance to referent, or, since Kaplan thinks that names are directly referential and hence that the content of an indexical *is* its referent, as a function from context of utterance to content.

Yet importantly, this referent-determining descriptive meaning is no part of what gets said when a sentence containing an indexical is uttered; that is, it is no part of the *content* of an indexical. When Mandela utters *I am angry* he does not utter a sentence with the same content as the sentence *the agent of this context is angry*. If he *did* then what he says would be true even if *he* were not angry and some other angry person were speaking. But it would not be. What Mandela says when he utters *I am angry* is not true in any context of evaluation in which he is not angry. It follows that indexicals must have more than one kind of meaning. There is the content, and there is something else, the descriptive meaning that determines the content. Kaplan calls this second kind of meaning *character* and for him character plays two roles: it is the aspect of meaning that determines the content of an indexical, given a context of utterance, and it is the part of the meaning that a speaker must know in order to count as competent with the word. Thus on this view the content of an expression is different from its character. The content of *I*, for example, is always an agent. The character (the thing that a speaker must know to count as competent with the expression) is a rule for determining that content given a context of utterance: the content of *I* is always the agent of the context of utterance. So on Kaplan's picture of indexicals, character and content are distinct.

These distinctions between different kinds of meaning will be important in Sections 2.3 and 6.5. In Section 6.5 they will be used to defend truth in virtue of meaning against objections due to Harman and Putnam, and in 2.3 they will be used to distinguish sentences which are true in virtue of meaning from those which express necessary truths. But first I wish to draw attention to one other relevant feature of Kripke's and Kaplan's work.

The contingent analytic

The work of Kaplan and Kripke on rigid designation and direct reference raised the issues of the necessary a posteriori, contingent a priori, and of course, the contingent analytic. Kaplan's examples of the contingent analytic involve indexicals and his invented operator *dthat*:

(D1) I am here now

(D2) α = dthat [α]

(D3) I exist.

(D4) $\Phi \leftrightarrow$ actually, now Φ

Dthat takes a description, α, and forms a directly referential singular term. As with an indexical, the description is part of the character of the resulting term, but it is no part of the content. For example *dthat[the shortest spy]*, used in a context in which Austin is the shortest spy, refers to Austin, but unlike the description *the shortest spy* its content is also just that referent.

Kaplan's diagnosis of what these examples have in common is that they are all logical truths of the logic of demonstratives. Logical truth in the logic of demonstratives is truth in every admissible context of every LD-structure. We can think of such a structure as involving a set of circumstances of evaluation (a set of possible worlds) and a number of possible contexts of utterance, with features such as an agent, a time, place and a circumstance of evaluation. Agents must be located at the time and place of the context in the circumstance of evaluation of the context. (This restriction is essential for Kaplan's explanation of the status of the contingent analytic.) An occurrence of a sentence will be true with respect to a context if and only if the content it expresses in that context is true in the circumstance of evaluation of that context. A sentence is true in a structure if it is true with respect to every context in the structure, and a logical truth if it is true in every structure. The informal, intuitive idea is that a logical truth of the logic of demonstratives is a sentence that you could not utter falsely; no matter what the context of utterance, the sentence will come out true.

I am here now, for example, will be true with respect to a context just in case the agent of the context is at the place and time of the context in the circumstance of evaluation of the context. Now it is a constraint on being a context that this is the case. So the sentence will come out true with respect to every context in every structure, and this is what it is to be a truth of the logic of demonstratives. Kaplan thinks that this captures the sense in which *I am here now* is "deeply, and in some sense, . . . universally, true" (1989*b*: 509). Yet '□ (I am here now)' is *not* a logical truth of the logic of demonstratives, for there are contexts (most of them) in which the content expressed by the sentence '□ I am here now' is not true. Though the truth of 'I am here now' is, in some sense, guaranteed by its meaning, I need not have been here now; I might have been somewhere else.

2.3 TRUTH IN VIRTUE OF REFERENCE DETERMINER

In this section I will argue that the meaning in 'true in virtue of meaning' is not content but reference determiner (with respect to expressions in which content and reference determiner are identical it will be content too.) Moreover, that the world in the two-factor story is not necessarily the context of evaluation but may also be context of utterance or a different kind of context that I will call *context of introduction*.[5]

It is a familiar thought from Frege that the meaning of a sentence is determined by the meaning of its parts. Suppose that the sentence meaning which plays a role in the two-factor story is also determined by the meaning of the sentence's constituent expressions. Then, in a synthetic sentence, we might expect that we could vary the value (extension) of a subexpression in two ways: by varying the meaning of the expression, and by varying the way the world is.

But now observe that if we assumed that by *meaning* here we mean the *content* of the expression, the two-factor story breaks down for some expressions. It works fine for an expression like *bachelor*: as it happens, *bachelor* applies to Chris Mole. If *bachelor* had meant something different, like *unmarried woman* it would not have applied to him. And if the world had been different and Chris had married last week, it would not have applied to him then either.

But the two-factor story does not work for a directly referential expression like *Hesperus*. Yes, if *Hesperus* had meant Mars, it would apply to Mars and not to Venus. But this is a strange thing to say, because the way you get *Hesperus* to mean Mars is by changing the *referent*. Here, as Kaplan noted, it is the referent that determines the content and not the world and content which together determine the referent. And the other aspect of the story fails completely: you cannot hold the meaning of *Hesperus* fixed and change the referent by changing the world of evaluation. *Hesperus* denotes Venus with respect to all contexts of evaluation—it is a rigid designator.

The two-factor story in terms of content and context of evaluation fails for indexical directly referential terms too. The content of *I* varies given the context of utterance, so suppose we have settled the context of utterance and hence settled the content. Let's say the referent of *I* in that context is Gil Harman. Then, yes, changing the content of *I* can change the referent, but, as in the case of names, this is only because in order to change the content of *I* you have to change the referent and

---

[5] Kaplan had some useful terminology for showing when he was referring to contexts of evaluation and when to contexts of utterance. He called the former *circumstances (of evaluation)* and the later *contexts (of utterance)*. The word *context* was thus reserved for contexts of utterance. I like this convention but I've run out of appropriate 'c'-words for naming world-states. Hence *context* of evaluation, *context* of utterance, *context* of introduction.

not because the content of *I* determines its referent together with the world of evaluation. The world of evaluation is completely irrelevant to determining the referent of *I*, as is brought out by the fact that if we hold the content of *I* fixed and vary the world of evaluation, this will have no effect at all on its referent.

On the other hand, the reference determiner for *I* says that *I* always refers to the speaker or writer of the context of utterance. If by *meaning* we mean reference determiner, and by *world* we mean context of utterance, then there is a real two-factor story to be told: there were two things that made it the case that this particular use of *I* referred to Gil Harman. The first is the reference determiner: if *I* referred to the time of the utterance then *I* would not have referred to Gil Harman but to (say) 10 a.m. The second is the context of utterance. If it had been Paul that uttered *I* then it would have referred to Paul.

A similar thing can be said about names like *Hesperus*, though this time the salient world state is the state when the word is introduced to the language in the first place, which I will call the *context of introduction*. *Hesperus* refers to Hesperus and there are two things that go into making this the case: the reference determiner for *Hesperus* and the context of introduction. If the reference determiner of *Hesperus* were expressed by the description *the red planet* then *Hesperus* would refer to Mars. But if we hold the reference determiner fixed as the condition expressed by *the bright speck on the horizon in the morning on such and such an evening* but change the context of introduction so that Mars is the bright speck that the introducer can see, then the word *Hesperus* would refer to Mars.[6]

Moreover, the expressions for which a two-factor story can be told in terms of content are, I conjecture, the expressions for which content and reference-determiner coincide. The above considerations lead me to the following two thoughts:

(1) The meaning which plays a role in the two-factor story is *reference determiner*.

---

[6] It seems to me that the paradigm cases of expressions whose referents are functions of the context of introduction are names and natural kind terms and that most other expressions are not sensitive to context of introduction at all. Even if someone introduced the word *I* in a certain context of introduction using the description *the utterer of the context of utterance*, it does not follow that the meaning of *I* depends on who fulfilled the condition expressed by that description in the context of introduction. The reference determiner for *I* is a different kind of condition, in that it has different sensitivities: it is sensitive to context of utterance rather than to context of introduction. See §5.2 for more on this topic.

(2) The world state which plays a role in the two-factor story can be the context of evaluation (in the case of *bachelor* (and in fact, most predicates)) or the context of utterance (in the case of *I*, and other indexicals and demonstratives) or the context of introduction (in the case of directly referential words with constant character (in Kaplan's sense here) like names.)*

Given (1) and (2) it seems wise to revise my M-function to a function M' which takes account of the fact that different kinds of world-state can play a role in determining reference and truth. We can think of M' as a quintuple, consisting of three contexts c_i (the context of introduction), c_u (the context of utterance), c_e, (the context of evaluation) and a reference determiner, R, as arguments, and a value (an object, a set of objects or a truth-value):

$$\langle c_i, c_u, c_e, R, V \rangle$$

With this richer understanding of the two-factor story we can see why not all non-indexical sentences which express necessary propositions, such as *Hesperus is Phosphorus* are true in virtue of meaning, in the sense given in Section 2. Though the truth of the sentence is fully-determined by the arguments c_i and R, varying the argument c_i can vary the value of the M-function. Hence the truth-value of the sentence is not fully-determined by the R-value alone and the sentence is not true in virtue of meaning, even though it expresses a necessary truth.

One more problem needs to be addressed. On the account given so far, the sentence *I am here now* is not true in virtue of meaning, since varying the context of evaluation can make it false.[7] But we were trying to develop an account on which *I am here now* comes out true in virtue of meaning. The solution to this problem was provided by Kaplan. Kaplan allows that contexts of utterance *contain* their own contexts of evaluation, and insists that the agent is always located at the place and time of the utterance in that context of evaluation. A context of utterance is then a quadruple

$$\langle a, p, t, w \rangle$$

---

* The *or* here is intended inclusively.

[7] This problem is similar to that faced by the initial 'double indexing' attempts to deal with indexicals.

in which the agent will be located at the place and time and in the world of evaluation of the context. The restriction is motivated by Kaplan's observation that a sentence is true iff it is true with respect to the context of evaluation in which it is uttered.

Definition 5 (context of utterance) *A context of utterance is a quadruple* $\langle a, p, t, w \rangle$ *in which a is an agent, p is a place, t is a time and w is a possible world in which a is located at t in p.*

Hence we will make one more adjustment and replace the M'-function with the M^*-function. M^* is a function from reference determiner, context of utterance and context of introduction to truth-value, that is, it is the set of all quadruples $\langle c_i, c_u, R, V \rangle$. A sentence is true with respect to a context of introduction, c_i, and a context of utterance, c_u, just in case, once the referent of any indexical terms has been fixed by c_u, and the referent of any names and natural kind terms has been fixed by c_i, the sentence is true *with respect to the context of evaluation of* c_u. A sentence is true in virtue of meaning just in case its reference determiner fully-determines the value 'true'—that is, just in case for all pairs of contexts of introduction and contexts of utterance, the sentence is true at the context of evaluation of the context of utterance (i.e. w in the quadruple $\langle a, p, t, w \rangle$).

Definition 6 (Truth in Virtue of Meaning (modal definition)) *A sentence S is true in virtue of meaning just in case for all pairs of context of introduction and context of utterance, the proposition expressed by S with respect to those contexts is true in the context of evaluation.*

Contraposing, a sentence is *not* true in virtue of meaning just in case there exists some pair of context of introduction and context of utterance such that the content which the sentence expresses with respect to that pair is false at the context of evaluation contained in the context of utterance.

I am here now will be true in virtue of meaning, for example, because according to the reference determiners for *I, here* and *now*, these expressions refer to the agent (c_A), location (c_T) and time of the context of utterance (c_T.) No expression in the sentence has a reference determiner which is sensitive to context of introduction, so we need not consider that. The entire sentence will be true just in case the referent of *I* is located at the referent of *here* at the time picked out by *now* in the world of evaluation c_W. Since only contexts of utterance in which the agent is located at the location of c_u at the time of the c_u in the world of evaluation of c_u are genuine, the sentence is always true with respect to that context of evaluation. Hence the truth-value of the sentence is fully-determined to be true by its reference determiner.

A sentence like *snow is white*, however, remains synthetic, since with respect to any pair of context of introduction, c_i and context of utterance $\langle a, p, t, w \rangle$ in which w is a world where snow is black (and not white), the sentence will be false. Hence the reference determiner of *snow is white* does not fully-determine its truth-value.

2.4 EXAMPLES OF ANALYTIC TRUTHS

At this point it might be illuminating to look at some more examples of sentences which do, and do not, have their truth-values fully determined by their reference determiners.[8] But in providing these examples I face two problems. The first is that which sentences are true in virtue of meaning depends on what the sentences mean (what their reference determiners are), and this in turn depends on what the reference determiners of their component expressions are. But for many interesting kinds of expression, such as names, indexicals, natural kind terms, quantifiers and descriptions, this is controversial. Two dimensionalists like Jackson and Chalmers think that natural kind terms have reference determiners which are sensitive to context of utterance. (e.g. my twin on Twin Earth speaks English but in her context of utterance the English word *water* picks out $X_Y Z$ instead of H_2O.) (Jackson 1998; Chalmers 2004). Others, such as Soames, think that the English *water* refers to H_2O regardless of the context of utterance. Traditional Fregeans think that the referent of a name is determined by a descriptive content known to the speaker, whereas direct reference theorists think that the referent of a name is standardly determined by a mechanism unknown to the speaker and which is no part of the name's content. Some hold that the extension of a unary quantifier is a set of sets, others that it is a Second-order property. Since my aim is merely to clarify the notion of truth in virtue of meaning, I intend to tackle this problem by force. I will assume a theory (often a simplified version of my current favorite theory) of reference determination for the different kinds of expression, and show which sentences would turn out to be true in virtue of meaning on

---

[8] If you are a certain kind of philosopher it might also be illuminating to examine the extension of Kaplan's formal framework in Appendix A .

those assumptions. Repeating the exercise with his own favorite theories
of reference determination is left as an exercise for the reader.

2nd problem

The second problem is that, even if we have settled on, say, a Millian
conception of names, I do not really know how the referent of, say,
Hesperus was determined, since it is not required of me as a competent
speaker. So where I don't know the real story, I'm just going to make one
up. (Suppose someone in 1242 pointed to Hesperus and said *Let's call
that 'Hesperus'* etc . . .) So what follows are the stipulations about kinds
of reference determiners for kinds of expressions, and some specific
reference determiners for specific expressions. Perhaps the next section
contains nothing but elaborate fiction, but that would be okay, since the
the aim of the examples that follow is clarificatory, and the assumptions
are merely being used to provide some examples of sentences that would
be true in virtue of meaning, if the assumptions were true.

Names (Hesperus, Phosphorus, Mohammed Ali, Cassius Clay):

I will assume that names are directly referential. One gives a name a
meaning, and hence introduces it to a language, by giving it a referent.
This can be done using a description (e.g. *Let 'Hesperus' refer to the
evening star.*) The referent of the name is then whatever single object
falls under this description in the context of introduction, so long as
there is one, and if there is not then the expression is meaningless. The
name will refer to that object regardless of the agent, time or place
specified in the context of utterance (in this names are unlike indexicals)
and regardless of the context of evaluation (names are rigid designators).
I will assume that the name *Hesperus* was introduced when someone
pointed to a bright speck near the horizon one evening and said: *Let's
call that bright speck 'Hesperus'*. *Hesperus* thus refers to whatever (if
anything) the baptiser demonstrated whilst saying this in the context of
introduction. The story for *Phosphorus* is similar, except that the baptiser
was pointing at a bright speck in the sky one *morning*. *Phosphorus* thus
refers to whatever (if anything) it was the baptiser was pointing to in the
context of introduction for *Phosphorus*. I will also consider two more
names that will be important in the discussion of the epistemic status
of analytic sentences. We'll stipulate, in order to have a clear example,
that the name *Cassius Clay* was introduced when Cassius Clay's parents
baptised him (*Let's call him* (pointing) *'Cassius Clay'.*) The referent of
Mohammed Ali was introduced in a slightly different way, when Elijah
Muhammad, the leader of the Nation of Islam, said *Let's use 'Mohammed*

Ali' to name Cassius Clay. Mohammed Ali thus refers to whatever object, if any, *Cassius Clay* refers to.

Pure Descriptions (the shortest spy):

Like the truth-value of a sentence, the referent of a description will depend on the referents of its parts. In natural languages there are descriptions that contain names (*the father of Anais and Josh*) and descriptions that contain indexicals (*the closest cafe to here*), and in these cases the referent of the description will be sensitive to the context of introduction and the context of utterance (in addition to the context of evaluation) respectively. But for now I am interested in a simpler kind of description and when I talk about a pure description I will mean a complex singular term whose referent is fully-determined by its reference determiner and the context of evaluation. I will assume that *the shortest spy* is such a description.

Purely Descriptive Predicates (bachelor):

What I will call *purely descriptive predicates* work the way you might once intuitively have thought that all predicates work. There is a set of properties associated with the predicate, and whether the predicate applies to an object is determined by whether or not the object has those properties in the context of evaluation. What makes them *pure* is that—like pure descriptions—their referent is fully-determined by their reference determiner and the context of evaluation.[9] I will assume that *bachelor* is a purely descriptive predicate and that for all x, *bachelor* applies to x just in case x has the property of being a man and also the property of being unmarried, in the context of evaluation. To keep things simple I am going to ignore any complications that might arise from the fact that *man* could be a natural kind term.

Simple Natural Kind Predicates (water):

Again, to avoid unnecessary complications, I will assume that a natural kind predicate is introduced when someone points at a sample of the kind and says *Let's use the word 'N' to refer to any substances that have the same underlying structure as that stuff.* If all goes well with the baptism

---

[9] Once again, it is not *obvious* that there are any such predicates in natural languages. Perhaps all natural language predicates smuggle in some indexical or natural kind-style element, making context of utterance or context of evaluation relevant to determining referent.

and there really is just a single chemical substance there, then 'N' will apply to a sample of something just in case, in the context of evaluation, it is a sample of that same stuff that was pointed out in the context of introduction. We will assume that *water* is of this kind. The extension of *water* is thus sensitive to context of introduction (because it could have been a sample of $X_Y Z$ at the baptism) and sensitive to context of evaluation, (because that stuff in your glass now could be vodka) but insensitive to the identity of the agent, time or place of the context of utterance.

Complex Natural Kind Predicates ($H_2 0$)

These have reference determiners which are a bit like descriptive predicates in one way—whether or not '$H_2 0$' applies to an object is a matter of whether, in the world of evaluation, it has certain properties, like the property of being a molecule made of two hydrogen atoms and an oxygen atom—but the reference determiner of a complex natural kind predicate is also sensitive to context of introduction. I will suppose that *hydrogen* was introduced when someone pointed to a sample and said *Let's call stuff that has the same chemical make up as that 'hydrogen.'* Now if that is the reference determiner for *hydrogen* then the reference of *hydrogen* will vary with context of introduction. If the sample had really been (what we call) lithium then *hydrogen* would have referred to lithium. Complex natural kind predicates differ from purely descriptive predicates in that the properties a sample needs to have in order to fall under the predicate may vary with context of *introduction*. And this means that the referent may vary with context of introduction. In a world where that initial sample was lithium and not hydrogen, '$H_2 0$' applies to samples of dilithium oxide ($Li_2 O$), not samples of water.

Singular Indexicals (I, here):

Indexicals work as Kaplan suggests in "Demonstratives." The reference determiner for *I* is something like: for all x, *I* refers to x iff x is the agent of the context of utterance. Thus the referent of *I* depends on the context of utterance. Indexicals are rigid designators (insensitive to context of evaluation) and, I will assume, insensitive to context of introduction.

Truth-functional Connectives (if . . . then, $\wedge$):

We can think of truth-functional connectives like '$\wedge$' as applying to ordered n-tuples of truth values—the extensions of sentences. The extension of a truth-functional connective is then the set of n-tuples of truth-functions which it applies to, for example, '$\wedge$' applies to a pair of truth-values in case they are both true. '$\wedge$' is a kind of super-duper-rigid designator; its extension is the same regardless of context of evaluation, or context of utterance, or context of introduction—changing the environment just won't make it apply to something else. But the reference determiner of sentence containing '$\wedge$' (a compound expression) probably will be sensitive to different contexts, because other expressions in the sentence will be; a sentence of the form $\ulcorner S \wedge T \urcorner$ is true just in case the reference determiner of S and the reference determiner of T both give the value 'true' at the context of evaluation. The truth-value of a conjunctive sentence such as *I am tired $\wedge$ Hesperus is a planet* will depend on both the context of utterance and the context of introduction for *Hesperus*. Other n-ary truth-functions will be treated in the same way.

Quantifiers (all, some):

We will suppose that the extension of a quantifier is a relation on sets.[10] In particular *all* has its reference determined by the condition *being an ordered pair of sets such that the first is a subset of the second*, and *some* has its reference determined by the condition *being an ordered pair of sets with non-empty intersection*. The reference determiner of a quantifier picks out the same pairs of sets with respect to every context of evaluation, or indeed any other context. However the extension of a quantified *sentence* may change depending on the context of evaluation, since other expressions in the sentence may pick out different sets on different occasions. In a context of evaluation in which the set of spies, S_1, is a subset of the set of women, W_1, *all* applies to the ordered pair $\langle S_1, W_1 \rangle$. But in a context of evaluation in which some spies are male, the set of all spies will be a different set, say S_2 one which is not a subset of W_1 and so *all* does not apply to $\langle S_2, W_1 \rangle$ (even though the original pair $\langle S_1, W_1 \rangle$ remains in the extension of *all*.) For simplicity we will assume that *all* is not sensitive to changes in the agent, time or place of the context of utterance.

Extensionless Expressions:

It is not always natural to think of expressions as having extensions. While some adjectives can be thought of as picking out a set of objects, e.g. *red* could be thought of as having the set of red things as its extension, adjectives such as *alleged* in *alleged communist* are different. What exactly would the set of *alleged* things be? *Alleged* is more naturally

---

[10] See (Glanzberg 2006) for more about this approach to quantification.

thought of as systematically modifying the reference determiners of the expressions it is attached to. Whereas *communist* might have as its extension the set of objects which meet condition C, *alleged communist* has as its extension the set of objects which meet a different condition: being alleged to meet condition C—an entirely different set whose intersection with the original set could be null.

Example sentences

With these assumptions made, we can take a look at some sample sentences:

(2.1) All bachelors are bachelors.

This sentence is true in virtue of meaning. To see why we consider whether it is true, and whether we can make it false by varying either the context of introduction, or the context of utterance. The sentence is true, since the set of bachelors is a subset of the set of bachelors (though not a proper subset.) By assumption, none of the expressions in the sentence have reference determiners which are sensitive to the identity of the agent, time or place of the context of utterance, (they are not indexicals and we are assuming that quantifiers are not sensitive to these things), or to context of introduction (there are no names or natural kind terms in the sentence.) However, as we noted above, the extension of the quantifier *all* will not vary with context of evaluation, but the extension of the component expression *bachelor* does; given a context of evaluation where Fred and Sid are unmarried men, *bachelor* applies to them, but given a context of evaluation in which Fred got hitched and Sid has had a sex change, *bachelor* does not. Nevertheless, despite the fact that the referents of at least these component expressions vary with context of evaluation, the extension (truth-value) of the sentence does not. How can this be? Although the extensions of the first and second occurrences of *bachelor* vary from world to world, they (of course) never vary in such a way as to make it the case that the two occurrences have different extensions.[11] So the extension of the first occurrence of *bachelor* is *always* a subset of the extension of the second occurrence of *bachelor* since it is always identical to it, and hence though the

---

[11]   I do not mean to make the empirical claim that two occurrences of the same syntactic word type in a sentence must always have the same interpretation, only that given the way I am in fact interpreting *all bachelors are bachelors*, both occurrences of *bachelor* have the same intension.

extension of the quantifier *all* varies with context of evaluation, it always contains whatever pair consists of the extensions of the first and second occurrences of *bachelor*. We have now seen that (2.1) is true and that varying the contexts of introduction and utterance does not affect the truth-value of the sentence and so the truth-value of the sentence is fully-determined by its reference determiner, which is to say that it is true in virtue of meaning.

(2.2) All bachelors are men.

This sentence is true in virtue of meaning too. The reasoning is as above except that we appeal to the fact that although the extensions of *bachelor* and *men* both vary with context of evaluation, the extension of *bachelor* is always a subset of that of *men*. This is a consequence of my assumption that *bachelor* applied to all and only things that had the property of being men and the property of being unmarried.

(2.3) Snow is white.

We noted in Section 2.3 that (2.3) is not true in virtue of meaning, since there are contexts of evaluation (contained in admissible contexts of utterance) for which it is false, e.g. any $\langle a, p, t, w_b \rangle$, where w_b is a possible world in which snow is black.

(2.4) Hesperus is Hesperus.

Sentence (2.4) is not true in virtue of meaning, though it does possess an interestingly similar property. Though the reference determiner of *Hesperus* is not an indexical, and is not even sensitive to changes in the context of evaluation (it is a rigid designator), consider a context of introduction in which what had seemed to be a bright spot near the horizon was really an illusion—the speaker only thought he could see such a thing because of a problem with his perceptual cognition (maybe Bugs Bunny bashed him on the head and he is seeing stars). Then nothing fits the reference determiner for *Hesperus* and so the expression is meaningless.[12] And if *Hesperus* is meaningless, then (2.4) is not true. Nevertheless, *Hesperus is Hesperus* does have a property very like truth in virtue of meaning—namely, it will be true whenever its reference determiners succeed in picking something out, as the reference determiners for *Hesperus* and *Hesperus* are (of course) identical, and so pick out the same objects with respect to all contexts. All that is required

---

[12] This is a result of the stipulation above.

for the truth of *Hesperus is Hesperus* with respect to a pair of contexts c_i, c_u is that *Hesperus* picks out an object which is identical, in the context of evaluation to the referent of *Hesperus* and this is guaranteed by the reference determiners so long as the names refer. Can we shore up the *Hesperus is Hesperus* example to get a sentence that is true in virtue of meaning? What about (2.5)?

(2.5) If Hesperus exists, then Hesperus is Hesperus.

This whole sentence will be true if there is no context of evaluation in which the antecedent is true and the consequent is not (we know this from thinking about the reference determiner for the conditional.) The only way the consequent could fail to be true is if nothing met the condition provided by the reference determiner for *Hesperus* in the context of introduction (as in the illusion case.) But if that is the case then *if Hesperus exists* doesn't mean anything either. If the possible failure of *Hesperus* to refer is what keeps *Hesperus is Hesperus* from being true in virtue of meaning then we should not think that *if Hesperus exists, Hesperus is Hesperus* fares any better.

(2.6) The shortest spy is the shortest spy.

The case of (2.6) is similar to that of (2.4), though there are two main differences. The first is that the reference determiner of the description *the shortest spy* is sensitive to changes in the context of evaluation, rather than to changes in the context of introduction (unlike that of *Hesperus*). Nevertheless the first and second occurrences of the description will always pick out the same object with respect to any one context of evaluation. The second difference is that *the shortest spy* is a contentful expression even if it has no referent, since, unlike the directly referential expression *Hesperus*, its sense is not determined by its referent, but rather it is composed of meaningful parts. The central aspects of the case are the same however: though the sentence contains no indexicals and is insensitive to context of introduction, it will be true in circumstances of evaluation in which the referent of the singular terms exists, but not in those in which it does not. The fact that *the shortest spy* is meaningful even when it fails to refer has the consequence that the conditional sentence *is* true in virtue of meaning.

(2.7) If there is a shortest spy, then the shortest spy is the shortest spy.

(2.8) Hesperus is Phosphorus.

We noted previously that (2.4) is not true in virtue of meaning, since varying the context of introduction can result in *Hesperus* and *Phosphorus* referring to *different* objects. For this reason, *Hesperus is Phosphorus* is not even nearly true in virtue of meaning (as *Hesperus is Hesperus* is.) But the reason that we cannot shore the case up in this way is not just that *Hesperus* and *Phosphorus* are different *words*. Consider an identity sentence containing our specially interlocked names:

(2.9) Cassius Clay is Mohammed Ali.

This sentence is not true in virtue of meaning, just as *Hesperus is Hesperus* is not, but its *modal profile* has more in common with that sentence than with *Hesperus is Phosphorus*. *Cassius Clay is Mohammed Ali* only fails to be true when the names have no referent. There is no way, given these reference determiners, to assign them *different* referents, as we can with *Hesperus is Phosphorus*.

As noted in the previous section, the truth of (2.10)

(2.10) I am here now.

is fully-determined by its reference determiner.

(2.11) Everything that is (an instance of) water is (an instance of) water.

This sentence has a similar status to *Hesperus is Hesperus*. Should the baptism have failed, the sentence will be meaningless. But within a context of evaluation, the predicates *is (an instance of) water* and *is (an instance of) water* will pick out the same things (of course). Varying the context of introduction (to say, Twin Earth) can make the predicates pick out something different ($X_Y Z$) in every context of evaluation, but the two predicates will still pick out the same objects. So the sentence is not true in virtue of meaning, but it will have the similar property of being true if its reference determiners pick out something.

(2.12) All instances of water are instances of H_2O.

This sentence is, unsurprisingly, not true in virtue of meaning, but neither is it such that with respect to any context of introduction and context of utterance pairs in which *water* and 'H_2O' refer it will be true. The reference determiner for water says that it will apply to anything that has the same underlying chemical make-up as the initial sample. Similarly for *hydrogen, oxygen* etc. (I'm assuming that 'H_2O' is shorthand for something like *a molecule consisting of two hydrogen and one oxygen atom*.) Now suppose that *water* is introduced in a context of introduction in which the sample is (what we call) H_2O. Then *water* will apply to all and only samples of H_2O in all contexts of evaluation. If *hydrogen* is introduced using a sample of (what we call) hydrogen, (similarly for *oxygen*) then all is well and 'H_2O' will apply to all and only samples of (what we call) H_2O in all contexts of evaluation. Given those contexts of introduction, the sentence will express a necessary proposition. But consider a more deviant context of introduction for *hydrogen* that makes it refer to lithium. Then *all instances of water are instances of H_2O* is false (no instances of water are instances of dilithium oxide), so the sentence is not true in virtue of meaning.

Table 2.1. Examples

True in Virtue of Meaning	True if Referring	Not (True in Virtue of Meaning)
All bachelors are bachelors	Hesperus is Hesperus	Snow is white
If there is a shortest spy then the shortest spy is the shortest spy	If Hesperus exists, then Hesperus is Hesperus	Hesperus is Phosphorus
	Cassius Clay is Mohammed Ali	
	The shortest spy is the shortest spy	
All bachelors are male		
	Everything that is an (instance of) water is (an instance) of water	
I am here now		Everything that is an (instance of) water is an (instance of) H_2O

2.5 TWO OBJECTIONS AND A SERIOUS PROBLEM

One might worry about whether the notion of truth in virtue of reference determiner described here can really be the notion of truth in virtue of meaning which underlies analyticity. Here are two objections.

The first objection is based on the observation that reference determiners are not always *meanings*. The reference determiner for a name, for example, is no part of the *meaning* of a name; it is no part of what gets said when a sentence containing a name is uttered, and a competent speaker can be completely oblivious to the manner in which the referent was determined. Rather the reference determiner for a name belongs to what Kaplan calls *metasemantics*. (1989b) Facts about reference determiners are facts about how the meanings of words get fixed, not meaning facts themselves. So following Kaplan we should say that the fact that the reference of *Hesperus* was determined by the description *the morning star* belongs with other metalinguistic facts such as:

. . . the fact that *nauseous* used to mean *nauseating* but is coming to mean *nauseated*. (1989b: 574)

It does not belong with the real semantic facts which state what words mean, because the reference determiners of names are not their meanings. So truth in virtue of reference determiner, whatever it is, is not really truth in virtue of meaning, and so it isn't really analyticity.

The second objection is epistemological in character. Even if truth in virtue of reference determiner were a kind of truth in virtue of meaning, it would not be analyticity. Analytic sentences are supposed to be knowable by anyone who understands them, but a speaker can be competent with *Mohammed Ali* without knowing how its referent is determined. So it seems that for such a speaker *Mohammed Ali is Cassius Clay* has just the same status as *Hesperus is Phosphorus* does. (Simplifying for a moment to ignore the case in which 'Cassius Clay' has no referent) the sentence comes out as true in virtue of reference determiner, but it has no hope of meeting any kind of special epistemic condition. So truth in virtue of reference determiner is not analyticity.

Basically, I agree with both of these objections. The reference determiner for an expression is sometimes a part of the meaning and sometimes not. In the case of a name it is not. In the case of an indexical such as *I* it is. But the discovery that the reference determiner of a word need not be part of the meaning of the word was a huge step forwards in the philosophy of language and it was a discovery that still lay in the future during much of the debate over the analytic/synthetic distinction. I believe that when supporters of the analytic/synthetic distinction spoke of truth in virtue of meaning they had truth in virtue of reference determiner in mind. They didn't know enough to distinguish reference determination from content, or from character, so they weren't more specific about what kind of meaning they were talking about. They were content to call it *meaning* because they were not aware of the pressures that have caused us to refrain from calling it meaning in some cases (it is not part of the content, speakers need not be aware of it.) This is why they referred to the phenomenon they were talking about as 'truth in virtue of *meaning*.' We are aware of these pressures and so may want to refrain from referring to it as 'truth-in-virtue-of-meaning.' This is not to say that we are not talking about exactly the same phenomenon.

I also agree with the second point: not all sentences that are true in virtue of reference determiner are going to have the epistemic properties traditionally attributed to analytic sentences. If we wanted to put this more catchily we might call it the *analytic a posteriori*. But it is only because philosophers conflated character and reference determiner that they thought that sentences that were true in virtue of meaning would be sentences that would grant knowledge to anyone who understood them. The very sketchy reasoning went something as follows: (P1) sentence A is true because of what it means. (P2) But any competent speaker knows what sentence A means, so (C) should he not be able to tell that it is true? But even if the other holes in this 'argument' can be filled, it equivocates on the word *meaning*. *Meaning* in premise 1 refers to reference determiner, *meaning* in premise 2 refers to character (the meaning that a speaker has to know to be competent.) So we shouldn't think that a sentence that is true in virtue of meaning will automatically be such that anyone who understands it can know that it is true. Nonetheless, *sometimes character and reference determiner coincide*, for example with descriptions and indexicals. Where this happens it might turn out that we can get sentences with special epistemic properties.

A left-over Problem:

But one serious objection to the definition of truth in virtue of meaning given and illustrated in this chapter remains. This chapter proposed a solution to a general problem raised at the end of Chapter 1. The general problem was that the account presented appeared to suggest that the notion of an analytic sentence was really just the notion of a sentence which expresses a necessary truth. This was bad because we have examples of sentences which are analytic, though they express contingent truths and two kinds of examples of sentences which express necessary truths though they are not analytic. By equating the meaning referred to in *truth in virtue of meaning* with reference determiner, rather than content, we have avoided the general problem and *two* of the three specific problems: that is we have clearly distinguished the properties of analyticity and expressing a necessary truth (the general problem) and, in particular, I explained the details of how *I am here now* comes to be analytic, and how *Hesperus is Phosphorus* fails to be. But what about substantive necessities, such as the one in my fictional example *the evening star is the morning star*? Suppose, just for the sake of the example, that *the evening star is the morning star* is an identity statement involving two pure descriptions, and that, as our modal realist believed, it expresses a necessary truth. Then the sentence contains no expressions which are sensitive to context of introduction and no expressions which are sensitive to context of utterance. And so—since it expresses a necessary truth—it always expresses a proposition which is true with respect to all contexts of evaluation; its reference determiner *fully determines* the truth-value true. And *that* is still the wrong result.

3

Beyond Modality

3.1 THE PROBLEM

In the previous chapter I gave the following modal definition of truth in virtue of meaning:

Definition 7 (Truth in Virtue of Meaning (modal definition)) *A sentence S is true in virtue of meaning just in case for all pairs of context of introduction and context of utterance, the proposition expressed by S with respect to those contexts is true in the context of evaluation.*

There is a problem with the definition. There is a class of sentences which it classifies as true in virtue of meaning—and hence analytic—but which are, intuitively, *synthetic*. Consider, for example, any sentence which does not contain any expressions whose reference determiners are sensitive to context of utterance (such as indexicals or demonstratives) or sensitive to context of introduction (such as names, or natural kind terms) but which expresses a necessary truth. Some theists might think *there is a god* meets these criteria and our hyper-realist about possible worlds who thinks that the evening star is the morning star in every possible world is committed to a view that implies that *the evening star is the morning star* is such a sentence. If any of the sentences in the right-hand column of the table below express necessary truths, then all the sentences in the table will count as true in virtue of meaning on the definition above. But the sentences in the right-hand column are *synthetic*. So the definition is wrong.

Table 3.1. Two kinds of constant sentence

All bachelors are unmarried	the evening star is the morning star
I am here now	there is a god
Cassius Clay is Mohammed Ali	

This problem is a natural consequence of the fact that the definition of truth in virtue of meaning is given in modal terms; given that, it should not surprise us that it is vulnerable to the modal facts. If the proposition expressed by a sentence like *there is a god* or *the evening star is the morning star* turn out to be necessary—as a matter of substantive modal fact—then the sentence will count as true in virtue of meaning on the modal definition, even though, intuitively, it ought not to.

In this chapter I argue that we have run into a problem which besets recent semantic theory as a whole, not just the present account of analyticity: the familiar modal tools for analysing meaning—though undoubtedly powerful—are too coarse. I then propose a solution to this problem by presenting a refinement of the account developed so far.

3.2 SEMANTICS AND MODALITY

In the wake of the twentieth century it has become natural to reach for possible worlds when attempting to analyse or define semantic notions. Seminal work by Carnap, Montague, Lewis, Kripke, Kaplan, Stalnaker and others has provided a framework for thinking about semantic properties in terms of possible worlds and the basic notions from logic and set theory (Carnap 1958*b*; Lewis 1973; Montague 1974; Lewis 1976; Kripke 1980; Kaplan 1989*b*; Stalnaker 1999). But like all good theories, possible worlds accounts of semantic concepts are amenable to counterexample, and the counterexamples have been piling up since the early days. They have not instituted a full-scale stampede away from possible worlds semantics, but this is true in part because some have hoped that a refinement of the powerful possible worlds style accounts can avoid the counterexamples, and in part there hasn't been any very firm ground to stampede *to*.[1] What follows is a review of some semantic properties which have resisted analysis in modal terms. In the case of only two of them do we have a proposal about how they could be

[1]   Richmond Thomason writes: "We have not tried to disguise the fact that difficulties can be found with possible world semantics. But the worst of these, far from illustrating an unhealthy isolation from linguistic evidence, consists of a tension with this evidence. . . . On the other hand, possible worlds semantics has succeeded in producing solutions to semantic puzzles of long standing, in the form of generalisations of widely accepted mathematical theories. In view of this achievement, and taking into account the theoretical attention the topic is now receiving, the problems arising with awareness cannot be said to justify abandoning the framework, at least until a better one has been proposed." (1974: 56)

analysed instead. None of them is a knock-down counterexample, but together they add weight to the case for seeking an alternative way to think about meanings.

3.2.1 Direct Reference

On Kaplan's view in *Demonstratives*, names and indexicals are directly referential and, as a consequence, the referent of a name or indexical is insensitive to the world in a certain way; regardless of the context of *evaluation* the name will refer to the same object. Following Kripke, we call this property—the modal property which is a consequence of direct reference—*rigidity*, and terms which have this property *rigid designators*.

The fact that names are rigid designators is explained by the fact that they are directly referential. A directly referential term has no sense (and specifically no descriptive content) which might pick out a new referent relative to different worlds. Its only content is its referent and so, for want of an alternative, this object is the referent relative to every possible world.

> . . . the intuitive idea is not that of an expression which *turns out* to designate the same object in all possible circumstances, but an expression whose semantical *rules* provide *directly* that the referent in all possible circumstances is fixed to be the actual referent. In typical cases the semantical rules will do this only implicitly, by providing a way of determining the *actual* referent and no way of determining any other propositional component. (Kaplan 1989*b*: 493)

As a result, rigidity can act as a rough and ready test for direct reference. We know that *the shortest spy* is not directly referential because it is not rigid; it can refer to different people with respect to different contexts of evaluation. But the rigidity test is not perfect because it returns false positives; there are at least two kinds of expression which are rigid, even though they are not directly referential.

First, there are descriptions which pick out the same object in every possible world as a result of substantial modal facts. For example, the description *the sum of 2 and 4* refers to the number 6, regardless of the context of evaluation. The reason for this is not that it is directly referential. Number 6 satisfies the expression *the sum of 2 and 4* because it fits the criterion specified. It satisfies it with respect to every possible world because the number 6 is an object with unusual modal properties (they are not unusual for numbers, of course). Alternatively, suppose you are a modal realist who believes that Venus is the evening star in every

Table 3.2. Three kinds of rigid designator

directly referential	substantively rigid	rigidified
Hesperus	the evening star	dthat[the evening star]
π	the sum of 2 and 2	the actual sum of the angles of a triangle
God	the creator of the universe	the actual creator of the universe
I	the agent of this context	dthat[the agent of this context]

possible world. It would follow from your view that the description *the evening star* is rigid—it picks out Venus in every possible world—but then it would be a rigid designator as a result of substantial modal facts, not because it is directly referential. I will call such designators *substantively rigid designators.*

Second, there are rigidified descriptions, such as *the actual evening star*. The most common ways to rigidify descriptions are using an actuality operator, and by using Kaplan's operator *dthat*. Combined with a description α, $\ulcorner$ dthat[α] $\urcorner$ will be an expression which refers rigidly to the object which fits α in the actual world, though—at least on one of Kaplan's interpretations—its content is a complex composed of the contents of the operator and the description. Rigidified descriptions are rigid designators, but they are not directly referential, and they need not be rigid as a consequence of substantive (non-actual) modal facts.[2]

Kaplan emphasises the inability of the modal account to define direct reference:

> When we think in terms of possible worlds semantics, this fundamental distinction [between directly referential terms and rigid designators] becomes subliminal. This is because the style of the semantical rules obscures the distinction and makes it appear that directly referential terms differ from ordinary definite descriptions only in that the propositional component in the former case must be a *constant* function of circumstances. In actual fact, the referent, in a circumstance, of a directly referential term is simply *independent*

---

[2] Perhaps *the actual sum of 2 and 2* is rigid for *both* reasons: it contains a rigidifying operator, but even if it didn't, it would be rigid as a consequence of substantive modal fact. We might say its rigidity is over-determined. Certainly, it seems we should say that the two kinds of non-directly referential rigid designator are not exclusive.

of the circumstance and is no more a function (constant or otherwise) of circumstance, than my action is a function of your desires when I decide to do it whether you like it or not. (Kaplan 1989*b*: 497)

3.2.2 Content

Standard possible worlds accounts of content identify the content of an expression with its intension—a function from circumstances of evaluation (usually possible worlds, sometimes pairs of possible worlds and times) to the extension of the expression at that world. So, for example, the content of a predicate like *is a father* might be a function which maps each possible world to the set of fathers at that world, the content of a name like *Hesperus* is a function which maps each possible world to the object which is Hesperus at that world, and the content of a sentence like *snow is white* is a function which maps each world in which snow is white to the truth-value 'true', and each world in which it is not the case that snow is white to the truth-value 'false.' Equivalently, the intention of a sentence (the proposition it expresses) can be identified with a set of possible worlds—the set at which the sentence is true.

Jeff King (2005) identifies two different sources of dissatisfaction with this view. First of all, all sentences which express necessary truths have the same intension—the set of all possible worlds. (3.1)–(3.4), for example, are all taken to express the same proposition:

(3.1) Hesperus is Hesperus.

(3.2) $2 + 2 = 4$.

(3.3) Triangles have three sides.

(3.4) All bachelors are unmarried.

This is the wrong result and it has unfortunate consequences for propositional attitude reports, such as:

(3.5) John believes that $2 + 2 = 4$.

(3.6) John believes that Fermat's Last Theorem is true.

If we construe belief as a relation between epistemic agents and propositions, and belief ascriptions like those above as reporting such relations, then if (3.5) is true, so is (3.6), since on the view that propositions are sets of possible worlds, (3.5) and (3.6) report John as being in the belief relation to the *same* proposition.

(3.7) Mary believes that snow is white.

(3.8) Mary believes that snow is white and that Fermat's Last Theorem is true.

(3.9) $7 \times 8 = 62$

Moreover, anyone who believes a proposition—as reported in (3.7)—must believe the conjunction of the proposition with any necessary consequences of it—for example, as reported in (3.8)—since these propositions will be true at the same worlds. But it is plausible that belief distributes across conjunction, that is for example, if Mary believes that snow is white and grass is green, then Mary believes that snow is white, and Mary believes that grass is green. But now, on the possible worlds view of propositions, we are committed to the view that everyone believes all the necessary consequences of their beliefs. Moreover, since the impossible proposition has every proposition as a necessary consequence, anyone who believes it (e.g. anyone who has believed some false arithmetical proposition, such as (3.9)) believes every proposition. (Soames 1987: 198–9) This is another false consequence of identifying propositions with sets of possible worlds.

King's other reason for dissatisfaction with the modal characterisation of the content of sentences comes from thinking about direct reference again. Since the view that names and indexicals are directly referential implies views about their contents, it also has consequences for the contents of sentences containing names and indexicals. Kaplan proposed an alternative, more metaphysical picture, not just of the meanings of directly referential terms, but of the contents of sentences:

If I may wax metaphysical in order to fix an image, let us think of the vehicles of evaluation—the what-is-said in a given context—as propositions. Don't think of propositions as sets of possible worlds, but as structured entities looking something like the sentences which express them. For each occurrence of a singular term in a sentence there will be a corresponding constituent in the proposition expressed. [. . .] In general, the constituent of the proposition will be some sort of logical complex, constructed from the various attributes by logical composition. But in the case of a singular term which is directly referential, the constituent of the proposition is just the object itself. (Kaplan 1989*b*: 494)

And:

The distinction [between rigidity and being directly referential] that is obscured by the style of possible worlds semantics is dramatised by the structured propositions picture. That is part of the reason why I like it. (Kaplan 1989*b*: 497)

As King emphasises, while Kaplan is clear about the drawbacks of the modal picture, he is circumspect about his commitment to the structured propositions picture. Yet:

Many current direct reference theorists take the structured proposition account much more seriously. It *is* part of *their* theory in the sense that when they say that an expression is directly referential they are *literally* saying that it contributes its referent to the propositions expressed by sentences containing it. (King, 2005: 7)

3.2.3 Kaplanian Character

A third semantic notion that resists analysis in terms of possible worlds is character *in Kaplan's sense*. The Kaplanian character of an expression is—intuitively—a rule known to competent speakers which tells them, given the context in which an expression is uttered, what its content is.[3] The character of the indexical *I*, for example, is known to speakers and stipulates that the content of the expression is the agent of the context in which it is uttered. Within his two-dimensional modal logic, however, Kaplan has to make do with a modal version of K-character as a function from contexts of utterance to intensions, which are themselves functions from possible worlds to extensions. For example, the K-character of the indexical *I* becomes a function that maps contexts of utterance to constant functions from possible worlds to individuals, and the K-character of the whole sentence *I drink tea* becomes a function from contexts of utterance to a function which maps possible worlds in which the agent relative to that context of utterance drinks tea to the True, and possible worlds in which he does not drink tea to the False. Similarly, the character of ⌜ dthat[α] ⌝, for a description α, is a function which maps contexts of utterance to constant functions from possible worlds to the referent of α with respect to the context of utterance.

But now consider the character of *dthat[the sum of 2 and 4]* and the character of *dthat[the x: x = 6]*. Both the descriptions *the sum of 2 and 4* and *the x: x = 6* pick out the number 6 with respect to all contexts of utterance. So the character of both *dthat[the sum of 2 and 4]* and *dthat[the x: x = 6]* is a function which maps every context of utterance

---

[3] I will refer to character, understood Kaplan's way, as 'K-character' to distinguish it from character in the sense of what a speaker has to know to understand an expression, which is what I use *character* to express elsewhere in this book.

Table 3.3. Two kinds of K-character synonymy

K-character synonymy	modal K-character equivalence
I	dthat[the sum of 2 and 4]
me	dthat[the x: x = 6]
we	the sum of 2 and 4
us	the x: x = 6

to a constant function from possible worlds to the number 6. As far as the modal account is concerned, they have the same K-character. Even without a rival picture of character to jump to, we can see that the modal account has got it wrong. Intuitively, speakers do not follow the same rule in working out the content of *dthat[the x: x = 6]* as they do in working out the content of *dthat[the sum of 2 and 4]*. Similarly, since the descriptions *the sum of 2 and 4* and *the x: x = 6* are substantively rigid and contain no indexicals, they too share a single (modally construed) K-character. The modal account makes no distinction between these examples, and examples of genuine synonymy of K- character. It seems to me that *I* and *me* might well have the same K-character, since both are understood by speakers to pick out the agent of the context of utterance, and the same might be said for *we* and *us*.

Here again the problem of substantive necessity has appeared for the modal definition of a semantic concept.

3.2.4 Reference Determiner Synonymy

Synonymy is sameness of meaning, but given that we are distinguishing four different senses of *meaning*, there will be four different kinds of synonymy: sameness of referent, sameness of content, sameness of character and sameness of reference determiner. Quine (1951) claims that there is a set of semantic concepts, each member of which can be defined in terms of the others, which includes the concepts of meaning and synonymy, as well as necessity, self-contradictoriness, semantic rule, definition and analyticity. In Chapter 2 I argued that the kind of meaning in terms of which analyticity can be defined is reference determiner and while I shall not claim that this is a way of breaking into Quine's circle—I imagine Quine would have been as suspicious of reference determiners as he was of meanings in general—we might still wonder whether we can give definitions of the other terms in

Quine's circle in terms of reference determiners. It will turn out that there are two obvious notions of synonymy available: a strict notion, and a slightly looser notion which can be defined, as Quine suggested, in modal terms. The strict notion of synonymy is the more obvious one:

Definition 8 (Strict Synonymy) *Two terms are synonymous just in case they have the same reference determiner.*

However, Quine also suggested that *necessity* could be used to define synonymy. On Quine's definition, two expressions are synonymous just in case they are always intersubstitutable within the context *it is necessary that. . . without change of truth-value.*

This is not true, even if we are not attempting to approximate the notion of sameness of reference determiner. I may substitute 'half of 4 + 4' for '4' within the context 'it is necessary that . . .' salve veritate but these expressions do not have the same meaning. The description is semantically complex, and it is implausible that '4' is an abbreviation of the expression 'half of 4 + 4'.

Even putting these problems aside, the notion of synonymy that Quine has defined here is not coextensional with our notion of strict synonymy, since *Hesperus* and *Phosphorus* are intersubstitutable within the context *it is necessary that* . . . and they do not have the same reference determiner.

Nevertheless, we can understand Quine's definition as an attempt to capture the idea that *words with the same meaning have the same modal profile,* so that when a word in a sentence is replaced with a word with the same modal profile, the new sentence will have the same modal profile as the original. Our new framework allows for a more complicated notion of modal profile, on which we can think of the modal profile of an expression as a set of triples in which the first member is a context of introduction, the second a context of utterance and the third the extension of the expression with respect to those contexts. Expressions with modal properties like rigidity, constancy etc. or with properties which determine modal properties like being directly referential, or being true in virtue of meaning, have distinctive modal profiles.

Definition 9 (Sameness of Modal Profile) *Two expressions have the same modal profile just in case, with respect to the same contexts of introduction and utterance, they always have the same extensions.*

Table 3.4. Two kinds of reference determiner synonymy

strictly synonymous	same modal profile
I	dthat[the sum of 2 and 4]
me	dthat[the x: x = 6]

This suggests a new, recognisably Quinean definition of synonymy:

Definition 10 (Loose Synonymy) *An expression* E₁ *is loosely synonymous with an expression* E₂ *just in case a sentence* S₂*, which has been formed by replacing one or more occurrences of* E₁ *in the arbitrary sentence* S₁*, has the same modal profile as the original sentence,* S₁*.*

The notions of strict and loose synonymy are not coextensive. All pairs of expressions which are strictly synonymous are also loosely synonymous, but the converse does not hold. Since reference determiner determines modal profile, if two words have the same reference determiner, they have the same modal profile—all pairs of strictly synonymous expressions are loosely synonymous. So, for example, if someone introduced the names *Hesperus* and *Phosphorus* by pointing at Venus and saying *Let's give that object two names, let's call it both* Hesperus *and* Phosphorus, then substituting *Hesperus* for *Phosphorus* in a sentence would never change the modal profile of that sentence. But we can achieve exactly the same result without identity of reference determiner, as a result of substantial modal facts. Suppose that the names were introduced separately in the normal way but that it is actually *impossible* that the bright light in the sky in the morning is anything other than the bright light in the sky in the evening, so that there was no context of introduction which would result in *Hesperus* or *Phosphorus* referring to anything other than Venus. Then the two names would have the same modal profile—both would refer to Venus in every context of evaluation, utterance and introduction—though they would have different reference determiners.

This is really a version of the problem with 'half of 4 + 4' and '4' that I raised for Quine's attempt to define synonymy in terms of necessity. Expressions may be necessarily coextensive because they mean the same thing, but they may also be necessarily coextensive because of substantial modal facts; maybe the thing that fits description 1 just *has* to be the thing that fits description 2.

3.2.5 Analyticity and Modality

In providing a modal definition of truth in virtue of meaning in the previous chapter, we ran into the problem of substantive necessity. But, as I have argued, this is just one more manifestation of a larger, recurrent problem in semantics: if you define semantic notions in modal terms, you just are going to end up with a definition that is vulnerable to the problem of substantive necessity. We have one model for how to deal with this problem—Kaplan's "metaphysical picture" (though in truth possible world semantics might also, without strain, be called a "metaphysical picture") of direct reference and structured propositions containing the referents of expressions—and this is a model that I intend to follow. Just as Kaplan, when he needs to, distinguishes content conceived of modally (a function from circumstances of evaluation to extensions) from the stricter, more metaphysical conception of content, so I will distinguish truth in virtue of meaning conceived of modally (as in the previous chapter) from a stricter, more metaphysical conception of truth in virtue of meaning, to be developed in the rest of this part of the book.

I claim that the strict, metaphysical truth in virtue of meaning stands to the modally explicated truth in virtue of meaning isolated in the last chapter as direct reference stands to rigidity, and as strict content stands to functions from circumstances of evaluation to referents. That modal notion is, if you like, the best modal approximation to analyticity. It will be useful to have a separate name for it, so where necessary for the purposes of disambiguation, I will call it *constancy*.

Definition 11 (Constancy (sentences)) *A sentence is constant just in case it is true in all contexts of utterance and introduction.*

To speak more evocatively, yet a bit loosely for a moment, constant sentences are the ones which cannot be uttered falsely, even if the speaker is on Twin Earth, speaking Twin Earthese. Constancy, like direct reference, is a property of expressions. All analytic sentences are constant, but some synthetic sentences are constant as well, and so constancy can act only as a rough test for analyticity. Constancy is different from rigidity in some important respects.[4] It is a property of sentences, not terms, and it is a matter of having *true* as one's extension regardless

---

[4] If there were a sentential version of direct reference it would presumably be a sentence whose extension was the True, though that fact was not mediated by the proposition the sentence expressed but identical with it. The only candidate I can think

of context of utterance or introduction, whereas rigidity is a matter of taking an object as one's extension, regardless of context of evaluation.

Now we are faced with a question: what can we say about the property that stands to the modal conception of truth in virtue of meaning as direct reference stands to rigidity? What could the underlying metaphysical picture possibly look like?

3.3 STRICT TRUTH IN VIRTUE OF MEANING

How should the strict notion of truth in virtue of meaning be defined? The looser modal notion was defined in terms of the modal profile of a sentence, but, as we discovered, the modal profile of a sentence can be dependent on substantial modal facts as well as on the meaning of the sentence. What we require, then, is a property of the sentence which is independent of such facts—or even stronger, something intrinsic to the meaning of the sentence—which guarantees the sentence's truth, just as something about the meaning of a directly referential term guarantees the rigidity of that expression.

A sentence like *Hesperus is Hesperus* is true in virtue of meaning because of a certain relation which holds between the reference determiners of the two names: identity. The first and second occurrences of *Hesperus* in this sentence have the *same* reference determiner—they are strictly synonymous. As a result, though the first occurrence of *Hesperus* might have referred to Mars, and the second occurrence might have referred to Venus, those two possibilities are not *co*-possible. Whatever the first occurrence of the name refers to, the second refers to it too. Similar points might be made about *all bachelors are bachelors*, or *today is today*. Strict synonymy—that is, identity of reference determiner—occurring appropriately in a sentence, can guarantee truth, independently of the modal facts.

But so can something else. Consider the expressions *Cassius Clay* and *Mohammed Ali*, as introduced in Chapter 2:

Cassius Clay was introduced when Cassius Clay's parents baptised him (*Let's call him (pointing) 'Cassius Clay.'*) The referent of *Mohammed Ali* was introduced

---

of is the symbol 'T' (top) as it is sometimes used in formal languages, yet, even here, sometimes that symbol is taken as a definitional abbreviation of the conjunction of all the tautologies (in which case its content would seem to mediate its extension), and even where this is not the case, it is not clear to me that the True is a suitable candidate for a sentential *content*. But perhaps that is just my over-tutored prejudice.

in a slightly different way, when Elijah Muhammad, the leader of the Nation of Islam, said *Let's use 'Mohammed Ali' to name Cassius Clay. Mohammed Ali* thus refers to whatever object, if any, *Cassius Clay* refers to.

Although their reference determiners are not *identical*, these two names will have the same modal profile, regardless of the modal facts, since *Mohammed Ali* is determined to refer to whatever *Cassius Clay* refers to. It seems clear what is going on here. The reference determiners of *Cassius Clay* and *Mohammed Ali* are not identical, but the reference determiner of *Cassius Clay* is a part of that of *Mohammed Ali* (so that the reference determiner of *Cassius Clay* is identical to part of that of *Mohammed Ali*). This, too, is sufficient for a sameness of modal profile which is not hostage to the modal facts. Once we recognise this we can see that identity of reference determiner (strict synonymy) is just the limit case of one reference determiner being a part of another.

The relation of containment between meanings—often referred to as *conceptual containment*—has a large place in the history of attempts to explain analyticity, as we can see from the following early characterisations in Locke and Kant:

. . .*when a part of the complex* idea *is predicated of the name of the whole* (Locke 1993[1690]: Book IV, Chapter VIII, 350)

Either the predicate B belongs to the subject A, as something that is (covertly) contained in this concept A; or B lies outside the concept A, although it does indeed stand in connection with it. In the one case I entitle the judgements analytic, in the other synthetic. (Kant 1965*a*: A7/B11)

The idea that analyticity could arise when the meaning of one expression in a sentence is contained in the meaning of another was central to both Locke and Kant's accounts. Yet thanks to influential criticisms of Frege, the positivists, and Quine, those old-style 'conceptual containment' accounts are now widely ridiculed. But I want to suggest that we can get our metaphysical picture by rehabilitating something like the Kantian account.

A simple, but naive, approach would be to simply replace the mention of concepts in Kant's definition with mention of reference determiners, giving us a kind of neo-Kantian definition of analyticity: a sentence is analytic just in case the reference determiner for its predicate is contained in the reference determiner for its subject. This would address one of Frege's main worries, namely that the definition—in making reference to concepts—was too psychological, but the unsympathetic are likely to object that they have no more of an idea what reference determiners are than they had of what concepts were. Moreover other traditional objections remain and ultimately they make this simple adaptation of Kant's definition untenable. Still, I will eventually want to propose a metaphysical picture which does feature reference determiners and containment relations between them. But instead of appealing just to containment relations between the reference determiners of the subject and predicate expressions in the sentence, the account I present will appeal to both containment *and exclusion* relations between the reference determiners of expressions, and moreover, *three* parts of speech will be involved: what I'll call the logical subject expression, the logical predicate expression, and a third thing: the sentence's modifier.

3.3.1 Obstacles to a Neo-Kantian approach

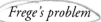

Frege's problem

One of Frege's criticisms of Kant's definition of analyticity was that it only applied to judgements composed of a restricted subject-predicate form. This is not so dire a consequence as it might at first sound to modern readers. Kant's account is not restricted to sentences which we might translate into the language of first-order logic with the sentence Fa. Sentences which Kant would have regarded as being of subject-predicate form include sentences like:

(3.10) Gold is a yellow metal.

(3.11) All bodies are extended.

which we teach introductory logic students to translate into the language of first-order logic as something like:

(3.12) $\forall x(Gx \rightarrow (Yx \wedge Mx))$.

(3.13) $\forall x(Bx \rightarrow Ex)$.

But there *are* sentences which apparently have neither subject nor predicate even in this extended sense, including many sentences which contain other sentences as proper parts, such as certain sentences containing sentential connectives or modal operators:

(3.14) All bachelors are unmarried *and* snow is white.

(3.15) *If* all bachelors are unmarried *then* all bachelors are unmarried.

(3.16) *It is not the case that* any bachelors are married.

(3.17) *It is possible that* snow is white.

These sentences seem not to be of subject-predicate form, and even where we might identify a unique subject in the case of (3.16) the Kantian definition seems to give the wrong result, since, plausibly (3.16) is analytic if *all bachelors are unmarried* is.

Katz' Problem

A second problem, often pointed out by Katz, is that there seem to be analytic sentences in which, while there is a subject and a predicate, it is not remotely plausible that the reference determiner of the predicate is contained in that of the subject, such as:

(3.18) Mary walks with those with whom she herself walks.

(3.19) Mary walks with those with whom she herself strolls.

(3.20) Poor people have less money than rich people.

(3.21) Rich people have more money than poor people.

Sentence (3.18) is putatively analytic and it has a subject, namely *Mary*, but the reference determiner for *Mary* need make no reference at all to walking, or even to other people, so the reference determiner for the predicate will not be contained in the reference determiner for *Mary*. Moreover it seems implausible to suppose that the reference determiner for *poor people* contains something so complex as that of *have less money than rich people*, and even if it did, how would we explain the analyticity of (3.21) without making the reference determiners of *rich people* and *poor people* circular? So two major difficulties of merely adapting Kant's definition so that it makes reference to reference determiners rather than concepts are, first, that there seem to be analytic sentences which are not of subject-predicate form—call that Frege's problem—and second, that there seem to be analytic sentences which *are* of subject-predicate form, but where the predicate concept does not seem to be contained in the subject concept—call that Katz' problem.

Given these two problems, the naive neo-Kantian definition fails on its own terms, even before critics begin to protest that they don't understand words like *reference determiner* and *containment*. Can we rework the definition so that it might at least appeal to non-skeptics?

I think that the solution to both problems lies with *four* insights. The first is a recasting of the definition of analyticity so that it is a matter of relations between the reference determiners of *three* different parts of the sentence, what I will call the *logical subject expression* (LSE), the *logical predicate expression* (LPE), and the *modifier* of the sentence. The second is the admission of an additional relation; since we use the *containment* relation between reference determiners to define analyticity, why not also exploit an *exclusion* relation? The third is a generalisation of the notion of analyticity on the model of a generalisation of logical truth due to Gentzen, and the fourth is the recognition of a distinction: Locke's distinction between a set of core analytic truths and their consequences.

3.3.2 Parts of Sentences

One way to approach Frege's problem would be by rethinking the notions of a sentence's subject and predicate. Perhaps they can be conceived of in such a way that sentences like those above have subjects and predicates after all. Kant's conception of a subject-predicate sentence might not be perfectly clear, (though I'm sure it's clearer to proper Kant scholars than it is to me) but it does have *some* intuitive content. Each of the simple assertoric sentences below can be seen as composed of a subject expression (in italics) and a predicate expression.

(3.22) *All bachelors* are male.

(3.23) *Some gold* is yellow.

(3.24) *All gold* is not yellow.

(3.25) *Some gold* is not yellow.

(3.26) *John* is a bachelor.

(3.27) *John* is not a bachelor.

(3.28) *The tallest boy in the class* is handsome.

(3.29) *The tallest boy in the class* is not handsome.

The subject-predicate distinction is not just a remnant of an old folk theory of meaning. It has an analogue in contemporary linguistics, and, simplifying somewhat, sentences like those above are analysed syntactically into noun phrases (NP) and verb phrases (VP):

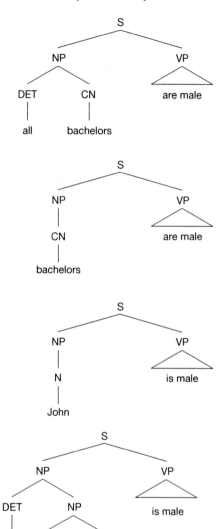

So if we're looking for ways to identify subject and predicate expressions today, we *might* look to recent theories of syntax to provide them for us. The subject expression would be whatever the best syntactic theory identifies as the highest noun phrase in the syntactic tree for the sentence, and the predicate expression would be whatever that same theory identifies as the highest verb phrase.

One shadow over this approach is that it doesn't seem to help much with sentences containing sentential connectives and modal operators. (3.14) and (3.17) would most likely get analysed along the following lines, with (3.14) having *no* highest noun or verb phrases, and with (3.17) having only the pleonastic pronoun *it* as the highest noun phrase.

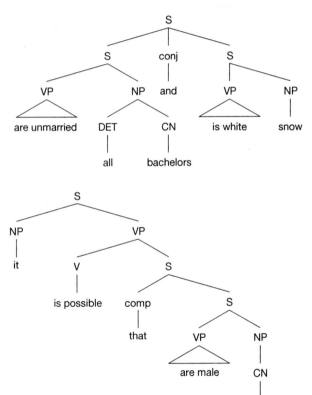

The semantic approach

There is another, more semantic, approach that we might take to classifying parts of sentences into subject and predicate expressions. It is fairly natural to gloss the idea of the subject and predicate of a sentence as follows: the subject picks out the object or objects about which the sentence makes a claim and the predicate expression specifies a condition which that object (or those objects) have to meet for the sentence to be true. Thinking of the subject and predicate this way has two advantages over the syntactic approach: first, it generalises more naturally to complex sentences and second, it makes it easier to connect our eventual metaphysical picture to the modal account. (If you recall, the underlying metaphysical picture is meant to *explain* that distinctive modal profile.)

Generalising to other sentence types

One might think that just about every assertoric sentence has to specify some object or objects and claim that they meet a condition, since that's pretty much what it is to make a claim about the world. And indeed, with a little ingenuity, we can analyse lots of sentences that way. For example, in a complex sentence we can often think of the main connective or logical constant in the sentence as being the predicate; it specifies a condition that the ordered pair (or n-tuple) of the referents of the simpler sentences will have to meet if it is to be true, (e.g. they must both be true (conjunction) or the first must be false or the second true (material conditionals)). In atomic sentences containing predicates of arity greater than one, we can often think of the subject as an ordered n-tuple of the referents of the predicate's argument expressions. This way of thinking of the 'subject' and 'predicate' of sentences is likely to come fairly easily to logicians, but it isn't perhaps all that intuitive in some ways, so to avoid confusion with the intuitive notion, I'll refer to the predicate, conceived of this way as the LPE (logical predicate expression) and the subject as the LSE (logical subject expression).

A first stab (soon to be revised) at analysing some simple sentences into LPE and LSE might look something like this.

(3.30) Bachelors are male.

[are male]$_{LPE}$ [bachelors]$_{LSE}$

(3.31) Poor people have less money than rich people.

[have less money than]$_{LPE}$ [⟨ poor people, rich people ⟩]$_{LSE}$

(3.32)   Hesperus is Hesperus.

       [is]$_{LPE}$ [⟨ Hesperus, Hesperus ⟩]$_{LSE}$

(3.33)   Mohammed Ali *is* Cassius Clay.

       [is]$_{LPE}$ [⟨ Mohammed Ali, Cassius Clay ⟩]$_{LSE}$

(3.34)   If snow is white then snow is white.

       [if . . . then . . .]$_{LPE}$ [⟨snow is white, snow is white⟩]$_{LSE}$

(3.35)   If snow is white and grass is green then snow is white.

       [if . . . then . . .]$_{LPE}$ [⟨snow is white and grass is green, snow is white⟩]$_{LSE}$

(3.36)   It is necessary that snow is white.

       [is necessary]$_{LPE}$ [that snow is white]$_{LSE}$

But here we hit *another* problem. All but the last of the above sentences are candidates for analyticity, and on this analysis there is something odd about many of them. While there often does seem to be a clear containment relation between parts of the sentence, it is not between the reference determiners of the LPE and the LSE, as expected, but rather *between parts of the LSE reference determiner*. For example between the two occurrences of 'Hesperus' in *Hesperus is Hesperus*, and between the antecedent and the consequent of *if snow is white and grass is green then snow is white*.

Quantified sentences seem particularly tricky to analyse, perhaps in part because here we can have genuine conflict between the intuitive notion of a subject expression and the idea of the LSE.

(3.37)   All bachelors are male.

In (3.37) the intuitive subject might be *all bachelors*, but given an extended Mostowskian generalised interpretation of binary quantifiers, on which quantifiers take binary relations on sets as their extensions and on which the clause of the truth-definition for *all* reads:

     Where X and Y are sets, ⌜All(X, Y)⌝ is true iff $X \subseteq Y$.

---

all can be though of as having a reference determiner which is met by a pair of sets just in case the first member of the pair is a subset (possibly improper) of the second. After this analysis it seems natural to take *all* as the LPE and the ordered pair ⟨*bachelor, male*⟩ as the LSE. Once again, if we analyse the sentence into parts using the approach from (3.30)–(3.36) the containment relation is, if anywhere, between the reference determiners of *bachelor* and *male*, but these are not the reference determiners of the LSE and the LPE, but rather those of different parts of the LSE.

This might seem to point to a novel way to revise the Kantian definition of analyticity by stipulating that the containment relation must be between the different parts of the LSE, and not between the subject and predicate after all. But this is a dead-end: containment relations between different parts of the reference determiners of the LSE are not sufficient for analyticity. They are not even sufficient for truth. (3.38), for example, features the same containment relations as (3.37) and is false:

(3.38) No bachelor is male.

       no (⟨ bachelor, male⟩)

Yet I think this example also gives us a clue to the correct account. It suggests a tripartite reclassification of the parts of sentences like those in the above sample—and this will be the approach I actually take. On this approach to analysing sentences into parts, there is the LSE, which picks out the object or objects about which the sentence makes a claim, there is the LPE, which specifies a condition, and there is often a *third* part to the sentence which says something about whether or not, and how, the condition is satisfied by the objects—I'll call this the sentence modifier. Here are the sentences above re-analysed along these lines:

(3.39) Bachelors are male.

       [are]$_M$ [bachelor]$_{LSE}$ [male]$_{LPE}$

(3.40) Poor people have less money than rich people.

       [have less money than]$_M$ [poor people]$_{LSE}$ [rich people]$_{LPE}$

(3.41) Hesperus is Hesperus.

       [=]$_M$ [Hesperus]$_{LSE}$ [Hesperus]$_{LPE}$

(3.42) Mohammed Ali *is* Cassius Clay.

       [=]$_M$ [Mohammed Ali]$_{LSE}$ [Cassius Clay]$_{LPE}$

(3.43) If snow is white then snow is white.

[if . . . then . . .]$_M$ [snow is white]$_{LSE}$ [snow is white]$_{LPE}$

(3.44) If snow is white and grass is green then snow is white.

[if . . . then . . .]$_M$ [snow is white and grass is green]$_{LSE}$ [snow is white]$_{LPE}$

(3.45) It is necessary that snow is white.

[is necessary]$_{LPE}$ [that snow is white]$_{LSE}$

The simplest kinds of sentences are true just in case any object which satisfies the reference determiner for the LSE (which specifies the subject) also satisfies the reference determiner of the LPE. But the way in which the LPE is used to provide a condition on the referent of the LSE can be modified by the modifier.

Three kinds of modifier interest us in particular. Positive modifiers tell us that the sentence will be true *if* all the objects which satisfy the LSE also satisfy the LPE.[5] Examples of positive modifiers include, *all*, = (the *is* of identity), *is/are* (the *is* of predication), *if . . . then* and *. . . if, and only if . . .* .

Negative modifiers tell us that the sentence will be true if *none* of the objects which meet C_{LSE} meet C_{LPE}. Negative modifiers include *no*, and *if . . . then not . . .* .

Neutral modifiers do neither of the above. A large number of modifiers are neutral, and to see this one need only consider that *four* in *four bachelors are male* is neutral, as is *five* in *five bachelors are male*. Other examples include *and* and *or*. *Most* is also neutral, as is *a few*.

Though simple sentences like those below might seem at first glance to only have explicit LSEs and LPEs,

(3.46) Bachelors eat.

[ ] [bachelor]$_{LSE}$ [eat]$_{LPE}$

(3.47) Runners run.

[ ] [runner]$_{LSE}$ [runs]$_{LPE}$

(3.48) Mary eats.

[ ] [Mary]$_{LSE}$ [eats]$_{LPE}$

---

[5] This is definitely intended to be an *if* and not an *if, and only, if* since that would exclude the conditional from being a positive modifier. Consider the case where the antecedent determines the false, and the consequent the true.

it is nevertheless *as if* they had positive modifiers; the sentence will be true just in case every object which satisfies the LSE satisfies the LPE. A simple way to have our theory deal with this is to say that all such sentences have *positive* modifiers, the modifiers simply aren't represented explicitly in the surface structure of the sentence.

As noted previously, *no* in *no bachelors are married* requires a different relation between the extensions of the predicates involved than the *all* in *all bachelors are male* does:

 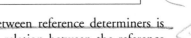

> Where X and Y are sets, $\ulcorner$No $(X, Y)\urcorner$ is true iff $X \cap Y = \emptyset$

and so a different kind of relation between reference determiners is needed to explain its analyticity. One relation between the reference determiners which could guarantee this would be *exclusion*.

3.3.3 Inter-part Relations: Containment and Exclusion

Connecting the metaphysical and modal pictures

Why would a metaphysical picture, on which one part of the reference determiner of a sentence was contained in another part, *explain* the truth of a sentence? Why would it explain the modal property of constancy? The answer is that its explanatory power is a consequence of two facts, one about containment, one about the truth-conditions of sentences of subject-predicate form.

Whatever else is true of the containment relation on reference determiners, it ought to satisfy the following principle:

Containment Principle
If the reference determiner for an expression E contains the reference determiner for an expression F, then for all x, if x satisfies E with respect to an ordered pair $\langle c_i, c_u \rangle$, where c_i is a context of introduction and c_u a context of utterance, then x satisfies F with respect to $\langle c_i, c_u \rangle$.

More loosely: where A and B are reference determiners, if A contains B, then B is satisfied by any object that satisfies A. For example, since the reference determiner for *bachelor* contains that of *is a man*, anything which satisfies *bachelor* also satisfies *is a man*. Similarly, since the reference determiner for *Mohammed Ali* contains that of *Cassius Clay*, anything which satisfies *Mohammed Ali* satisfies *Cassius Clay*.

Taking the containment principle as a necessary condition on containment narrows down the interpretation of *containment* quite a bit, and it allows us to say that certain pairs of expressions do not provide examples of containment as it is intended here. For example, it is not the case that the reference determiner for *former communist* contains the reference determiner for *communist*, since there are objects which satisfy the former without satisfying the latter. Similarly the reference determiner for *unmarried* does not contain the reference determiner for *married*, since nothing which satisfies the former satisfies the latter.

The second fact we need in order to see how containment can explain constancy is a fact about what has to be the case for a subject-predicate sentence with a positive modifier to be true. The reference determiner of the subject expression is a condition which picks out which object or objects the sentence is making a claim about and, given that the sentence has a positive modifier, the reference determiner for the predicate is a condition which picks out the objects of which the claim holds. The sentence will be true just in case the object or objects picked out by the former condition are also picked out by the latter condition. *But this is just what containment of the predicate reference determiner in the subject reference determiner guarantees.*

It is traditional to appeal to containment relations in discussions of analyticity, but it seems to me that another notion has just as much right to be used: exclusion. If it makes sense to talk about containment relations between reference determiners, then it ought to make sense to talk about exclusion relations as well, and in fact this is required to make sense of the analyticity of sentences with negative modifiers.

Reference determiners are conditions and conditions can be put together in different ways in order to build new, more complex conditions. Suppose I'm trying to specify a condition, D. I can say that in order to meet condition D an object has to meet the following conditions: *being red, being a painting* and *being simple*, in which case D will contain each of those three component conditions. But I could also use those same conditions in a different way, and construct a complex condition, E, by saying that some simpler conditions must be met, or that some simpler conditions must *not* be met. For example, meeting E might be a matter of an object's meeting the conditions *being a painting, being simple* and **not** meeting the condition *being red*. In that case I will

ANALYTICIT*Y*

containment relation ⟹ exclusion ⟹ complementary ??

say that condition E contains the conditions *being a painting,* and *being simple* and *excludes* the condition *being red.*

The reference determiner for *bachelor* excludes that of *married* and that can help to explain the intuitive analyticity of:

(3.49) No bachelor is married.

Whatever else is true about the exclusion relation, it should satisfy the following principle:

Exclusion Principle

If the reference determiner for an expression E excludes the reference determiner for an expression F, then for all x, if x satisfies E with respect to an ordered pair $\langle c_i, c_u \rangle$, where c_i is a context of introduction and c_u a context of utterance, then x does not satisfy F with respect to $\langle c_i, c_u \rangle$.

I think it is natural to say that the reference determiner for $\neg$ *snow is white* excludes that of *snow is white,* that the reference determiner for *bachelor* excludes that of *married,* that the reference determiner for *unexpected* excludes that of *expected* and that the reference determiner for the predicate expression *not red* excludes that of *red.*

Since sentences with negative modifiers will be true (with respect to c_u and c_i) if *none* of the objects that satisfy the LSE satisfy the LPE (with respect to c_u and c_i), and this is just what exclusion guarantees, the exclusion relation between the reference determiners of the LSE and LPE explains the constancy of sentences with negative modifiers.

We are now ready to give a definition of analyticity and some related notions. This definition will be in terms of reference determiners, and I want to say a little more about what reference determiners are before we get to the definition.

3.3.4 More about Reference Determiners

At a first stab, the reference determiner for an expression is a condition which any object must meet in order for the expression to apply to it (and such that the expression will apply to any object which meets it.) But this first stab does not accurately capture my intended meaning; here is a condition which an object must meet in order to be the referent of *Hesperus:*

H x must be the bright spark in the evening sky in 1845 which was
noticed by the man who introduced *Hesperus*, to which he intended
the name to refer.

And here is another

H′ x must be the referent of *Hesperus*,

and another

H″ x must be the referent of *Phosphorus*.

Only H is the reference determiner of *Hesperus* in my intended sense
of the expression *reference determiner*.⁶

The problem with H′ is that it is circular. One can never determine (in
either epistemological or metaphysical senses of *determine*) the referent
of *Hesperus* by stipulating that the referent of *Hesperus* is whatever
the referent of *Hesperus* is. Circular conditions like this one determine
nothing—neither metaphysically or epistemologically. So we can rule
H′ out by stipulating that reference determiners must be non-circular
conditions.

The problem with H″ is that it is only a condition on being the
referent of *Hesperus* in virtue of the fact that H is a condition on
being the referent of *Hesperus*. *Being the referent of 'Phosphorus'* is a
condition which the referent of *Hesperus* meets because (i) *being the
evening star noticed by the man in 1845* is a condition on being the
reference determiner for *Hesperus* and (ii) the referent of *Phosphorus* is
the evening star noticed by the man in 1845.

This has the *consequence* that the following counterfactual is true: if
Hesperus did not apply to the evening star noticed by the man in 1845,
(suppose instead that it applied to the best band in Britain) then *being the
referent of 'Phosphorus'* would not be a condition which an object would
have to meet to be the referent of *Hesperus*. But this counterfactual is
not: if *Hesperus* did not apply to the referent of *Phosphorus*, then *being*

⁶ One might also think that x *must be Hesperus* and x *must be Phosphorus* are
conditions which an object must meet to be the referent of *Hesperus*, but this just isn't
true. In a context of introduction in which Mars is the bright star in the sky in the evening
noticed by the introducer of *Hesperus*, *Hesperus* refers to Mars, and not to Hesperus.
Similarly, one might imagine that *being a horse* (or *being water*) is a descriptive condition
which any object would have to meet to fall under the reference determiner for *horse* (or
water)—but it isn't: with respect to contexts of introduction in which horses are robots
sent from Mars, *horse* applies to robots, and not to our equine familiars (on Twin Earth,
water applies to XYZ, and not to water.)

the evening star noticed by the man in 1845 would not be a condition which an object would have to meet to be the referent of *Hesperus*. This is because *being the referent of 'Phosphorus'* is a condition which an object must meet in order for *Hesperus* to apply to it *in virtue of* the fact that *being the evening star noticed by the man in 1845* is a condition on which an object must meet in order that *Hesperus* apply to it. We can rule out conditions like H″ by stipulating that reference determiners are conditions which objects must meet to be in the extension of an expression, such that no other such condition explains its holding.

One other remark about that first stab: the 'must' was too weak on its own, in two ways. Firstly, meeting the condition is not merely a necessary condition for satisfaction of the expression by an object, it is also sufficient. And secondly, the 'must' suggests necessity and our definition was supposed to go beyond such coarse-grained modal notions. Yet notice, once it is added that the reference determiner is the condition in virtue of which all others hold, our definition already goes beyond the modal conception, even though it contains the modal concepts of necessity and sufficiency. Recall the modal realist who has come to believe that necessarily, the morning star is the evening star. For him there is no context of introduction (or utterance) with respect to which the names *Hesperus* and *Phosphorus* designate different entities, and so the reference determiners of the two expressions have the same modal profiles: for any pair of contexts of utterance and introduction, *Hesperus* and *Phosphorus* pick out the same objects. Yet with our new conception of reference determiner in hand, *Hesperus* and *Phosphorus* still do not have the same reference determiners. It is true, assuming the modal realist is right, both *being the bright shape visible in the morning* and *being the bright shape visible in the evening* accurately specify necessary and sufficient conditions for satisfaction of the name *Hesperus*, and for *Phosphorus* as well—that is, they determine the same function from context of introduction and utterance to extension. And so both the following are true: For all x, 'Hesperus' applies to x iff x was the bright shape visible in the *evening*, and for all x 'Hesperus' applies to x iff x was the bright shape visible in the *morning*. And yet the latter conjunct is only true because the former is. If the bright shape in the evening had been Mars, rather than Venus, then it would still be true that for all x, *Hesperus* applies to x iff x is the bright shape visible in the evening, but it would not apply to the bright shape visible in the morning—Venus. But to falsify the first conjunct is to falsify the second, since the second is only true in virtue of the first: if it were not the case that for all x, *Hesperus* applies to x iff x is the bright shape visible in the evening, (say if instead, for all x, *Hesperus* applies to x iff x is Saul Kripke's pet aardvark) it would not be the case that for all x *Hesperus* applies to the bright shape visible in the morning. Hence 3.51 is the reference determiner for Hesperus, whereas 3.50 is not:

(3.50) x was the first bright shape visible in the morning sky.

(3.51) x was the first bright shape visible in the evening sky.

Here is a second stab at defining the reference determiner for an expression, which takes the above remarks into account:

Definition 12 (Reference Determiner) *A reference determiner for an expression is a non-circular condition, such that any object which meets it satisfies the expression and does so in virtue of meeting that condition. If there are other such non-circular conditions, then the reference determiner is the one in virtue of which the others all hold.*

Reference determiners are met by individual objects. The set of all objects which meet a reference determiner for an expression is the extension of that expression. So ⌐ red ⌐ is met by the largest tomato in my refrigerator, but not by the set of all red things—no set meets the conditions for being red, or any other color. Rather the set of all red things is the extension of the expression *red*.

Similarly, n-ary reference determiners are met by sequences of n-objects. The set of all sequences of n-objects which meet a reference determiner for an expression is the extension of that expression. So ⌐ is larger than ⌐ is met by the ordered pair ⟨Jupiter, Mercury⟩ and the set of all pairs in which the first member is larger than the second member is the extension of the expression *is larger than*.

Not every expression has a complete reference determiner to call its own. Some expressions are better thought of as modifying the reference determiners of other expressions in order to form a new reference determiner for a complex expression. Good examples include adjectives like *former* and *allegedly*. It is difficult to imagine either of these expressions having an extension, because there doesn't seem to be a good answer to the question *which objects does* former *apply to?* in the way that there is to the question *which objects does* red *apply to?* Nonetheless, it plays an important role in modifying the reference determiner of *communist* to form one for the complex expression *former communist*. There *is* a good question *what objects does* former communist *apply to?*

Many assertoric sentences can be understood as claiming that an object, or a certain kind of object, meets a condition, for example, *Hesperus is a planet* says that the object *Hesperus* meets the condition of being a planet, and *all bachelors are married* claims that objects of the kind *bachelor* meet the condition of being married. A natural way to specify a condition is by replacing a referring term in a sentence with a variable, as in examples (3.52) and (3.51) above. We can also refer to the same reference determiners using noun phrases such as *being the first bright shape visible in the morning sky* or *being the first bright shape visible in the evening sky*, as in *being the bright shape visible in the evening sky is a condition on being the referent of the expression* Hesperus. It will be useful to have a further convention for referring to the reference determiner for a particular expression and I so will write '↓' on either side of an expression to form a name of the expression's reference determiner. For example, '↓ Hesperus ↓' is a name for the reference determiner of the expression *Hesperus*—the condition of being the first bright shape visible in the evening sky; '↓ I ↓' is a name for the reference determiner of the expression *I*—the condition of being the agent of the context of utterance; and ↓ I am here now ↓ is a name for the reference determiner of *I am here now*—a complex condition with the interesting property of picking out 'true' relative to all contexts of introduction and utterance.

A natural way to attribute a reference determiner to an expression is by use of a biconditional such as this:

(3.52) for all x, 'Phosphorus' applies to x iff x was the first bright shape visible in the morning sky.

But this attribution is a little rough. If we understand the 'iff' in the usual truth-functional way, then this claim is weaker than the claims.

(3.53) Being the bright shape visible in the evening sky is the reference determiner for *Hesperus*.

3.4 THE DEFINITION OF ANALYTICITY

For our purposes, sentences which are candidates for analyticity can be analysed into three parts. The LPE specifies a condition, which, by default, anything that satisfies the LSE has to meet. Sometimes the LSE is the intuitive subject of the sentence, namely, *Hesperus* in *Hesperus is Phosphorus* or *bachelors* in *all bachelors are male*. Sometimes it is an entire subclause, as in the first *snow is white* in *if snow is white then snow is white*. The LPE specifies a condition on the referents of the LSE, but the relation required between the referents of the LSE and the condition specified by the LPE in order for the sentence to be true can be modified by the modifier. Positive modifiers require that any individual which meets the LSE meets the condition specified by the LPE. Negative modifiers require that it not meet that condition. Neutral modifiers require neither.

If a sentence's modifier is positive, then it is a condition on the truth of the sentence that any objects which satisfy the LSE satisfy the LPE. If $\downarrow$ LPE $\downarrow$ is contained in $\downarrow$ LSE $\downarrow$ this is guaranteed by the containment principle. If a sentence's modifier is negative, then it is a condition on the truth of the sentence that any objects which satisfy the LSE *not* satisfy the LPE. If $\downarrow$ LPE $\downarrow$ is excluded by $\downarrow$ LSE $\downarrow$, this is guaranteed by the exclusion principle. The consequences of this fact will depend on another fact about the sentence: whether it can be true even if the LSE is not met by any object. *All bachelors are male* can be, whereas *Hesperus is Hesperus* cannot.

Definition 13 (Analyticity (metaphysical picture)) *A sentence that consists of modifier (M), logical subject expression (S) and logical predicate expression (P), is analytic if (i) the sentence can be true even if (S) is not met by anything, and either (ii) (M) is positive and $\downarrow(S)\downarrow$ contains $\downarrow(P)\downarrow$ or M is negative and $\downarrow(S)\downarrow$ excludes $\downarrow(P)\downarrow$.*

Though this definition differs from Kant's in many ways, I hope it is clear that in some senses it is a generalisation of the Kantian definition. Kant's definition applies only in the case where we have the null modifier or some positive modifier, and then only to sentences of traditional subject-predicate form.

Some sentences, though not analytic, have a property very like analyticity. Though their reference determiners do not guarantee their truth, they do guarantee something like the following: if their subject expression is satisfied, then they are true. *Ali is Clay* is such a sentence. When we drop the simplifying assumption that Ali has a referent, it is not really true in virtue of meaning; its reference determiner does not even fully determine its truth, since there are possible contexts of introduction in which nothing is the baby pointed at by Mrs Clay. Nonetheless, whenever *Clay* successfully claims a referent, the sentence will be true, and this is guaranteed by the reference determiners for the expressions:

Definition 14 (Pseudo-Analyticity) *A sentence consisting of modifier (M), logical subject expression (S) and logical predicate expression (P) is pseudo-analytic if it is not analytic but i) if M is positive, $\downarrow(S)\downarrow$ contains $\downarrow(P)\downarrow$ and ii) if M is negative, $\downarrow(S)\downarrow$ excludes $\downarrow(P)\downarrow$.*

These definitions do not account for the analyticity of any sentences which cannot be analysed as consisting of a modifier, (LSE) and (LPE) (a less acute version of Frege's problem), or any sentences in which the reference determiner of the LPE is not contained or excluded from that of the LSE (Katz' problem), or any sentences which have neutral modifiers. But as yet we have only looked at two of the four points which were intended to help with these worries.

3.4.1 Generalising Analyticity

Gentzen's "Investigations into Logical Deduction" (Gentzen 1964) generalised the notion of a logical theorem so that it no longer applied just to *sentences*, but also to pairs of sets of sentences and sentences, pairs that are naturally thought of informally as arguments. Where once the theorems of a logic were all things like this:

$$\vdash A \vee \neg A$$
$$\vdash A \rightarrow A$$
$$\vdash (A \wedge B) \rightarrow A$$

Now they could also look like this:

$$\{A\} \vdash A$$
$$\{A \wedge B, C\} \vdash A$$
$$\{A \vee B, \neg A\} \vdash B$$

This counts as a generalisation because the theorems in the first group are a special case of the theorems in the second: the case when the first member of the pair is the empty set.

It seems to me that analyticity admits of a similar generalisation. It's not just sentences that can be analytic, but ordered pairs in which the first member is a set of sentences and the second is an individual sentence: arguments. Just as some sentences are true in virtue of meaning, so some arguments are valid in virtue of meaning. Such a notion of validity in virtue of meaning can be given a modal definition, just as analyticity was given a modal definition in Chapter 2.

Definition 15 (Validity in Virtue of Meaning (modal version)) *A pair* $\langle \Gamma, A \rangle$, *where* Γ *is a set of sentences and* A *is a sentence, is valid in virtue of meaning just in case for any pair of context of introduction and context of utterance with respect to which each member of* Γ *is true,* A *is also true with respect to that pair.*

The following are examples of rules of implication (both schematic rules and interpreted instances of schematic rules) which would satisfy that description:

$$\frac{\text{Snow is white.}}{\text{Snow is white.}} \qquad \frac{A \to B, A}{B} \qquad \frac{\text{dthat[the shortest spy]} = \text{Austin}}{\text{The shortest spy} = \text{Austin}}$$

Yet just as certain analytic sentences seem ripe for a more fine-grained explanation in terms of containment relations between the reference determiners of their parts, so some instances of the implication relation seem especially apt for explanation in terms of containment relations between the reference determiners of *their* parts. For example,

$$\frac{A \wedge B}{A}$$

and perhaps even:

$$\frac{\forall x (Fx)}{Fa} \qquad \frac{\Box A}{A}$$

Just as in the case of putatively analytic sentences, the validity of some arguments does not look so amenable to explanation in this way:

$$\frac{A \wedge \neg A}{B} \qquad \frac{A \wedge B, \neg B}{\neg A} \qquad \frac{A}{B \to A}$$

So a tentative definition of analytic validity might go something like this:

Definition 16 (Analytic Validity (arguments)) *A pair* $\langle \Gamma, A \rangle$, *where* Γ *is a set of sentences and* A *is a sentence, is analytically valid just in case the reference determiner for the conclusion is contained in the reference determiners for the premises.*

3.4.2 Locke's Distinction

The fourth insight we need is that if we define analyticity in terms of containment there is no reason to think that the set of analytic sentences is closed under logical consequence, and this leaves room for a *distinction* between the analytic sentences and their consequences. In fact, given that we are also identifying a distinctive analytic consequence relation, we might be particularly interested in the analytic consequences of analytic sentences.[7]

Definition 17 (Wide Analyticity (sentences)) *A sentence is widely analytic just in case it follows by analytically valid rules from a set containing only analytic sentences.*

These two observations—that analyticity can be generalised to apply to arguments and that containment-style accounts then allow for a distinction between core and wide analytic truths—make room for the class of wide analytic sentences. Wide analytic sentences are true in virtue of meaning in the sense that the explanation for their truth appeals to containment relations between reference determiners, (and they will also have the modal profile associated with truth in virtue of meaning) but it is not necessarily the case that the reference determiner for the sentence's own predicate is contained in the reference determiner for the sentence's own subject. This allows for there to be a kind analytic truth which is not of subject-predicate form—thus making space for a broader solution to Frege's problem—and it allows for there to be a kind of analytic truth which is of subject predicate form, though the reference determiner of the predicate is not contained in the reference determiner for the subject—thus making space for a solution to Katz' problem.

The details of particular cases will—as ever—depend upon one's views about reference determiners, but the sentence (3.18) would seem to be an analytic consequence of (3.54), which should hopefully admit

---

[7] We can also think of some rules of implication as being derived from others. It is not obvious that this means that there is a non-trivial distinction between core analytically valid rules and their consequences however. Perhaps the containment relation is transitive, and if it were, then all consequences of core analytically valid rules would themselves be core analytic rules. Yet if there were a distinction to be drawn here we would be able to distinguish analytic truths even more finely, since there would be those that followed from core analytic truths by core analytically valid rules, and those that followed from core analytic truths by wide analytically valid rules.

of the same explanation as (3.55), and similarly (3.19) would seem to be an analytic consequence of (3.56), which should admit of the same explanation as (3.57).

(3.54) $\forall x$(Mary walks with x $\rightarrow$ Mary walks with x)

(3.55) $\forall x$(bachelor x $\rightarrow$ bachelor x)

(3.56) $\forall x$(Mary walks with x $\rightarrow$ Mary strolls with x)

(3.57) $\forall x$(bachelor x $\rightarrow$ man x)

We might also allow that a wider class of sentences still can be *Frege-analytic*, where a Frege analytic sentence is a logical consequence of an analytic sentence. This property may go some way towards explaining the appearance of analyticity in the cases of some intuitively analytic sentences which do not fit the definitions above.

3.5 EXAMPLES

As always, which sentences turn out to be true in virtue of reference determiner will depend on the reference determiners of the expressions involved, and these matters can be controversial. I wish for my definition of analyticity to be neutral between rival accounts of the reference determiners of different expressions, but examples often make definitions easier to understand, and so here I will give some examples of sentences that turn out to be analytic, given some plausible assumptions about reference determiners.

Examples of Analytic Truths

(3.58) Bachelors are male

[are]$_{+ve}$ [bachelor]$_{LSE}$ [male]$_{LPE}$

The modifier is the 'is' of predication, which is positive. $\downarrow$ bachelor $\downarrow$ contains $\downarrow$ male $\downarrow$ and so the sentence is analytic.

(3.59) All bachelors are male.

[All]$_{+ve}$ [bachelor]$_{LSE}$ [male]$_{LPE}$

The modifier *all* is positive, $\downarrow$ bachelor $\downarrow$ contains $\downarrow$ male $\downarrow$ and so the sentence is analytic.

(3.60) Runners run.

    [ ]$_{+ve}$ [runners]$_{LSE}$ [run]$_{LPE}$

This sentence is analytic because it has a positive (though null) modifier and ↓runner↓ contains ↓runs↓.

(3.61) If snow is white and grass is green then snow is white.

    [if. . . then . . .]$_{+ve}$ [snow is white and grass is green]$_{LSE}$ [snow is white]$_{LPE}$

The modifier *if . . . then . . .* is positive, and the reference determiner of the LSE (snow is white and grass is green) contains that of the LPE (snow is white), and so the sentence is analytic.

(3.62) If snow is white then snow is white.

    [if. . . then . . .]$_{+ve}$ [snow is white and grass is green]$_{LSE}$ [snow is white]$_{LPE}$

The modifier *if . . . then . . .* is positive, and the reference determiner of the LSE (snow is white) contains that of the LPE (snow is white), and so the sentence is analytic.

Examples of pseudo-analytic sentences

(3.63) Hesperus is Hesperus.

    [=]$_{+ve}$ [Hesperus]$_{LSE}$ [Hesperus]$_{LPE}$

The modifier is the relational identity predicate, which is positive, and the reference determiner for the LPE ↓ Hesperus ↓, is contained in that of the LSE, ↓ Hesperus ↓. Yet sentences with the modifier '=' require that the LSE is satisfied, so this sentence is merely pseudo-analytic.

(3.64) Ali is Clay.

    [=]$_{+ve}$ [Hesperus]$_{LSE}$ [Hesperus]$_{LPE}$

The modifier is the relational identity predicate, which is positive, and the reference determiner for the LPE ↓ Clay ↓, is contained in that of the LSE, ↓ Ali ↓. Yet sentences with the modifier '=' require that the LSE is satisfied, so this sentence is merely pseudo-analytic.

(3.65) The red book is red.

    [is]$_{+ve}$ [the red book]$_{LSE}$ [red]$_{LPE}$

The modifier is *is* which is positive, and the reference determiner for the LPE ↓ red ↓, is contained in that of the LSE, ↓ the red book ↓. Yet sentences with LSE *the* require that the LSE is uniquely satisfied, so this sentence is merely pseudo-analytic.

(3.66) I am here.

$[=]_{+ve}$ [I]$_{LSE}$ [here]$_{LPE}$

[am]$_{+ve}$ [I]$_{LSE}$ [here]$_{LPE}$

I think that this sentence is very tricky and I offer this analysis merely as an illustration. It is hard to see how Kaplan's *I am here now*, or, for simplicity, just *I am here*, will fit into the pattern, since Kaplan's reference determiner for *I* does not actually contain that of *here*; if it did the containment principle would guarantee that the two words always apply to the same thing—but no *location* is an *agent*.

But Kaplan's reference determiner for *here*, which makes it a singular term picking out a *place*, doesn't seem correct anyway for the word as it appears in *I am here*. The *am* in *am here* seems to be a species of the 'is' of predication, rather than the 'is' of identity. To say that something *is here* is similar to saying that something *is red*, and, just as *is red* is satisfied by all the objects which are red, so *is here* is satisfied by all the objects which are here. Of which I am one. On this understanding the reference determiner of *here* in (3.66) is *not* Kaplan's rule: *the place of the context*.[8] (Encouragingly, we can say, *there are lots of people* in *Maidstone* where Maidstone picks out a place, but not *I am Maidstone* to mean *Maidstone is the place where I am*. Are there any ways to construe the reference determiners for *I* and *here* such that the sentence is analytic? Perhaps if the reference determiner for *I* is *the x: x is speaking in the place and time of the context* and that for *here* is *x is in the place of the context* it is plausible that ↓ I ↓ contains ↓ here ↓, and in that case, since the 'is' of predication is a positive modifier, the sentence is pseudo-analytic. But I have little confidence in my analysis of the reference determiners in this case.

(3.67) dthat[the shortest spy]= the shortest spy

$[=]_{+ve}$ [dthat[the shortest spy]]$_{LSE}$ [the shortest spy]$_{LPE}$

---

[8] Though that might be a more plausible reference determiner for the *here* in *there are lots of people in here*.

This sentence is pseudo-analytic, since the modifier is positive and the reference determiner of the LSE contains that of the LPE and it could not be true if the LSE were to fail to refer.

Examples of sentences which are neither analytic nor pseudo-analytic

(3.68) Snow is white.

$[\text{is}]_{+ve}$ [snow]$_{LSE}$ [white]$_{LPE}$

This sentence is not analytic because (let us assume) $\downarrow$ snow $\downarrow$ does not contain $\downarrow$ white $\downarrow$.

(3.69) Snow is black.

$[\text{is}]_{+ve}$ [snow]$_{LSE}$ [black]$_{LPE}$

This sentence is not analytic because $\downarrow$snow$\downarrow$ does not contain $\downarrow$black$\downarrow$.

(3.70) Snow is black and snow is black.

$[\text{and}]_n$ [snow is black]$_{LSE}$ [snow is black]$_{LPE}$.

This sentence is not analytic because its modifier is neutral.

(3.71) Bachelors are male and bachelors are male.

$[\text{and}]_n$ [bachelors are male]$_{LSE}$ [bachelors are male]$_{LPE}$

This sentence is not analytic because its modifier is neutral.

(3.72) Bachelors are male or bachelors are male.

$[\text{or}]_n$ [bachelors are male]$_{LSE}$ [bachelors are male]$_{LPE}$

This sentence is not analytic because its modifier is neutral.

(3.73) Bachelors are frustrated.

$[\text{are}]_{+ve}$ [bachelor]$_{LSE}$ [frustrated]$_{LPE}$

This sentence is neither analytic nor pseudo-analytic because, although the modifier is positive, the reference determiner for *frustrated* is not contained in that of *bachelor*.

(3.74) Hesperus is Phosphorus.

$[=]_{+ve}$ [Hesperus]$_{LSE}$ [Phosphorus]$_{LPE}$

This sentence is neither pseudo-analytic nor analytic because the reference determiner of *Hesperus* does not contain that of *Phosphorus*.

Examples of analytic entailment

> Snow is white and grass is green.
> ————————————————————
> Grass is green.

is analytically valid. The reference determiner for the premise *Snow is white and grass is green* contains the reference determiner for *Grass is green*; if the former is true, it will be at least in part because the latter is true.

APPENDIX A

The Formal System

A.1 PRELIMINARIES

A formal model theory for a subject matter need not answer all the questions that one might ask about it. We now have a formal way of thinking about modality, but we still cannot claim to have a good understanding of modality, or to have solved all the puzzles surrounding modal claims. But sometimes a formal approach can help to fix ideas, and can make subtle mistakes and equivocations more obvious. It is in the hope of achieving greater consistency and precision that I propose an extension of Kaplan's two-dimensional logic of demonstratives and indexicals, (LD) to a three-dimensional logic (3D), which models the distinctive roles of names and natural kind predicates. I make no claims for its elegance, nor for its technical innovation, but I do hope to clarify and fix ideas.

A.1.1 What a third dimension would add

One might wonder whether a three-dimensional logic is really required. Standard modal logics already handle some of the distinctions between analytic and non-analytic sentences involving names, such as *Hesperus is Hespersus* and *Hesperus is Phosphorus* and provide them with appropriate modal properties.[1] The first is analyzed as '$a = a$', which is necessary, and a truth of the logic, the other as '$a = b$', which is not a logical truth, though it has the interesting modal profile of being, within any model, true at all possible worlds if true at any.[2] The semantics for an ordinary modal logic explains this interesting status:[3] names are assigned referents without respect to possible worlds (outside of the possible worlds, if you like), and so, once a name is assigned its referent in the model, the state of the possible world with respect to which we are evaluating the sentence is irrelevant; if *Hesperus* refers to the same object as

---

[1] I'll ignore the worry about Hesperus not existing here.

[2] I will refer to the property of having this distinctive modal profile—as is commonplace—as the property of being *necessary if true.*

[3] My use of *explaining* here might seem a little odd. To what extent does a description of different models containing different "possible worlds", an accessibility relation and a story about interpretation constitute an explanation? Well, in one sense it can't, but in another it does: it shows that these differences between the sentences are *predicted* by the semantic theory.

Phosphorus in some model, they will both refer to that object with respect to all the possible worlds of that model and the sentence will be true with respect to all the possible worlds of the model, even if it is false in other models where *Hesperus* and *Phosphorus* are assigned different referents. Hence the sentence is *necessary if true.*

I think it's true that one-dimensional modal logic does a good job of accounting for these modal and logical properties of sentences containing names, but that there are also properties which it does not account for. Two things that I hope a three-dimensional modal logic could capture are:

- the sense in which *Hesperus is Phosphorus* could have been false, (and not simply by being interpreted as saying that Tom Stoppard solved the Liar paradox in Bratislava—the sense in which it can be false, even if we keep the reference determiners constant.)
- the fact that *Ali is Clay* could never have been false in the same way.

Modest aims, perhaps, but my aims here nonetheless.

First I will argue that these facts that I want to capture are true. *Hesperus is Phosphorus* (the *sentence*) could have been false. Here's how:

The name *Hesperus* was (let us suppose) introduced in 1845 when a man pointed at a bright star in the sky in the evening, and said, *Let's call that bright star 'Hesperus.'* The name *Phosphorus*, (our story continues) was introduced in 1700 when a woman pointed at our own morning star and said, *Let's call that bright spot 'Phosphorus.'* *Hesperus* thus, was determined to refer to whatever bright star the man was distracted by one morning in 1845 and *Phosphorus* to whatever bright spot the woman noticed in 1700.[4] As it happened these were the same object, and so the sentence *Hesperus is Phosphorus* expresses a proposition which is necessarily true, namely the proposition that Hesperus is Phosphorus. This *proposition* cannot be false, except (maybe) in a merely epistemic sense of *can*. Nonetheless the sentence *Hesperus is Phosphorus* might have been false, because the bright spot in the sky in the morning in 1845 might have been Mars. In that case *Hesperus is Phosphorus* would have expressed a different proposition, namely the proposition that Mars is Phosphorus.[5] This proposition is necessarily false, so the sentence would have been false.

So there is a way the world could have been which would have made the sentence *Hesperus is Phosphorus* false, consistent with it having the same reference determiners as it actually has.

But the same thing cannot be said of the sentence *Muhammed Ali is Cassius Clay*, given the way I have imagined it introduced. If *Muhammed Ali is*

---

[4] I do not, of course, mean to suggest that 'Hesperus' *means* 'what the bright spark was distracted by in 1845' means, nor that speakers in general know such a thing, nor that it plays a role in the proposition asserted when the sentence is uttered assertorically. I *do* mean to suggest that (prescinding from considerations about linguistic corruption) what our word *Hesperus* refers to depends on which object distracted the spark in 1845. It depends on *which* object he named.

[5] Assuming that the morning star in 1700 was still Venus.

introduced to refer to whomever *Cassius Clay* refers to, then (given that the names are introduced successfully) there is no way the world could be that would make the sentence *Muhammed Ali is Cassius Clay* false. Taking account of the context of introduction will allow us to account for this difference.

A.1.2 Could we do this without a third dimension?

A context of introduction is, in a sense, just a part of an ordinary possible world (a context of evaluation). The state of the world in which *Madonna* was introduced is just a past time-slice of the actual world. Do we really need a third kind of context when we might just make reference to part of one we are already considering?

Kaplan considers a similar objection to his two-dimensional logic. Kaplan's critic suggests that all we need is a slightly more general notion of a possible world—an index—that provides not merely a world but also a time, place, agent, etc. in that world:

$$i = \langle w, t, p, a, \ldots \rangle$$

"All these coordinates can be varied, possibly independently, and thus affect the truth-values of statements which have indirect references to those coordinates." (Kaplan 1989*b*: 508)

Kaplan's response is that this fails to capture what is special about the sentence *I am here now*. For many choices of index (i.e., those at which the agent is not located at place of the utterance), the sentence will be false. A logic of indexicals that does not capture the intuitive difference between this sentence and ordinary contingent sentences "has bypassed something essential to the logic of indexicals", says Kaplan. (1989*b*: 509)

A refinement of the rival solution that Kaplan also considers and rejects involves restricting the admissible indices to the *proper* ones, i.e. those $\langle w, t, p, a \rangle$ in which the agent a is located at the position p at t and with respect to w. The problem with this more restricted version of the proposal is that the falsehood

$$\Box \text{ (I am here now)}$$

comes out as a logical truth. We need the two different kinds of possible worlds–the two dimensions of the logic—to capture what is special about *I am here now*: the sentence is true with respect to all contexts of utterance, but not with respect to all contexts of evaluation. Hence the need to distinguish the two clearly.

The parallel criticism of my proposal would be that we do not need to make our models three-dimensional in order to correctly evaluate sentences involving names. Kaplan used the sentence *I am here now*, a logical truth which expressed contingent propositions, in order to show that truth with respect to a context of utterance differed from truth with respect to a possible world. Is there a sentence which could do similar work for me in the case of context of introduction and possible world? An obvious choice is the sentence *Hesperus is Phosphorus*, since here too the logical properties of the sentence come apart from the modal properties of the proposition it expresses: whether it says that Venus is Venus, or that Mars is Venus, it expresses a proposition which has the same truth value with respect to all possible worlds, but which is neither a logical truth, nor a logical falsehood. So let's consider two proposals for a semantics which takes account of the reference determiners of proper names without the use of a separate context of introduction, and ask whether they deal with *Hesperus is Phosphorus* appropriately.

We begin with the observation that two different names in the same sentence, such as *Hesperus* and *Phosphorus* in *Hesperus is Phosphorus*, will routinely have been introduced when the world was in different states; Hesperus was introduced at one time, Phosphorus at another.[6] Both those states were states in the same possible world and they were states of that world at different times. The neatest way to deal with this will be to let a context of introduction be an entire world history, and build a reference to time into the reference determiner for the name. The reference determiner for *Hesperus* can be thought of as a function from a context of introduction (a kind of world history) to an object—the bright star in the evening sky in 1845. Given the same context of introduction, the reference determiner for *Phosphorus* picks out the bright spot in the morning sky in 1700. With respect to the actual world history the functions take the same value, but given a different context of introduction—one where the bright star in the evening sky in 1845 is Mars—the functions have different values.

So here's the first of two non-3D proposals: Why not evaluate sentences with respect to an index, consisting of the following coordinates: a possible word history (the context of evaluation); a time; a series of objects, including a bright star in the evening sky in 1845, and a bright spot in the morning sky of 1700:

$$i = \langle w, t, e, m, \ldots \rangle$$

A sentence will be true at an index if, once the names have been assigned appropriate referents (*Hesperus* will denote the evening star of the index e, *Phosphorus* the morning star m, etc.) the resulting proposition is true in world

---

[6] I suppose it is possible to imagine a similar thing happening with the state of the world in which a sentence is uttered. ('I want *you* to start . . . 1, 2, 3 . . . NOW!'—clearly it is not permitted for the addressee to start as soon as the sentence is begun) but this is a special case, whereas with context of introduction it is routine for the context of introduction for names and natural kind terms to be centuries apart.

w of the index at time t of the index. On this version of the proposal, indices in which the evening star in w is not e are permitted. A model is a collection of indices and an interpretation function. A sentence is true in a model if true in all indices of the model, and a sentence is a logical truth if it is true in all models. So far, so intuitive. The problem with this proposal is that *Hesperus is Phosphorus* has lost the special modal character of being necessary if true. There are models in which *Hesperus is Phosphorus* is true at some index (say, $\langle w_1, t, e, e \rangle$) but false at another (say, $\langle w_1, t, e, f \rangle$). Since undoubtedly $w_1 R w_1$, '$\Box$(Hesperus = Phosphorus)' will not be true at the first index, though 'Hesperus = Phosphorus' is true.)

An alternative proposal is to restrict the admissible indices to those in which the referent of *Hesperus* is the object which is the bright star in the evening sky in 1845 *in the context of evaluation*, and the referent of *Phosphorus* is the bright spot...etc. In some ways this is an intuitive restriction: after all, we know that however *Hesperus* and *Phosphorus* were introduced, the world of their introduction was the actual world.

However it does not solve our problem: *Hesperus is Phosphorus* will still be false with respect to worlds accessible from this one, namely those at which the evening star is not the morning star. Moreover it causes new problems: the true modal claim:

(A.1) Hesperus might not have been the bright spot in the evening sky in 1845

is true at no index! This is to say that its negation comes out as a logical truth—a horrible result. In order to get (A.1) to come out true we need to fix its referent with one world (it will be the bright spot in the evening sky in 1845 in that world) but evaluate the truth of the resulting proposition with respect to a different possible world. So long as the indices are restricted to those in which the reference-fixing context matches the world of evaluation, this is impossible.

So, just as Kaplan argues that context of utterance and context of evaluation are different, we can give a similar argument that context of introduction and context of evaluation are different. But that is not sufficient to show that we need *three* dimensions, since once might think that context of introduction is just a feature of the context of utterance.[7]

A.1.3 A Two-Dimensionalist Strategy

Another two-dimensional strategy would proceed by allowing that the context of *utterance*, in addition to supplying an agent, and a time and a place, supplied

---

[7] Indeed, that strategy was urged upon me by Brendon Murday in his very useful commentary on my paper at the Syracuse Summer Workshop on the a priori in 2004.

a series of additional objects, such as a bright shiny object in the sky in the evening of 1845 and a bright shiny object in the sky in the morning of 1700:[8].

$$C = \langle a, t, p, e, m \ldots \rangle$$

The reference determiner for a name like *Hesperus* could then be modelled on Kaplan's one for *I*:

$$|I|_{cftw} = c_A$$

This can be read: the denotation of *I* in the context c under the assignment f at time t and at the world w is the agent of the context c. The "semantics" for the names *Hesperus*, *Phosphorus*, *Clay* and *Ali* might be:[9]

$\lvert\text{Hesperus}\rvert_{cftw}$	$= c_E$	where c_E is the bright shiny object in the sky in the evening of 1845 of the context.
$\lvert\text{Phosphorus}\rvert_{cftw}$	$= c_M$	where c_M, where c_M is the bright shiny object in the sky in the morning of 1700 of the context.
$\lvert\text{Clay}\rvert_{cftw}$	$= c_B$	where c_B is the first born baby of Mrs Clay of the context.
$\lvert\text{Ali}\rvert_{cftw}$	$= \lvert\text{Clay}\rvert_{cftw}$	

Given the reference determiner for *Hesperus*, the two-dimensionalist might want *Hesperus is the bright shiny object in the sky in the evening of 1845* to be true with respect to every context in which Hesperus gets a non-alien referent, but we definitely would not want the sentence to be necessary. (Hesperus might have been destroyed by the Vogons in 1840.) We can achieve this by allowing only proper contexts, those in which the object which the context assigns as the bright shiny object in the sky in the evening of 1845 (h) is the object which fits that description in the world of the context, w. (And likewise for the other names in the language.)

This is a view according to which names are a bit like indexicals, and as such, I don't like it very much. It's hard to believe that the reference determiner for a name somehow gets to be sensitive to the context in which the name is uttered, especially when speakers generally don't know the reference determiners for the names they use.

---

[8] We can perhaps imagine that sometimes the object provided is the null set, or perhaps Kaplan's alien {†}.

[9] The scare quotes around the word *semantics* are in acknowledgement of the point made in §2.5: that the study of the reference determiners of the names is not really a part of semantics, merely of metasemantics.

A reason that relies less on my own predilections is that having a separate context of introduction suggests an interesting way to define a *language*, namely as an assignment of reference determiners to expressions, plus a context of introduction:

Definition 18 (Language) *A language is an ordered pair* ⟨f, c⟩ *in which* f *is a function from expressions to reference determiners, and* c *is a possible world history (the context of introduction).*

Since reference determiners can be thought of (at the modal level) as functions from contexts of introduction to functions from context of utterance to intensions (themselves functions from possible worlds to extensions) such a pair provides a function from context of utterance to intension for each expression in the language.

One more intuitive reason for keeping contexts of introduction and utterance separate in the formalism is that we can consider cases in which the two vary independently of each other. Putnam's Twin Earth thought experiment is sometimes thought of as containing a description of a way the Earth might have been, that is, as describing an alternative universe. Thought of this way, there is no prospect of any of us actually visiting Twin Earth—even on construals of possibility on which such a Twin Earth would be a concrete place, it is not spatio-temporally connected to our spacetime. But another way to think about Twin Earth is as a planet very far away from our own which just happens to be very similar to the Earth. On this version of the thought experiment, it would be possible for two ordinary Earthlings—call them Oscar and Orlando—to go on holiday to Twin Earth. Let us suppose that while they are there Oscar visits the Science Museum in Twin London, and finds an exhibit which teaches him that the clear potable liquid which falls from the sky and fills the rivers, lakes and oceans on Twin Earth is not, as he had assumed, H_2O, as it is on Earth, but the foreign chemical compound X_YZ. Returning to their holiday chalet, he tells Orlando: "The stuff in the rivers here isn't actually water—it's something called X_YZ." Our version of the externalist intuition says that what Oscar tells Orlando is true, or more simply, that the following English sentences are true:

(A.2) The stuff in the rivers on Twin Earth is not H_2O.

(A.3) The stuff in the rivers on Twin Earth is not water.

(A.4) The stuff in the rivers on Twin Earth is X_YZ.

Intuitively, the context of introduction of the English word *water* has not changed (it was introduced on Earth), even though the context of utterance has. Suppose that the reference determiner for water states that *water* applies to the clear potable liquid found in the nearest to the baptiser in 1242. We are considering a case—on Twin Earth—in which the clear potable liquid found in the nearest lake in 1242 was X$_Y$Z, and yet Oscar's word *water* still picks out H$_2$O. It follows that the reference determiner for *water* is not sensitive to context of utterance—if it were, *water* would have to pick out X$_Y$Z. Yet it is okay for it to be sensitive to context of introduction, for that has not changed. The English word *water* was not *introduced* on Twin Earth, but on Earth.

Those who reject the externalist view and who think that names and natural kind terms are more like indexicals, so that, for example, the English word *water* is associated with a description such as *the actual clear potable liquid which fills streams, rivers and oceans* will think that *water* picks out X$_Y$Z when used on Twin Earth, and so might argue that we do not need contexts of introduction to account for the behaviour of that expression. But even if the natural language expression *water* does not work that way, it surely makes sense to imagine that some expression does, and even to define a new expression which does. And as Jim Pryor suggested to me, we can also define a one-place functor *superdthat*, on the model of Kaplan's regidifying functor *dthat*.[10]

Definition 19 (dthat[α]) *If α is a description, the denotation of ⌜dthat[α]⌝ with respect to the context of utterance ⟨a, p, t, w⟩ is the denotation of α at time t with respect to the context of evaluation w.*

For example, uttered on 4 December, 2005 *dthat[the shortest spy]* refers to whoever is the shortest spy on 4 December, 2005, and the sentence (A.5) is true just in case the person who is the shortest spy *in the context of utterance* is middle-aged *ten years later*.

(A.5) Ten years from now, dthat[the shortest spy] will be middle-aged.

Similarly, (A.6) could be true, even if it were necessary that there are at least two spies of differing heights, because *dthat[the shortest spy]* refers to whoever the shortest spy is in the world of the context of utterance—and there is surely a possible world in which *that person* is the tallest spy.

(A.6) It might have been the case that dthat[the shortest spy] was the tallest spy.

Definition 20 (Superdthat[α]) *Where α is a description, the denotation of* superdthat[α] *with respect to the context of introduction* c_i *is the denotation of* α *with respect to* c_i *for* α

(A.7) Superdthat[the watery stuff] is X$_Y$Z.

(A.8) Superdthat[the watery stuff] is H$_2$O.

---

[10] As Kaplan notes in "Afterthoughts" (1989*a*), his expression *dthat* originally (and unintentionally) received two interpretations in "Demonstratives". In the main body of the text *dthat[α]* had a complex character but simple content; the content of the expression was the referent of the description in the context of utterance.

(A.9) Water is $X_Y Z$.

(A.10) Water is not H_2O.

For example (A.7) would be false on Twin Earth, since *superdthat[the watery stuff]* refers to $H_2 0$ regardless of the context of utterance, and (A.8) is true on Twin Earth for the same reason, even if, as some maintain, (A.9) and (A.10) would be true there.

A.1.4 The Three-Dimensional Approach

So now, hopefully, I have said enough to justify exploring the three-dimensional approach. On this approach names and natural kind terms have reference determiners that are as insensitive to context of utterance as they are to context of evaluation. The fact that the sentence *Hesperus is Phosphorus* might have been false is a consequence of the fact that the reference determiner for a name is sensitive to something else: the context of introduction. This does not mean that names are just a different kind of indexical. The content of an indexical term varies with context of utterance. But, with respect to a language at least, the contents of names do not actually vary at all. The meaning of a name is determined at its introduction and it remains constant. It's just that had the context of introduction been different, the content of the name might have been different.

Here is how this might play out more formally:[11]

A.2 THE LANGUAGE

A.2.1 Primitive Symbols

(0) Punctuation: (,), [,]
(1a) Variables:
     (i) An infinite set of individual variables: V_i
     (ii) An infinite set of position variables: V_P
(2a) Predicates:
     i. An infinite number of m-n-place predicates, for all natural numbers m, n.
     ii. The 1-0-place predicate: Exist
     iii. The 1-1-place predicate: Located
(3) Functors:

---

[11] Much of what is presented here is already present in Kaplan's Logic of Demonstratives. Where practical, I indicate where this system differs from Kaplan's in bold type.

    i. An infinite number of m-n-place i-functors (functors which form terms denoting individuals)

    ii. An infinite number of m-n-place p-functors (functors which form terms denoting positions)

(4) Sentential Connectives: $\quad \wedge, \vee, \neg, \rightarrow, \leftrightarrow$

(5) Quantifiers: $\forall, \exists$

(6) Definite Description Operator: the

(7) Identity: $=$

(8) Modal Operators: $\square, \Diamond$

(9) Tense Operators: F, P, G

(10) Three 1-place sentential operators:

        N (it is now the case that)

        A (it is actually the case that)

        Y (yesterday, it was the case that)

(11) A 1-place functor: dthat

(12) An individual constant (0-0-place i-functor): I

(13) A position constant (0-0-place p-functor): Here

(14) **Individual constants: Ali, Hesperus, Phosphorus, Clay**

(15) **A one place functor: superdthat$_f$**

A.2.2 Well-Formed Expressions

The well-formed expressions are of three kinds: formulas, position terms (p-terms) and individual terms (i-terms).

(1)   i. If $\alpha \in \mathcal{V}_i$, then α is an i-term

      ii. If $\alpha \in \mathcal{V}_p$, then α is a p-term

(2)   If π is an m-n-place predicate, $\alpha_1, \ldots, \alpha_m$ are i-terms, and $\beta_1, \ldots, \beta_n$ are p-terms, then $\pi \alpha_1, \ldots, \alpha_m \beta_1, \ldots, \beta_n$ is a formula

(3)   i. If η is an m-n-place i-functor, $\alpha_1, \ldots, \alpha_m$ are i-terms, and $\beta_1, \ldots, \beta_n$ are p-terms, then $\eta \alpha_1, \ldots, \alpha_m \beta_1, \ldots, \beta_n$ is an i-term

      ii. If η is an m-n-place p-functor, $\alpha_1, \ldots, \alpha_m$ are i-terms, and $\beta_1, \ldots, \beta_n$ are p-terms, then $\eta \alpha_1, \ldots, \alpha_m \beta_1, \ldots, \beta_n$ is a p-term

(4)   If ϕ, ψ are formulas, then $(\phi \wedge \psi), (\phi \vee \psi), \neg \phi, (\phi \rightarrow \psi), (\phi \leftrightarrow \psi)$ are formulas.

(5)   If ϕ is a formula and $\alpha \in \mathcal{V}_i \cup \mathcal{V}_p$, then $\forall \alpha \phi$ and $\exists \alpha \phi$ are formulas

(6)   If ϕ is a formula, then

    i. if $\alpha \in V_i$, then the $\alpha \phi$ is an i-term

    ii. if $\alpha \in V_p$, then the $\alpha \phi$ is a p-term

(7)   If α, β are either both i-terms or both p-terms, then $\alpha = \beta$ is a formula

(8)   If ϕ is a formula, then $\square \phi$ and $\Diamond \phi$ are formulas

(9)   If ϕ is a formula, then $F\phi$, $P\phi$ and $G\phi$ are formulas

(10)   If ϕ is a formula, then $N\phi$, $A\phi$ and $Y\phi$ are formulas

(11)   i. If α is an i-term, then dthat$[\alpha]$ is an i-term

      ii. If α is a p-term, then dthat$[\alpha]$ is a p-term

(12)   i. If α is an i-term or a p-term, then $\ulcorner$'α'$\urcorner$ is an i-term

      ii. If α is an i-term, then superdthat$[\alpha]$ is an i-term

      iii. If α is a p-term, then superdthat$[\alpha]$ is a p-term

A.3 SEMANTICS

Definition 21 (3-D Structures) $\mathfrak{M}$ *is a 3D structure iff there are* $\mathcal{C}$, $\mathcal{H}$, $\mathcal{W}$, $\mathfrak{U}$, $\mathcal{P}$, $\mathcal{T}$ *and* $\mathcal{I}$ *such that:*

(1) $\mathfrak{M} = \langle \mathcal{H}, \mathcal{C}, \mathcal{W}, \mathfrak{U}, \mathcal{P}, \mathcal{T}, \mathcal{I} \rangle$

(2) $\mathcal{C}$ is a non-empty set (the set of contexts of use)

(3)   If $c \in \mathcal{C}$ then

       i. $c_A \in \mathfrak{U}$ (the agent of c)

       ii. $c_T \in \mathcal{T}$ (the time of c)

       iii. $c_P \in \mathcal{P}$ (the position of c)

       iv. $c_W \in \mathcal{W}$ (the world of c)

(4) $\mathcal{H}$ **is a non-empty set (the set of contexts of introduction) If** $h \in \mathcal{H}$, **then:**

       i. $h_E \in \mathfrak{U}$ **(the bright star in the evening sky in 1845 of** h**)**

       ii. $h_M \in \mathfrak{U}$ **(the bright spot in the morning sky in 1700 of** h**)**

       iii. $h_B \in \mathfrak{U}$ **(the first-born of Mrs Clay of** h**)**

       iv. $h_W \in \mathcal{W}$ **the world of** h**) (needed for 'superdthat')**

(5) $\mathcal{W}$ is a non-empty set (the set of contexts of evaluation)

(6) $\mathfrak{U}$ is a non-empty set (the set of all individuals)

(7) $\mathcal{P}$ is a non-empty set (the set of positions, common to all worlds)

(8) $\mathcal{T}$ is the set of integers (thought of as times, common to all worlds)

(9) $\mathcal{I}$ is a function which assigns to each predicate and functor an appropriate intension as follows:

       i. if π is an m-n-predicate, I_π is a function such that for each $t \in \mathcal{T}$ and $w \in \mathcal{W}$, $I_\pi(t, w) \subseteq (\mathfrak{U}^m \times \mathcal{P}^n)$

       ii. if η is an m-n-place i-functor, $\mathcal{I}_\eta$ is a function such that for each $t \in T$ and $w \in \mathcal{W}$, $\mathcal{I}\eta(t, w) \in (\mathfrak{U} \cup \{\dagger\})^{(\mathfrak{U}^m \times \mathcal{P}^n)}$ (Note: $\dagger$ is a completely alien entity, in neither $\mathfrak{U}$ nor $\mathcal{P}$, which represents an 'undefined' value of the function. In a normal set theory we can take $\dagger$ to be $\{\mathfrak{U}, \mathcal{P}\}$)

       iii. If η is an m-n-place p-functor, $\mathcal{I}_\eta$ is a function such that for each $t \in \mathcal{T}$ and $w \in \mathcal{W}$, $I_\eta(t, w) \in (p \cup \{\dagger\})^{(\mathfrak{U}^m \times \mathcal{P}^n)}$

(10) $i \in \mathfrak{U}$ iff $(\exists t \in T)(\exists w \in W)(\langle i \rangle \in \mathcal{I}_{\text{Exist}}(t, w))$

(11)   If $c \in \mathcal{C}$, then $\langle c_A, c_P \rangle \in I_{\text{Located}}(c_T, c_W)$

(12)   If $\langle i, p \rangle \in \mathcal{I}_{\text{Located}}(t, w)$, then $\langle i \rangle \in \mathcal{I}_{\text{Exist}}(t, w)$

A.3.1 Truth and Denotation

We write: $\vDash^{\mathfrak{M}}_{\mathsf{hcftw}} \phi$ for ϕ, when taken in the context of introduction h and in the context of utterance c (under the assignment f and in the structure $\mathfrak{M}$), is *true with respect to* the time t and the world w.

We write: $|\alpha|^{\mathfrak{M}}_{\mathsf{hcftw}}$ for   the denotation of α, when taken in the context of introduction h and the context of utterance c (under the assignment f and in the structure $\mathfrak{M}$), *with respect to* to time t and the world w.

In general we will omit the superscript '$\mathfrak{M}$', and we will assume that the structure $\mathfrak{M}$ is $\langle \mathcal{C}, \mathcal{W}, \mathcal{H}, \mathfrak{U}, \mathcal{P}, \mathcal{T}, \mathfrak{I} \rangle$.

Definition: f is an assignment (with respect to $\langle \mathcal{C}, \mathcal{W}, \mathcal{N}, \mathfrak{U}, \mathcal{P}, \mathcal{T}, \mathfrak{I} \rangle$) iff:

$$\exists \mathsf{f}_1 \mathsf{f}_2 (\mathsf{f}_1 \in \mathfrak{U}^{\mathcal{V}_i} \text{ and } \mathsf{f}_2 \in \mathsf{P}^{\mathcal{V}_p} \text{ and } \mathsf{f} = \mathsf{f}_1 \cup \mathsf{f}_2)$$

Definition:

$$\mathsf{f}^{\alpha}_{\mathsf{x}} = (\mathsf{f} \sim \{\langle \alpha, \mathsf{f}(\alpha) \rangle\}) \cup \{\langle \alpha, \mathsf{x} \rangle\}$$

(i.e. the assignment which is just like f except that it assigns x to α.)

Definition: For the following recursive definition, assume that $\mathsf{c} \in \mathsf{C}$, f is an assignment, $\mathsf{t} \in \mathcal{T}$, $\mathsf{h} \in \mathsf{H}$ and $\mathsf{w} \in \mathcal{W}$:

(1)   If α is a variable, $|\alpha|_{\mathsf{hcftw}} = \mathsf{f}(\alpha)$

(2) $\vDash_{\mathsf{hcftw}} \pi\alpha_1 \ldots \alpha_m \beta_1 \ldots \beta_n$ iff $\langle |\alpha_1|_{\mathsf{hcftw}} \ldots |\beta_n|_{\mathsf{hcftw}} \rangle$
$\in \mathfrak{I}_\pi(\mathsf{t}, \mathsf{w})$

(3)   If η is neither 'I' nor 'here', **nor 'Hesperus', 'Phosphorus', 'Clay' or 'Ali'**, (see 12–17 below), then:

$$|\eta\alpha_1 \ldots \alpha_m \beta_1 \ldots \beta_n|_{\mathsf{hcftw}} = \left\{ \begin{array}{l} \mathfrak{I}_\eta(\mathsf{t}, \mathsf{w})(\langle |\alpha_1|_{\mathsf{hcftw}} \ldots \\ \quad |\beta_n|_{\mathsf{hcftw}}\rangle) \\ \text{if none of } |\alpha_j|_{\mathsf{hcftw}} \ldots \\ \quad |\beta_n|_{\mathsf{hcftw}} \\ \text{are } \dagger; \\ \dagger, \text{ otherwise} \end{array} \right.$$

(4)   i. $\vDash_{\mathsf{hcftw}} (\phi \wedge \psi)$ iff $\vDash_{\mathsf{hcftw}} \phi$ & $\vDash_{\mathsf{hcftw}} \psi$
    ii. $\vDash_{\mathsf{hcftw}} \neg\phi$ iff $\nvDash_{\mathsf{hcftw}} \phi$ etc.

(5) i. If $\alpha \in \mathcal{V}_i$, then $\vDash_{hcftw} \forall\alpha\phi$ iff $\forall i \in \mathfrak{U}, \vDash_{hcf_i^\alpha tw} \phi$

ii. If $\alpha \in \mathcal{V}_p$, then $\vDash_{hcftw} \forall\alpha\phi$ iff $\forall p \in \mathcal{P}, \vDash_{hcf_p^\alpha tw} \phi$

iii. Similarly for $\exists\alpha\phi$

(6) i. If $\alpha \in \mathcal{V}_i$, then:

$$|\text{the } \alpha\phi|_{hcftw} = \begin{cases} \text{the unique } i \in \mathfrak{U} \text{ such that } \vDash_{hcf_i^\alpha tw} \phi, \text{ if} \\ \text{there is such;} \\ \dagger, \text{otherwise} \end{cases}$$

ii. Similarly for $\alpha \in \mathcal{V}_p$

(7) $\vDash_{hcftw} \alpha = \beta$ iff $|\alpha|_{hcftw} = |\beta|_{hcftw}$

(8) i. $\vDash_{hcftw} \Box\phi$ iff $\forall w' \in \mathcal{W}, \vDash_{hcftw'} \phi$

ii. $\vDash_{hcftw} \Diamond\phi$ iff $\exists w' \in \mathcal{W}, \vDash_{hcftw'} \phi$

(9) i. $\vDash_{hcftw} F\phi$ iff $\exists t'$ such that $t' > t$ and $\vDash_{hcft'w} \phi$

ii. $\vDash_{hcftw} P\phi$ iff $\exists t'$ such that $t' < t$ and $\vDash_{hcft'w} \phi$

iii. $\vDash_{hcftw} G\phi$ iff $\vDash_{hcf(t-1)w} \phi$

(10) i. $\vDash_{hcftw} N\phi$ iff $\vDash_{hcfc_T w} \phi$

ii. $\vDash_{hcftw} A\phi$ iff $\vDash_{hcftc_w} \phi$

iii. $\vDash_{hcftw} Y\phi$ iff $\vDash_{hcf(c_T -1)w} \phi$

(11) i. $|dthat[\alpha]|_{hcftw} = |\alpha|_{hcfc_T c_w}$

ii. $|superdthat[\alpha]|_{hcftw} = |\alpha|_{hcfth_w}$ (time is not supplied by h)

(12) $|I|_{hcftw} = c_A$

(13) $|Here|_{hcftw} = c_P$

(14) $|\mathbf{Hesperus}|_{hcftw} = h_E$

(15) $|\mathbf{Phosphorus}|_{hcftw} = h_M$

(16) $|\mathbf{Clay}|_{hcftw} = h_B$

(17) $|\mathbf{Ali}|_{hcftw} = |\mathbf{Clay}|_{hcftw}$

A.4 CONTENT, VALIDITY AND REFERENCE DETERMINERS

We can use this formal framework to provide definitions of content, truth in a context, and reference determiner. In general, sentences containing indexicals or names will express different propositions with respect to different contexts of utterance and introduction. But we can think of the content of a sentence with respect to a context of introduction and a context of utterance as the proposition it would express if the context of introduction sensitive expressions it contains had been introduced in the context of introduction, and the sentence were uttered in the context of utterance, and identify that (in our rough and ready modal framework) with a function from contexts of evaluation and times to truth-values (in the case of sentences) or extensions (in the case of non-sentential expressions).

Where Γ is either a term or a formula,

we write: $\{\Gamma\}^{\mathfrak{M}}_{hcf}$ for the Content of Γ in the context of introduction h and the context of utterance c (under the assignment f and in the structure $\mathfrak{M}$)

Definition 22 (Content) *If ϕ is a formula, $\{\phi\}^{\mathfrak{M}}_{hcf} = $ that function which assigns to each $t \in \mathfrak{T}$ and $w \in \mathcal{W}$, Truth, if $\vDash^{\mathfrak{M}}_{hcftw} \phi$, and Falsehood otherwise. If α is a term, $\{\alpha\}^{\mathfrak{M}}_{hcf} = $ that function which assigns to each $t \in \mathfrak{T}$ and $w \in \mathcal{W}$, $|\alpha|_{hcftw}$.*

Sentences containing indexicals and names will not express contents, and hence will not have truth-values, until they are embedded in contexts of utterance and introduction. The content thus determined will be true just in case it maps the time and world of the context of utterance to Truth.

Definition 23 (Truth with Respect to Contexts) *ϕ is true in the context of introduction h and the context of utterance c, in the structure $\mathfrak{M}$ iff for every assignment f, $\{\phi\}^{\mathfrak{M}}_{hcf}(c_T, c_W) = $ Truth.*

Definition 24 (Validity) *ϕ is valid in 3-D ($\vDash \phi$) iff for every 3-D structure $\mathfrak{M}$, and every pair of context of introduction h and context of utterance c of $\mathfrak{M}$, ϕ is true with respect to c and h (in $\mathfrak{M}$).*

A.5 SOME THEOREMS

Theorem 25 ($\vDash$ N(**Located I, Here**)) *The addition of contexts of introduction does not affect the status of this sentence at all. The referents of I, here and now are all functions of context of utterance alone and, as before, only contexts of utterance where the agent is located at the place p and time t are admissible.*

Theorem 26 ($\vDash$ **Hesperus = Hesperus**) *Though varying the context of introduction will allow Hesperus to pick out different objects, there is no context of introduction with respect to which the first occurrence of Hesperus in the above wff fails to pick out the same object as the second occurrence. So for all h, c in all structures $|Hesperus|_{hcftw} = |Hesperus|_{hcftw}$ and hence $\vDash$ Hesperus = Hesperus.*

In the context of this logic we do not need to worry about reference failure, since the semantics guarantee every name a referent. Hence in the formal system not only is the distinction between the modal and metaphysical conceptions of analyticity lost, but the distinction between analyticity and pseudo-analyticity as well.[12]

---

[12] *Exactly* what the relation between logical truth and analyticity is is something I'm not too sure about. But I think they are very closely related: both are properties that

Theorem 27 (*If* ⊨ *Hesperus* = *Phosphorus then*⊨ □(*Hesperus* = *Phosphorus*))
Suppose ⊨ (*Hesperus* = *Phosphorus*). *Then for all* $\mathfrak{M}$ *and* $c \in \mathcal{C}, h \in \mathcal{H} \in M$
$\vDash^{\mathfrak{M}}_{hcftw}$ (*Hesperus* = *Phosphorus*) *(if the sentence is valid, then it is true in all pairs of* c *and* h *in all models.) Then for all such* h *and* c $|Hesperus|_{hcftw} = |Phosphorus|_{hcftw}$ *and so* $h_M = h_E$. *So* $|Hesperus|_{hcftw'}$ *(where* w' *is arbitrary)* $= |Phosphorus|_{hcftw'}$ *(since the values of* c, f, t *and* w *are irrelevant to determining the referent of a name), and thus* $\vDash_{hcftw'}$ (*Hesperus* = *Phosphorus*) *and* $\vDash_{hcftw}$ □(*Hesperus* = *Phosphorus*)*(by the semantics for '*□*', since* w' *was arbitrary).*

Theorem 28 (⊨ **Ali** = **Clay**) *Whatever the value of* h *and* c, $|Ali|_{hcftw} = |Clay|_{hcftw}$, *(by the semantics for 'Ali'.) So* $\vDash_{hcftw}$ Ali = Clay *and* ⊨ Ali = Clay

Theorem 29 (⊭ **superdthat**[α] = α) *Although* **dthat**[α] = α *is valid, as in Kaplan's system, superdthat[α] = α is not, since the referent of 'superdthat[α]' is the referent of* α *with respect to the context of introduction, and that may no longer be the referent of* α *since we need no longer be in the context of introduction. This is why one can use a description* α *to provide a definition of a term* t *and later on have* t = α *fail to be true. (See Chapter 5 for more on Quine's views on the transience of definition)*

We can think of the reference determiner of an expression as a function from contexts of utterance, introduction and evaluation to objects, extensions or truth-values.

Where Γ **is either a term or a formula,**

we write: $\downarrow \Gamma \downarrow^{\mathfrak{M}}_{hcf}$ for   the reference determiner of Γ (under the assignment f and in the structure $\mathfrak{M}$)

Definition 30 (Reference Determiner) *If* α *is a term,* $\downarrow \alpha \downarrow^{\mathfrak{M}}_{hcf} =$ *that function which assigns to each structure* $\mathfrak{U}$, *assignment* f, *context of introduction* h, *context of utterance* c *and context of evaluation* w, $|\alpha|_{hcftw}$.
If ϕ *is a formula,* $\downarrow \phi \downarrow^{\mathfrak{M}}_{hcf} =$ *that function which assigns to each structure* $\mathfrak{U}$, *assignment* f, *context of introduction* h, *context of utterance* c *and context of evaluation* w, *Truth if* $\vDash^{\mathfrak{M}}_{hcftw}$ ϕ

Given the definition of content, if the reference determiner of an expression is insensitive to context of utterance and context of introduction, its content and reference determiner will coincide.

Kaplan's formal system does not give a *semantic theory* for his language, in the sense of a theory that assigns meanings to expressions. Kaplan's formal

sentences have in virtue of their reference determiners, and I think that logical truth (and validity) admit of the same modal/metaphysical/wide distinctions as analyticity and direct reference. Our usual model theoretic characterisations of logical truth and validity look like attempts to capture the modal notion.

system is much more like the "semantics" (or model theory) for a traditional logic. (Burgess 2005) Within (LD) the meaning of a name, for instance, is provided by the model's interpretation function, and this means that different meanings may be assigned to the same name in different models. (3D) is not a semantic theory either, but the meaning of a name in (3D) is no longer assigned by the interpretation function. Rather (3D) assigns a reference determiner to each name, and that will determine its denotation. But the reference determiner of a name is not its meaning. If we were only interested in semantics, and so only interested in the meanings of expressions, we could allow (3D) to assign objects to names directly (instead of via a reference determiner). In assigning meanings via reference determiners, (3D) takes account of some elements of the pre-semantics of names—the way in which their meanings get determined—in addition to the semantics. It is this element that allows it to take account of the sense in which the sentence *Hesperus is Phosphorus* could have been false, even though (i) the proposition it expresses is necessary, and (ii) its meaning does not vary.

PART II

A DEFENSE

PART II (ABSTRACT)

"Quine's attack on intuitive semantics is no seamless web", wrote
Michael McDermott (2001: 977), and I am inclined to agree and
extend this remark to the case against the analytic/synthetic distinction
in general. There is no such thing as *the* argument against the distinction,
and though it is easy to get the impression that "Two Dogmas of
Empiricism" contains the most important arguments, perhaps with the
paper's skepticism about meaning supported by the book *Word and
Object*, in fact Quine's work contains a wealth of different attacks,
many of which can be found in the early paper "Truth by Convention"
(1935) and the later "Carnap and Logical Truth" (1954). In addition
to Quine's offensive, we have to contend with the rise of the picture
of language known as the causal theory of reference, with arguments
from externalism and vagueness, and with minor philosophical industry
of providing outlandish counterexamples to putatively analytic claims,
which began with Mill, and continues in the work of Putnam and
Harman. The three chapters of **Part II** defend my conception of
analyticity against a total of fourteen arguments against the distinction:
Chapter 4 focuses on the arguments from "Two Dogmas", Chapter
5 addresses a variety of Quinean arguments concerning the nature of
definitions and Chapter 6 confronts a mish-mash of other arguments,
including arguments from vagueness and content externalism.

4

The Spectre of "Two Dogmas"

4.1 THE CIRCULARITY OBJECTION

In "Two Dogmas of Empiricism" Quine argues that the expression *analytic* is defective. Its meaning is unclear and cannot be clarified because those expressions in terms of which it might have been clarified—*meaning, synonymous, necessary, semantical rule, self-contradictory* and *definition*—are themselves in need of clarification.[1] For example, Quine thinks that we can define an analytic sentence as one which can be converted into a logical truth by substitution of synonyms for synonyms, just as (4.1) below can be converted into the logical truth (4.1) by substituting the expression *bachelors* for *unmarried men*.

(4.1) All bachelors are bachelors.

(4.2) All bachelors are unmarried men.

Yet Quine maintains that this will not suffice to clarify analyticity, as the notion of synonymy—and hence the entire explanation—is itself unclear. We might say that two expressions are synonymous if they may always be substituted for each other within the contexts *it is necessary that*... and *necessarily*... without loss of truth-value. Yet this will not suffice to clarify synonymy, since the notion of necessity is also unclear. And worse:

The above argument supposes we are working with a language rich enough to contain the adverb 'necessarily,' this adverb being so construed as to yield truth when and only when applied to an analytic statement. But can we condone a language which contains such an adverb? Does the adverb really make sense? To suppose that it does is to suppose that we have already made satisfactory sense of 'analytic.' (Quine 1951: 29)

---

[1] Quine has a particular non-extensional sense of *meaning* in mind, a sense on which *the evening star* and *the morning star* mean different things.

Quine thinks that necessity can only be understood in terms of analyticity, and hence that the attempted explanation is *circular*. This is the circularity argument from the first part of "Two Dogmas of Empiricism."

The least contentious part of the argument is that semantic terms are inter-definable.[2] Let us also, for the sake of argument, grant that they cannot be defined without using expressions from Quine's circle. Then the argument is *still* enigmatic. What is wrong with analyticity that it requires this treatment? Why does Quine's failure to find an account of analyticity show that there is none? Why is supposing that necessity makes sense to suppose that we have already made sense of analyticity? And most puzzling of all, if Quine is right—if he does not understand semantic concepts, and there is no analytic/synthetic distinction—how come the bulk of his paper consists of pretty decent analyses of semantic concepts?

4.1.1 Appreciating the Circularity Argument

Soames has emphasised the need to see the circularity argument in its historical context in order to understand it. He points to two key assumptions which contemporary readers may not be making, but which were widely accepted at the time the paper was published.[3]

(T1) all necessary truths are analytic

(T2) if necessity can be explained, it can only be explained in terms of analyticity.

If one accepts (T2), then an explanation of analyticity in terms of necessity will be circular, but if, as some believe today, necessity can hold its own without a defense in terms of analyticity, the circularity can be avoided. Yet even once we accept that Quine was working with these assumptions, puzzles remain. Why was the explanation necessary in the first place? How can the failure of one explanation show that there is no

---

[2] Though it is still contentious. *Two* and *four divided by two* are intersubstitutable salve veritate within the context *it is necessary that . . .* but they are not synonymous. See §3.2.4 for more on this topic.

[3] Soames then maintains that since the circularity argument "presupposes the positivists' mistaken assumption that necessity . . . and analyticity make sense only if (T1) and (T2) are correct, it shares their error, and is largely irrelevant to contemporary understandings of these notions." (2003: 360--1) Here I retain Soames' names for the assumptions.

explanation? And how can Quine, given his professed beliefs, carry out the analyses he carries out?

Many of Quine's critics see his demand for an explanation as based on a special, but suspect, criterion of meaningfulness or clarity, which the critics then reject.

> . . . it would seem that Quine requires of a satisfactory explanation of an expression that it should take the form of a pretty strict definition but should not make use of any member of a group of interdefinable terms to which the expression belongs. We may well begin to feel that a satisfactory explanation is hard to come by . . . It would seem fairly unreasonable to insist *in general* that the availability of a satisfactory explanation in the sense sketched above is a necessary condition of an expression's making sense. It is perhaps dubious whether any such explanations can ever be given. (The hope that they can be is, or was, the hope of reductive analysis in general.) (Grice & Strawson 1956: 148)

> Our conclusion is that Quine's Socratic requirement on the legitimacy of concepts appears to be unreasonable and unmotivated. The fact that "analytic" does not meet that requirement does not establish that it is unintelligible."(Miller 1998: 123)

> It is a testimonial to how influential Quine has been with respect to some of his *other* philosophical ideas that this criticism of analyticity now seems so thin. Quine taught us that the main question we should ask about a theory is whether it is indispensable as a device for explaining and predicating phenomena . . . Quine's circularity argument against analyticity and necessity is a prime example of an appeal to 'first philosophy', a practice that Quine later criticised . . . (Sober 2000: 242)

Though Quine's criteria for a satisfactory explanation are not stated in "Two Dogmas of Empiricism", he does say in other places that a definition in terms of speakers' dispositions, or sometimes a definition in terms of extensional concepts, would be required to make analyticity respectable. Quine may then be understood as having thought that no expression which could not receive such an explanation was really meaningful, and as taking his careful but fruitless search for one as providing prima facie evidence that there was no explanation to be found in the case of analyticity. We might even explain Quine's use of analyses to challenge analyticity by thinking of the circularity objection as a kind of ad hominem argument, employing ideas accepted by his opponents to argue against them. It still seems odd that Quine was able to provide analyses of expressions which he professed not to understand, but if we think of him as employing a very restricted principle of meaningfulness, then we might maintain that although he *really* understood the expressions as well as anyone, he genuinely believed the deliverances of the overly restrictive principle, and hence concluded that he *couldn't* know what they meant, because they didn't mean anything.

However, it seems to me—now that we are better about distinguishing the different kinds of meaning—that we can do better justice to Quine's argument.

Circularity and reference determination

Expressions owe their referents to their reference determiners. And to the extent that an expression has no reference determiners, it will have no referent—referent acquisition is not a miracle.[4] To the extent that the reference determiners for an expression fail to legislate for particular cases, it will be undecided whether something falls into the extension (or anti-extension) of the expression.

It is possible to give the reference determiner for an expression by way of that of another expression. For example, we might introduce a new expression *ancle*, stipulating that something is an ancle just in case it is either an aunt or an uncle. Then, even if we are not sure about who is an aunt or an uncle, we will know that the extension of *ancle* will be the union of the extension of *aunt* and the extension of *uncle*. This introduction will go smoothly *unless* we have already used *ancle* to determine the referent for *uncle*. We might have done this, for example, by stipulating that an uncle is an ancle who is not an aunt. If this is how we introduced *uncle*, then we are in trouble. For consider what the reference determiner for *ancle* is: *ancle* applies to an object just in case either *aunt* does or *uncle* does. Suppose the world contains no aunts, does it contain any ancles? There is no answer to this question because the condition for being an ancle contains a circularity. The world contains ancles just in case it contains uncles (given that there are no aunts), and uncles just in case it contains ancles. So no matter what there is (so long as there are no aunts) we have no grounds for saying either that it is, or that it is not, an ancle. Reference determiners cannot contain circularities like this, because then they fail to determine referents.

So here is what I think Quine might have been thinking: he thinks that the reference determiner for *analytic* is circular. And if he is right,

---

[4] This, I suppose, need not mean that it is meaningless. Plausibly, *hello* has no referent, but it isn't meaningless. It just isn't a good fit in assertoric utterances.

then there is no fact of the matter, for any sentence, about whether it is analytic or not.

Part of the language myth is the thesis that speakers know how the referents of their words are determined and so Quine might expect himself to know—at least implicitly—the reference determiners of any word he understands, and in particular that his analysis of *analytic* (transformable into a logical truth by substitution of synonyms for synonyms) states *the* reference determiner for *analytic*. And similarly that his analysis of *synonymous* states *the* reference determiner for the expression. And if so, given that the reference determiner for *necessary* is parasitic on that of *analytic*, he will think that *the* reference-determiner for *analytic* is circular, in which case there is no fact of the matter, for any sentence, about whether it is analytic or not. There will be no sense in looking for other analyses, because we know that this is the one that gives the actual reference determiners for *analytic*. Moreover, Quine is able to give his analyses, even though he claims that the meaning of the expressions is unclear, because it is the *reference* of, say, *analytic* that is unclear (that is, it is unclear which things are analytic, because the reference determiner is faulty), not the mechanism by which the referent is determined (he thinks he knows what that is.) Thus this interpretation of Quine clears up the puzzles about why he thinks the failure of one explanation of the meaning of *analytic* shows that there is no explanation, about how he is able to argue that *analytic* is meaningless by giving analyses of words he doesn't understand, and it explains the importance of the circularity. It also explains why he thinks an explanation is required; if expressions don't have good reference determiners, then they do not have referents, and analytic is the kind of expression (unlike *hello!*), which is supposed to have a referent.

As we learned with the demise of the language myth, speakers do not always know the reference determiners for their words, and so relying on their intuitions—and even their philosophers' intuitions—to tell one about the reference of their words in certain cases is risky. It is certainly not the case that if one intelligent attempt at discovering the correct reference determiner for *analytic* turns out badly, no attempt can turn out well.

A further problem with the argument—squarely in the tradition of Grice and Strawson's and Sober's responses this time—is that Quine had some unusually strict ideas about the nature of reference determiners. He thought that the conditions under which an expression applies should be given in terms of speakers' dispositions to behave, or using only extensional concepts. I side with Grice, Strawson and Sober in holding that this is too restrictive. I am unable to give a definition of *bachelor* in terms of extensional concepts or speakers dispositions to behave, and if Quine's critique applies to this respectable word, as well to the racier *analyticity*, then there is something wrong with the critique—it proves too much.[5]

Finally, how does my own definition of analyticity fare with respect to the circularity objection? The reference determiner for *analytic* is not given in extensional terms, or in terms of speaker dispositions, but that is acceptable, since this requirement was too strong anyway. The important question is whether or not it provides a non-circular reference determiner for *analytic*. The definition ran as follows:

Definition 31 (Analyticity (metaphysical picture)) *A sentence that consists of a modifier (M), logical subject expression (S) and logical predicate expression (P), is analytic if (i) the sentence can be true even if (S) is not met by anything, and either (ii) (M) is positive and the reference determiner for (S) contains the reference determiner for (P) or M is negative and the reference determiner for (S) excludes the reference determiner for (P).*

Reference determiners are not obviously outside of Quine's circle of concepts, even though they cannot always be properly called *meanings*, and it is likely that Quine would have treated this appeal to reference determiners as an appeal to meanings. Nonetheless, failing Quine's excuse for thinking that reference determiners must be defined in terms of synonymy and synonymy in terms of necessity—none of these definitions appear to be the right way around to me—there is no reason to suspect that the reference determiner of *analytic* will be circular. In fact, I would hope the chain of dependencies would look something more like this:

---

[5] One worry about this way of understanding Quine: *analyticity* is not a natural kind term and its reference determiner does not seem to be sensitive to context of introduction, and so perhaps we don't have the same arguments available to show that speakers do not know the reference determiner of *analyticity*, as we do in the case of natural kind terms. In which case, there might be reason to think that Quine, since he knew the reference determiner for *analyticity*, was really giving the actual reference determiner for *analyticity* and that he has therefore shown that its reference determiner is circular and hence faulty. But there are ways in which this line of thought can be resisted. Making tacit knowledge explicit is a tricky business, so Quine might have made a mistake, and we can even suppose that he needn't have had the knowledge tacitly; perhaps he only possessed the concept through deference to other members of the community.

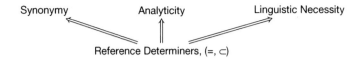

4.2 THE ARGUMENT FROM CONFIRMATION HOLISM

In the second half of "Two Dogmas of Empiricism," Quine attacks a traditional version of the verificationist theory of meaning, according to which the meaning of a statement is the "method of empirically confirming or infirming it" (1951: 35). He recognises that the theory is not widely held anymore, but claims that the spirit of the theory lives on in the "supposition that each statement, taken in isolation from its fellows, can admit of confirmation or infirmation at all." Quine claims that this supposition supports, "and is even identical with", the view that there is a distinction to be drawn between analytic and synthetic statements, since if we suppose that statements admit of confirmation and infirmation in isolation, then it seems natural to say that an analytic statement is one which is confirmed come what may.[6] It is not surprising then, that Quine objects to this view about meaning.

> My countersuggestion, issuing essentially from Carnap's doctrine of the physical world in the *Aufbau*, is that our statements about the external world face the tribunal of sense experience not individually but only as a corporate body. (1951: 38)

Quine uses a number of metaphors to introduce his alternative picture. He suggests that we think of our beliefs as forming a field of force, whose boundary conditions are experience. Statements or beliefs are at varying distances from the boundary of the field. Closeness to the boundary represents what Quine calls *germaneness* to experience. Statements with a high degree of germaneness to experience, though they will be *about* things such as physical objects (and not sense experiences),

---

[6] It is not clear to me how this shows that the "dogmas" of reductionism and the analytic/synthetic distinction are equivalent, never mind "at root identical" as Quine claims (1951: 38), nor even that the view that sentences may be infirmed or confirmed entails that there is a distinction between analytic and synthetic statements. One might believe, for example, that statements may be infirmed or confirmed but that it is a misunderstanding to think that some can be confirmed come what may.

are especially vulnerable to sense experience; we are especially likely to revise them in the light of certain experiences. Quine gives as an example: *there are brick houses on Elm street.* For other statements, such as statements in logic and mathematics, it is difficult to imagine any experience that would cause us to revise them. These statements appear in the metaphor as being towards the center of the field of belief.

Quine calls experiences which conflict with our beliefs "recalcitrant." Faced with a recalcitrant experience we will have choices about how to reform the field of belief, because there are many different fields that would accord with the same experiences. In practice, pragmatic considerations lead us to obey certain principles in revising our belief system; we try to keep it simple, and we try to change it as little as possible. Changes to some statements will induce changes to others because the statements have "logical interconnections." In particular, if we were to change statements from the center of the field—our logical principles—this will have repercussions throughout the web because these are statements about how other statements are allowed to interconnect.

This new picture, *when coupled with the thesis that the meaning of an expression is the experiences which would confirm it or infirm it* goes against the analytic/synthetic distinction in two ways. First, since the only objects which are infirmed or confirmed by experience are fields of belief, fields of belief are the only objects with meanings.[7] This makes it a kind of category error to say that a statement is true in virtue of its meaning—statements do not, on this picture, have meaning—and since a statement may appear in many different fields of belief, and no statement is guaranteed to have the same truth-value in every field, neither will a statement be guaranteed true in virtue of the meaning of a field of which it is a part. As Quine puts it: "the unit of empirical significance is the whole of science" (1951: 39).

The second way in which the picture undermines the analytic/synthetic distinction is by providing an alternative explanation of the intuitions that were thought to support it. Quine can explain *why* some statements have appeared to be unrevisable; we will nearly always refrain from revising them out of conservatism and our desire for simplicity.

There is more to the end of "Two Dogmas" than an argument against the analytic-synthetic distinction. A whole new picture is proposed, and

---

[7] There need not actually be someone who holds each belief in the field: Quine suggests we think of fields as the beliefs of imaginary men.

given its interest and power it might seem surprising that the argument against the analytic-synthetic distinction is really just this:

(P1) The meaning of a linguistic form is the sets of experiences which would directly confirm or disconfirm it.

(P2) A statement is analytic if it will be confirmed come what may. (Quine's definition from page 38)

(P3) Theories are the only objects for which there are sets of experiences which would directly confirm or disconfirm them. A statement will be indirectly confirmed if the theory of which it is a part is confirmed, but it is always possible to adopt a theory, consistent with any particular set of experiences, which does not include the statement. (Epistemological Holism)

(P4) Theories are not statements but structured fields of statements.

(C1) No statement has a set of experiences which would directly confirm or disconfirm it. (P3), (P4)

(C2) No statement has a meaning. (P1),(C1)

(C3) No statement is confirmed come what may. (P3)

(C4) No statement is analytic. (P2),(C3)

The problem with the argument is that premises P1, P2 and P3 are false.

4.2.1 P3: Sober, Epistemological Holism, and the Special Consequence Relation

According to Quine's epistemological holism, statements in all parts of a theory are indirectly confirmed when the entire theory is confirmed. For example, statements from pure mathematics are confirmed by evidence that confirms GTR, because those statements are an indispensable part of that theory. The upshot of this is that epistemological holism backs the special consequence condition on confirmation relations between theory and evidence, according to which anything worthy of being called a confirmation relation should validate the following inference form:

$$E \text{ confirms } T$$
$$T \vdash T'$$
$$\rule{4cm}{0.4pt}$$
$$E \text{ confirms } T'$$

In his 1945 article "Studies in the Logic of Confirmation" Hempel convincingly debunked this inference as a fallacy (1965) and Sober provides the following simple counterexample: suppose I pull a card from an ordinary pack at random. Consider the very simple theory, which contains only two sentences: *The card is a seven. The card is a heart.* Now imagine that we are told that the card is red. This confirms the theory; the probability of the theory increases from 1/52 to 1/26. This does *not*, even indirectly, confirm the sentence which says that the card is a seven. That is as probable as it ever was—1/13.

Sober points out that the theory has a further unfortunate consequence. Suppose my total theory includes statements X and Y, and yours includes statements X and $\ulcorner \neg Y \urcorner$. Then anything that confirms X confirms Y for me, but $\ulcorner \neg Y \urcorner$ for you. This is very odd.

Sober emphasises that epistemological holism should be distinguished from the Duhem thesis (sometimes called the Quine–Duhem thesis), which says that hypotheses, taken in isolation, do not have testable consequences. We must exploit *auxiliary assumptions*, which may state, for example, that our equipment works in a certain way. Quine makes this point in "Two Dogmas" when he says that statements in isolation do not admit of confirmation or infirmation. This thesis seems correct, so it is important to realise that Quine's epistemological holism is not a consequence of it. One may accept that a statement cannot be confirmed without making use of auxiliary hypotheses and still resist the claim that those hypotheses are also confirmed or infirmed in the testing.

Competing hypotheses typically make use of the *same* auxiliary assumptions, and that a datum O will be said to favour H_1 rather than H_2, given the auxiliary assumptions A iff $\Pr\dfrac{O}{H_1 \wedge A} > \Pr\dfrac{O}{H_2 \wedge A}$.

Sober maintains that hypotheses must always be tested against alternatives and the outcome O tells us nothing about the probability of A, since A is not being tested against an alternative. The normal case in science is that rival hypotheses are tested against a shared background of logic and mathematics, so that the results neither confirm nor infirm logic or mathematics.

The proper response to the Quine–Duhem thesis is indeed to give up the idea that statements may be confirmed or disconfirmed in isolation, but rather than accept Quine's epistemological holism, one should accept that confirmation is a *three*-place relation, between a piece of evidence, a hypothesis, and a set of background assumptions. O confirms H given background assumptions A, but this does not commit one to epistemological holism because it does not commit one to saying that the evidence confirms the background assumptions whenever it confirms some theory relative to them.

4.2.2 P2: The Verificationist Conception of Analyticity

P2 is Quine's characterisation of analyticity: a statement is analytic if it will be confirmed come what may. It is really more accurate to say that the characterisation is infected with the unclarity of its time, than to say that it is outright false, since it fails to distinguish clearly between necessity, analyticity and a priority. Which statements in the following list are confirmed come what may?

- Hesperus is Phosphorus
- water is H_2O
- I am here now
- stick S is one meter long at t
- Princeton University is the actual Princeton University

I do not know, and that is not because I do not know under which circumstances these sentences will be confirmed, but rather because of the unclarity of *come what may*. These complaints may seem a little unfair, given that Quine means P2 to capture the verificationist account of analyticity adopted by his opponents, but I mean to stress how primitive such a conception of analyticity—the one attacked in this argument—was in comparison to the one I defend.

4.2.3 P1: The Verificationist Conception of Meaning

And finally we reach the complaint most commonly leveled at the argument from confirmation holism, which is that it assumes the verificationist conception of meaning, according to which the meaning of an expression is the sets of experiences which would confirm or disconfirm it.

It is widely accepted in analytic philosophy that some kind of verificationism is false—verificationism is to the philosophy of language what Cartesianism is to the philosophy of mind, a position so deeply unfashionable that the name has currency as an insult. Yet there are weaker and stronger verificationist claims, and more and less sympathetic ways to interpret them (especially since most of them were made at a time when philosophy of language was not practiced with as much precision (or pedantry) as it is now) and there remains a thought at the heart of verificationism that is still plausible:

- Unless there are circumstances under which an expression could be said to apply, or be true, it doesn't express, or say, anything.

This idea might seem so plausible as to make one doubt whether it should really be counted as a weak kind of verificationism, but such theses were often expressed by positivist writers, and allowed to merge into stronger theses. Thus Moritz Schlick (Schlick 1932) wrote, "The meaning of a proposition consists, obviously, in this alone, that it expresses a definite state of affairs."

Several further theses lead us to stronger and more idiosyncratic versions of verificationism:

- such circumstances are to be expressed in terms of the sets of possible (qualitatively understood) experiences, (one kind of reductionist element)
- speakers know the set of circumstances under which their expressions correctly apply (the descriptivist element)
- the meaning of the expression not only determines, but is to be *identified* with, the set of circumstances (a different kind of reductionist element)
- the set of circumstances not only includes the circumstances to which the expression applies, but any circumstances which would provide confirming evidence in favour of those circumstances holding. (Thus the set of data which constitutes the meaning of *the newspaper has arrived* includes, not only the circumstance of the newspaper having arrived, but the sound of the letterbox snapping shut and the observation that it is 10 a.m., and also, since disconfirming evidence is also part of meaning, my background knowledge that the paperboy has smallpox.) (the most clearly verificationist element)

All five theses here are classic themes in verificationist thought, and we might wonder which are required for Quine's argument to go through. The specification of the conditions in terms of *experience*, for example, does not seem essential. Quine might allow a broader conception of the data which included things like readings on meters (rather than experiences of readings on meters), or positions of objects, without losing the point that there will always be multiple theories to explain such data. We may no longer be mad-dog reductionists, but this isn't what has saved us from the argument from confirmation holism.

Speaker knowledge of conditions does not seem to be at issue either. Quine can admit that speakers need not know the conditions which need to be met for their linguistic expressions to be confirmed without giving up the claim that sentences do not have meanings in isolation. Thus an appreciation of natural kind terms hasn't rescued us from Quine's argument either.

Is the identification required? Suppose we were to weaken premise 1 to

P1* In virtue of being meaningful, a linguistic form is associated with a set of circumstances. If those circumstances hold, then the linguistic form is true.†

This claim is something like the claim that appropriately meaningful theories and sentences have intensions—and there's nothing disreputable about that. But the argument formed by replacing P1 with P1* in Quine's argument from confirmation holism is invalid. P1*, with its use of *truth* rather than *confirmation*, does not engage appropriately with P2 and P3, which mention the properties of theories and analytic statements in terms of confirmation. We might adjust P2 and P3 to make the argument valid:

P2* A statement is analytic if it will be made true by every circumstance.

P3* Theories (not statements) are the only objects for which there are circumstances which would make them true.

From these starred premises and [P4] it follows that no statement is analytic and no statement is meaningful. This version of the argument is valid, and this time the first premise—the verificationist one—is weak enough to be plausible. However, we pay for these gains elsewhere. The third premise no longer even resembles the platitudinous Quine–Duhem thesis about confirmation. Instead it expresses a radical and implausible holism about truth-conditional content.[8]

---

† Note: Not merely *confirmed*, outright *true*.

[8] I believe that (at least at some time prior to the skepticism of *Word and Object*), Quine accepted such holism, but that he accepted it as a *result* of the argument from confirmation holism. This argument was never supposed to presuppose such a controversial thesis.

Thus it is not the *identification* of meaning with sets of circumstances which puts some forms of verificationism within the range of Quine's argument from confirmation holism, but the widening of those sets of circumstances to include, not only circumstances which will make a statement true, but also circumstances which will merely confirm it. Someone could identify the meaning of an expression with its intension and reject Quine's conclusions about meaning and analyticity by rejecting (P3*): the claim that only entire theories have such meanings. But if we allow the idea that, in virtue of being meaningful, any linguistic form is related to a set of circumstances which include those that merely confirm it, then, given Quine's (P3) and (P2), even denying the *identity* of meaning with those sets of circumstances will not save us, since statements do not (according to (P3)) have sets of circumstances which would confirm or disconfirm them.

Many of Quine's targets did maintain the kind of verificationism which brings them within range of his argument, and so it was very effective against them. But the conception of analyticity I advocate in this book had its roots in a very different conception of meaning.

5

Definitions

Definitions are sentences which ascribe meanings to linguistic expressions. They have sometimes been thought to be the key to understanding and defending analyticity; they have seemed to provide transparent examples of analyticity and synonymy (in terms of which Frege thought analyticity could be explained), and yet they are respectably entrenched in the practice of science and mathematics. Indeed, legislative definitions—those that are used to introduce new words (or new senses for old ones)—have seemed to provide *such* clear examples of synonymy that even Quine was provoked into an uncharacteristic admission of comprehension:

Here we have a really transparent case of synonymy created by definition; would that all species of synonymy were as intelligible. (1951: 26)

Since Quine believes that analyticity can be explained in terms of synonymy, it might seem as if this admission has made his position untenable. He maintains each of (5.1)–(5.3).

(5.1) *analyticity* does not make sense.

(5.2) there are no analytic sentences.

(5.3) legislative definitions are analytic.

Given the apparent triviality that some sentences are legislative definitions (5.3) entails the negation of (5.2) and pragmatically implies the negation of (5.1).

   Grice and Strawson think that Quine's claim about definition *does* make his position incoherent and charitably suggest that we ignore it in the interests of doing justice to the rest of his view:

Now if we are to take these words of Quine seriously, then his position as a whole is *incoherent*. It is like the position of a man to whom we are trying to explain, say, the idea of one thing fitting into another thing, or two things fitting together, and who says "I can understand what it means for one thing to fit into another, or two things to fit together, in the case where one was specially made to fit the other; but I cannot understand what it means to say this in any other case." Perhaps we should not take Quine's words here too seriously. (1956: 152-3)

Boghossian tries somewhat harder to accommodate (5.3) into the Quinean position as a whole, suggesting that the following is Quine's view:

Although there is such a thing as the property of synonymy; and although it can be instantiated by pairs of tokens of the same orthographic type; and although it can be instantiated by pairs of tokens of distinct orthographic types, provided that they are related to each other by way of an explicit stipulation; it is, nevertheless, in principle impossible to generate instances of this property in some other way, via some other mechanism. For example, it is impossible that two expressions that were introduced independently of each other into the language, should have been introduced with exactly the same meanings. (Boghossian 1997)

After attributing this unlikely-seeming view to Quine—apparently in desperation—Boghossian argues against it.

5.1 THE TRANSIENCE OF DEFINITION

I suspect that Quine's view of the relation between analyticity and definition was more innovative than this. His view of the use of definition in science was such that the kind of analyticity it could support was not the kind that could do any of the work that his targets wanted it to do—in particular it could not play an important role in the epistemology of science. He admits that there is some sense of *analytic* on which legislative definitions are analytic, but denies that this notion can be what his opponents and targets mean by *analytic*. They need a notion that will do more work.

The reason this notion cannot do enough work is that legislative definitions are in a certain sense *ephemeral, independent of meaning* and in the first place *properties of utterances* (which Quine thinks of as acts), rather than sentence types (Quine 1965[1954]). I will refer to this collection of Quinean theses as the doctrine of the transience of definition.

To begin with, Quine thinks that definitions are ephemeral. Though a word may be introduced using a definition and come to be an accepted part of the language; accepting the definition need be no part of accepting the word into the language. The definition might be completely forgotten, even by the person who introduced the word.

Next, Quine thinks that definitions are independent of meaning in the following sense: one can change the definition of a word without changing its meaning. There is a moderate and an extreme version of this view. On the moderate view one can change the definition of a word and so long as the word applies to the same objects, one can do it without changing the meaning. On the extreme view one can change the definition of a word in such a way that it now applies to objects to which it did not previously apply or fails to apply to objects to which it used to apply, and *still* not change the meaning of the word.

Third, it is acts of uttering sentences—not the sentences themselves—that are definitions. Quine writes:

> The distinction between the legislative and the discursive refers thus to the act, and not to its enduring consequence, in the case of postulation as in the case of definition . . . Conventionality is a passing trait, significant at the moving front of science but useless in classifying the sentences behind the lines. It is a trait of events not sentences. (1965[1954]: 112)

Prima facie these views about definitions are odd. Isn't ' 'bachelor' means *unmarried man*' a sentence type and a definition? I think what Quine has in mind are the kind of definitions used in mathematics, which philosophers call implicit definitions but mathematicians call explicit definitions.[1] Definitions of the form '$a = b$' or '$a =$ the F' or '$\forall x(Fx \text{ iff } Gx \wedge \neg Hx)$.[2] Sentences of this form are not such clear cases of sentences that are definitions and could never have been anything else.

Yet for someone who accepts the language myth this remains heady stuff. For, according to the language myth picture, a definition states the meaning of a word and the meaning of a word is what a speaker has to know in order to understand it. A linguistic community cannot accept the word introduced by a definition and then just forget about the definition—that would be to forget what the word means! So it seems that definition *cannot* be ephemeral. Secondly, since definitions ascribe meanings it is hard to see how the correct or accepted meaning ascription for a word can change without the meaning changing. Definitions do

---

[1] There is an explanation of this confusing terminology in §5.2.

[2] One reason to think this is that these definitions really are licenses to rewrite theories and Quine claims that that is the best way to think about definitions—as such licenses.

not seem to be independent of meaning. And finally Quine's claim about the kinds of objects that are definitions is baffling. Definitions would seem to be definitions in virtue of their content—their meaning ascribing content—and (so long as the sentence is not indexical) this will not change from utterance to utterance of the same sentence type. So why not allow that sentences types can be definitions?

From the perspective of the language myth, Quine's position looks crazy. How does it look if we reject that myth?

5.2 RETHINKING DEFINITIONS

If definitions are meaning ascriptions and there are four different kinds of meaning, then there are at least four kinds of definition: content ascriptions, referent ascriptions, reference determiner ascriptions and character ascriptions. But even before making these distinctions there are already a multitude of different kinds of definition: implicit, explicit (for mathematicians), implicit, explicit (for philosophers), legislative, discursive, explicative, impredicative, definitions in use and real definitions. So it is likely there are many different kinds of content ascribing definition, reference fixing description etc.

Definitions have been credited with all kinds of extraordinary properties: They have been said to be necessary, analytic, a priori, truth-valueless, meaningless, transient, trivial, mere licenses to rewrite theories, and epistemically equivalent to postulates and assumptions.[3] But many of these claims about definitions are only plausible for a restricted class of definitions, for example, reference-fixing definitions such as Kripke's (5.4) need not express necessary truths, nor need metalanguage definitions such as 'Snow' means *snow*, and impredicative definitions are not licenses to rewrite theories.

(5.4) The length of stick S at time t is 1 meter

I will argue that a good way to understand Quine's claims about definitions is as focusing on a particular kind of definition, namely reference ascriptions (a.k.a. reference-fixing definitions) for names and natural kind terms. I will claim that if we understand him this way then his claims about definitions make more sense than they seemed to

---

[3] Though never, I believe, all at once by one person. (Ayer 1990[1936]; Quine 1951: 24-6; Harman 1999*b*; Wittgenstein 1953: §50; Naess 1966: 44).

on the language myth picture. I will proceed by first discussing some kinds of definitions and their properties and then I will talk about how we might interpret Quine and where this leaves us in terms of using definitions to defend analyticity.

For the purposes of clarity I shall state what I mean by a definition. Below is a narrow sense, and then two extended senses of *definition*:[4]

Definition 32 (Definition (narrow)) *A sentence which semantically expresses a meaning ascription. e.g. '' 'bachelor' means the same as 'unmarried man' '' or ' 'bachelor' means unmarried man'.*

Definition 33 (Definition (extended)) *A sentence which can be used to ascribe meaning to an expression. e.g. 'x is a bachelor iff x is an unmarried man.'*

Definition 34 (Definition (hyper-extended)) *Anything that can be used to ascribe a meaning to an expression. e.g. pointing at Bill and saying 'Bill'.*

Explicit vs. implicit

The explicit/implicit definition distinction can be drawn in two different ways. Philosophers often use it to mark the distinction between definitions that mention the definiendum, and those that use it:

(5.5) 'Vixen' means *female fox*.

(5.6) A vixen is a female fox.

In this sense (5.5) is an explicit definition because it mentions the term to be defined and (5.6) is an implicit definition because it uses it. On this usage, explicit definitions are metalinguistic, whereas implicit ones are object language definitions.

In formal work the explicit/implicit distinction may be drawn differently. Definitions in mathematics are usually performed in the object language and *explicit* applies to definitions which take the form of identity statements or universally quantified biconditionals:

---

[4] Some people think that expressions are not the only things that can have definitions. They think that it is also possible to define objects. My characterisation does not allow for this. One reason for this is my dark and muddy suspicion that the sentences which have been taken to be definitions of objects are in fact reference-fixing definitions in disguise. But I would not really mind being wrong about this, and if it turns out that one really can define objects then I would be happy to admit that I have missed something that is ordinarily called a definition.

(5.7) Let $f(x) = 3y + 2$

(5.8) Let $v(a \wedge b) = 1 \Leftrightarrow v(a) = 1$ and $v(b) = 1$

(5.9) Let $(\forall x)(F(x) \Leftrightarrow G(x)) \wedge x \in S)$

In this sense of *explicit*, (5.7) is an explicit definition of the functor 'f' and (5.8) of 'v' and (5.9) of the predicate 'F'. The distinctive feature of definitions of this form is that they allow for the systematic replacement of the defined term with the definiens. They are, as Quine said, licenses to rewrite theories. Not all object language definitions are of this form, for example:

$$(5.10) \ \text{Let} f(x) = \begin{cases} y & \text{if } y \geq 5 \\ 2y & \text{otherwise} \end{cases}$$

Though implicit definitions may be converted into explicit definitions,[5] the definition above does not allow for straightforward replacement of '$f(x)$' with an alternative expression in the way that (5.7), (5.8) and (5.9) do.

For clarity I will refer to the kind of definition that mentions the definiendum as a *metalinguistic* definition, and the non-metalinguistic kind as an *object language* definition. Definitions, which allow replacement of defininendum with definiens or vice versa throughout a theory, will be *formally explicit* definitions and their counterparts *formally implicit*.

Stipulative, descriptive and explicative definitions

Carnap and Quine shared the view that there were three kinds of definition. *Stipulative* definitions are used to introduce new notations and purport to assign new meanings either to entirely new expressions, or to expressions that were previously used with different meanings.[6] Examples of such definitions are found in mathematics and in disciplines that make use of technical terms. For example,

Let $a = b^2$
$v(\alpha \wedge \beta) = 1$ iff $v(\alpha) = 1$ and $v(\beta) = 1$

Descriptive definitions purport to state (or in the case of implicit definitions, at least hold in virtue of) pre-existing meaning relations

---

[5] Frege offers one way to do this, Lewis another.
[6] Stipulative definitions are also referred to as *legislative* definitions by Quine.

between expressions.[7] The standard examples of such definitions are those found in dictionaries, for example, sentence (5.11) might be taken to say that the expression *vixen* means the same as the expression *female fox*.

(5.11) *vixen*, a female fox

Finally, on the Quine–Carnap picture, there are also *explications*:

There is also, however, a variant type of definitional activity which does not limit itself to the reporting of preexisting synonymies. I have in mind what Carnap calls *explication*—an activity to which philosophers are given, and scientists also in their more philosophical moments. In explication the purpose is not merely to paraphrase the definiendum into an outright synonym, but actually to improve upon the definiendum by refining or supplementing its meaning. (Quine 1951: 25)

An explicans purports to mean something similar to the expression it explicates, but to be more suitable for certain theoretical purposes, perhaps because it is simpler, or more precise. One controversial position is that Tarski's semantic conception of truth provides an explication of the word *true*.[8] On this view it is precise enough to use for many theoretical purposes, though it provides no account of why, for example, we might call pictures, or feelings *true*. The thought is that while this might be a barrier to Tarski's conception counting as a perfectly adequate descriptive definition of *true*, it is no barrier to the use of this definition in, say, mathematics.

For Carnap explication is an important task for philosophy:

The talk of making more exact a vague or not quite exact concept used in everyday life or in an earlier stage of scientific or logical development, or rather of replacing it by a newly constructed, more exact concept, belongs among the most important tasks of logical analysis and logical construction. We call this the task of explicating, or of giving an *explication* for, the earlier concept; this earlier concept, or sometimes the term used for it, is called the *explicandum*; and the new concept, or its term, is called an *explicatum* of the old one. (1958*b*: 8)

In a footnote Carnap notes that what he means by *explicandum* and *explicatum* seems to be very similar to what other philosophers have meant by *analysandum* and *analysans*, and indeed his examples of

---

[7] Descriptive definitions are sometimes called *discursive* definitions by Quine.

[8] See (Soames 1999*b*) for reasons to think it fails as an *explication*.

explications include Frege and Russell's analyzes of numbers in terms of sets and Russell's theory of descriptions, and both these definitions are standard examples of philosophical analysis.

Direction

It sometimes seems as if there is more to being an explication than being a good enough meaning ascription for scientific purposes. An explication is supposed to have a *direction*: the explicatum explicates the explicandum, and not vice versa.[9]

$$(\text{BOX}) \qquad v(\Box\alpha) = 1 \Leftrightarrow \forall w, \alpha \in w$$

is thought to explicate '$\Box$' in terms of the universal quantifier and possible worlds. Could it also be thought of as an explication of quantification over possible worlds in terms of truth and necessity? I'm inclined to think that it should not be thought of that way, though perhaps the feeling that the definition is directional like this could be explained by the fact that I am more *used* to taking it to be an explication of necessity and not an explication of quantification over possible worlds. Might something other than familiarity explain the feeling of direction?

Definitions do not *always* have a direction 'built in' like this. While a strict definition like ''vixen' means *female fox* does seem to have a direction built in—the sentence *has* to be a definition of *vixen* and not any expression used in the sentence—descriptive, content ascribing definitions of the form '$a = b$', or '*vixen* means the same as *female fox*' or *x is a vixen iff x is a female fox* ascribe meanings by stating or implicating that two expressions have the *same* content. Sameness is a symmetric relation and so, at least in principle, these sentences could be used to ascribe content to the expressions on either the left- or right-hand side of the '$=$' or 'iff'. '$a = b$' for example, could just as well be used to ascribe meaning to 'b' as it can to 'a'.

---

[9] It seems to me that Kit Fine endorses this intuition in his work on essence. (1994, 1995). He holds that the analytic truths are a special case of the essential truths. Essential truths are those whose truth flows from the nature of some object or collection of objects. Analytic truths are those whose truth flows from the nature of concepts, and within a proposition it may be that the truth flows from the nature of one concept rather than another. For example, in (Fine 1994) he suggests that *all bachelors are unmarried* is true in virtue of the meaning of *bachelor* rather than that of *unmarried*.

Here are three ways that we might explain the appearance of directionality in the definition of necessity above:

Explanation Explications and analyses might have an explanatory role; plausibly (BOX) tells us *what it is* for a proposition to be necessary. The 'what it is' locution has an explanatory reading and explanation—like justification—must be non-circular. So if I explain what it is to be necessary in terms of quantification over possible worlds, I shouldn't then attempt to explain quantification over possible worlds in terms of necessity. On this explanation (BOX) does not have direction built in—it is just that given the way we do use (BOX) (to explain necessity) we *ought not* to employ it in the other direction (to explain quantification over possible worlds.)

Complexity/Simplicity The analysans or explicatum ($\forall w, \alpha \in w$, *female fox, unmarried man*) of an analysis or explication is often complex while the analysandum and the explicandum are simple ('$\Box$', *vixen, bachelor*) and we are inclined to give the meanings of complex expressions in terms of the meanings of their parts—not in terms of different words or expressions altogether. For example, we should give the meaning of '$\forall w, \alpha \in w$' by giving a semantics for the universal quantifier and possible world variables, rather than by invoking equivalence with certain claims about necessity.

I think this is right but it does not get to the heart of the matter. The left-hand side of (BOX) is not a simple expression, even if '$\Box$' is. Rather it is a complex expression '$v(\Box\alpha) = 1$' containing the expression to be explained ($\Box$). Why couldn't (BOX) function as an analysis of the universal quantifier, or possible world variables?

Reference Determiner Ascription Some types of meaning ascriptions—even when they are of the form '$a = b$' or '$p \leftrightarrow q$'—*have* to be directional. Reference determination, for example, cannot be circular, so if the reference determiner of the expression A is correctly ascribed in the sentence '$\forall x(Ax \leftrightarrow Bx)$' then it cannot be the case that the reference determiner of B is correctly ascribed by the same sentence. Reference determiner ascriptions of the form $p \leftrightarrow q$ might be used to ascribe reference determiners to an expression in p or an expression in q. But only one such ascription could be correct.

Stipulative definitions and the environment

Sometimes when an expression is introduced with a stipulative definition, the environment (the context of introduction) plays an important role in determining what the expression means. One case in which this is true is when an object is baptised. Suppose Jeff introduces the name *Mendlow* for his newest pet fish. He points at it and utters sentence (5.12).

(5.12) I think I'm gonna call this new one *Mendlow*.

In doing so he sets up a condition on being the referent of the word *Mendlow*: *Mendlow* applies to something iff it is the new fish Jeff is pointing at in the context of introduction for the word *Mendlow*. Thus he provides reference determiner, referent and content for the word *Mendlow*.

Jeff did not literally say *let 'Mendlow' refer to an object just in case it is the new fish I am pointing at now*. He didn't even use the word *fish*. Yet in the context it was obvious that by *this new one* he meant *this new fish* and also that the *I think* in *I think I'm gonna call* . . . does not mean that he *merely* thinks he is going to call it *Mendlow*, it is just his low-key way of asserting that he's going to call it *Mendlow*. Jeff's sentence fits the extended definition of a definition: it is a sentence used to ascribe meaning to an expression.

This, I imagine, is a very common way for names to be introduced; one gets the word to mean something by picking out the thing in the environment to which it is to refer. Clearly, the environment plays an important role in determining the meaning of the expression.

It seems likely that a similar thing can happen with natural kind terms. Just as Adam is supposed to have named the animals, we can imagine that he named all the natural kinds in a similar way: Adam: I think I'll call these things *snakes* and this wet stuff *water*, and the things over there *trees* and these objects *apples*. Once again, the environment in the context of introduction is important for determining which kind the expression comes to denote. The kinds are already out there in the environment and Adam simply pairs them up with words.

The environment need not always play this role in the determination of the referent of a name. In introducing *Ali*, Cassius Clay's spiritual advisor says *Let's call Clay 'Ali'* and the environment at the time *Ali* is introduced is then unimportant to determining the referent of *Ali*. What matters is the environment at the introduction of *Clay*.

Similarly, if anti-Spanish feeling causes Americans to decide to use *tree-moss* to refer to what they now call *Spanish Moss*, then the environment at the time of deciding would be unimportant to the meaning of *tree-moss*.

This is just to observe that in the case of names and natural kind terms, it is possible to introduce them either by stipulating their referents directly or by giving a synonym. When stipulating the referents directly we need to somehow pick out the object or kind that is to be the meaning of the name. We can do this by pointing, or by giving a reference-fixing description. In these cases the environment is usually important, because without it to supply the thing pointed at, or the referent of the description, no referent gets fixed. When we give a synonym, the state of the world at the time of introduction is usually unimportant because there is no work for it to do. In introducing *tree-moss* as a synonym for *Spanish Moss*, I have no need to pick out the kind in the environment around me. In providing a synonym we provide the meaning for the new expression and no help from the environment there and then is required.

I have claimed that names and natural kind terms have reference determiners that are sensitive to context of introduction, but that other expressions, such as indexicals and the truth-functional connectives, do not. This is something one might doubt. Since all expressions are introduced at some time or other, shouldn't it always, or at least very often, be the case that what they apply to depends on what the world was like when they were introduced? Consider the following case: Delia writes out a truth-table on the board. Then she utters sentence (5.13).

(5.13) Let '∧' express the truth-function represented by that truth-table.

Is it not the case that relative to other contexts of introduction, in which a different truth-table is written on the board, '∧' expresses a different truth-function? And if it expresses a different truth-function, '∧' can apply to different pairs of truth-values. Thus the reference determiner for '∧' can be sensitive to context of introduction.[10]

The solution to this worry is to see that Delia and Jeff's definitions are of different kinds and that the role of the truth-table on the board in the definition of '∧' is different from the role of Jeff's fish in the definition of *Mendlow*. Recall that since there are four kinds of meaning, there are at least four kinds of meaning attribution, and hence four kinds of definition. Jeff's definition is a referent attribution: he gives the meaning

---

[10] I owe this example to a question from Jeff Speaks, and I would like to thank Mark Migotti, Nicole Wyatt and Richard Zach for impressing its importance upon me.

of *Mendlow* by giving its referent.[11] But Delia's definition is a reference determiner attribution. Her stipulation, understood as it is intended, is not that '∧' is a name for something represented by the truth-table on the board, (it is not a name and one does not give its meaning by giving a referent) rather she states the conditions for the correct application of '∧.' In doing so it is plausible that she also states the character of '∧' (something which you have to understand to be competent with the word). Her truth-table aids her in this project: it's an easy way for her to express the thought that '∧' correctly applies to two propositions just in case they are both true. But ultimately the correct way to understand her is as having asserted that '∧' applies to two propositions just in case both are true, not as having asserted that '∧' applies to whatever truth-function she has written on the board. If she had said that, then she would have stipulated a meaning for something else: a *name* for that function.

If the truth-table on the board had been different then, yes, '∧' would have applied to different pairs of truth-values. This does not show that the reference determiner of '∧' is sensitive to context of introduction however; had there been a different truth-table on the board, then the reference determiner for '∧' would have been different.

5.2.1 The Transience of Definition Again

Quine claimed that legislative definitions—though analytic—were ephemeral and meaning-independent (the definition can vary without the meaning varying) and that the *kind* of thing that could be definitional was an act of uttering. Certain definitions of names and natural kind terms *do* seem to fit this picture quite well. Consider a case where we legislatively introduce a name 'Sam' using the following object-language, reference-fixing definition:

(5.14) Sam is the tallest boy in the class.*

We learnt from Kripke that in order to be competent with *Sam* a speaker need not know anything about the description that was used to introduce the name. So the original legislative meaning ascription

---

[11] Since the content of a name is determined by (and identical with) its referent, it is also a content attribution.

* To avoid complications let's assume that the baptiser has *de re* acquaintance with the tallest boy in the class and knows that he is the tallest boy.

can be forgotten—the legislative definitions of names are *ephemeral*. Natural kind terms can be introduced by description in a similar way. Suppose someone introduces the word *water* using:

(5.15) (∀x)x is water if, and only if, x is a substance of the same underlying kind as the stuff that is falling from the sky right now.

A later speaker might learn and become competent with the word *water* without ever knowing the definition by which it was introduced. Legislative definitions for natural kind terms are ephemeral too.

Such definitions are also *meaning-independent*. We might provide a new and correct definition for a name without changing its meaning. The meaning of a name—both its content and referent, recall—is just the object it refers to. Though a community may have forgotten how the referent of a name was fixed, they can decide to re-legislate on the name. They decide that whatever it meant before, its new meaning will be fixed by the following definition:

(5.16) Sam is the manager of the West Port Inn.

Although there is now a new definition for the name *Sam*, the content and referent of *Sam* may be exactly as they were before. We can run this kind of story for natural kind terms as well. Presumably, the intensions of *water* and the German word *Wasser* were fixed in different ways, however this is no argument against their having the same intension and content. This kind of reference-fixing definition for a name or natural kind term is independent of meaning.

Finally, what is to be made of Quine's claim that analyticity is a property of acts of utterance? I think perhaps the best we can do with this is to say that it is an attempt to capture the same idea that Kripke was trying to capture when he allowed that the sentence (5.4) was a priori for the speaker who uses it to introduce the expression *meter* into English. Kripke notes that the sentence appears to afford some special epistemic access on that first occasion and not on later occasions. Analyticity is supposed to afford some kind of special epistemic access, so, says Quine, it can only be definitions on particular occasions that are analytic. I suspect that he thinks that this is more or less equivalent to saying that it is utterances of sentences on particular occasions that are analytic.

But given the definition of Part I, there is no such thing as the *ephemeral* analyticity of a sentence, because analytic sentences are true in all contexts of utterance and introduction. Thus I am not inclined to accept Quine's thesis that analyticity is a passing trait. Rather, reference-fixing sentences such as (5.14) were never analytic in the first place; if a giant joined Sam's class, we would be able to utter (5.14) falsely. The more explicit reference-fixing definition

(5.17) Sam is the tallest boy in the class at 9 a.m. on 3 September, 2004.

will be analytic, (at least in the modal sense) but then this definition does more than ascribe a referent; it also (implicitly) ascribes a reference determiner. What is a passing trait here is our epistemic access to the fact that it is a constant sentence and the ease with which it affords justification. This legislative reference-fixing definition will quickly be forgotten and without it, any analytic justification that it may have afforded will be unavailable.

However, Quine's doctrine of the transience of definition does not hold for definitions in general. Unlike the fact that *Sam* refers to the tallest boy in the class, the fact that *I* refers to the agent of the context of utterance is learned and remembered by speakers, and since this reference determiner, unlike the reference determiner for a name, *is* part of the *meaning* of the word, so that we could not change this definition without changing the meaning of the word, this definition is not meaning-independent. Recognisably analytic sentences, such as *I am here now*, unlike (5.14) and (5.17), are recognisably analytic because the reference determiners ensure that the sentence is true with respect to all contexts of utterance and contexts of introduction, and speakers may recognise that the sentence is analytic because those reference determiners are *not* forgotten by competent speakers: speakers have to know that *I* refers to the agent of the context in order to be competent with the word.

Thus I think that Quine's doctrine regarding the transience of definition is best regarded as providing some important insights about *meaning* and a certain class of definitions, insights which were not widely recognised at the time when he was writing. In particular, the reference-fixing definitions for names are quickly forgotten without the meaning of the name being lost by the linguistic community. This does not mean, however, that referent-ascribing definitions are only momentarily analytic. They were *never* analytic. Only a restricted class of definitions is transient.

5.3 DEFINITIONS AS POSTULATES

Quine thinks that some people who think definition is the key to analyticity misunderstand the significance of definitions in formalisations of theories. In "Carnap and Logical Truth" he explains that in formalising a theory we take some expressions as primitive, and use them to introduce other expressions, using the symbol '$=_{def}$' to mark the fact that the new expression is equivalent by definition to the old, for example,

$$F =_{def} ma$$

However there are different ways to formalise theories, and different formalisations may take different expressions as primitive and different expressions as defined. This will make different sentences of the theory 'true by definition'. Thus if analyticity is truth by definition, then which sentences are analytic will vary with how one formalises the theory. Which sentences get treated as true by convention is just a matter of preference at the time, so that "conventionality is a passing trait, significant at the moving front of science but useless in classifying the sentences behind the lines" (Quine 1965[1954]: 112).

This flexibility of the division between definitions and substantive postulates within a theory can lead to something that was originally introduced as a definition being given up as *false* in response to new evidence. Though *acid* might have been introduced via the stipulation 'an acid is a substance which turns litmus paper red,' later developments might result in our giving up this sentence of the theory in order to allow that acids do not always turn litmus paper red. So, writes Harman, "stipulative definitions are assumptions . . . the epistemological force of a stipulative definition is the same as the epistemological force of an assumption" (1999*a*: 152).

Once again, such claims are very hard to understand if we are assuming the language myth. On the language myth, a definition attributes a meaning and is true in virtue of that meaning, and that very meaning determines the truth of the sentence with respect to all possible worlds. So when Harman wrote (in 1967) "even if conventional assignments of truth or falsity determine meaning, it does not follow that a sentence is true by virtue of convention...[i]t does not even follow that the sentence is true," even Boghossian was puzzled:

> How might this happen?...Harman doesn't explain...how might it turn out that a sentence that is stipulated to be true, as a way of fixing the meaning of some ingredient term t, nevertheless fail to be true? One thing is, I think, certain: not by being false. (1997: 395)

But I think Harman *does* think that a sentence which is stipulated to true can turn out to be false; Harman thinks that definitions have the epistemological status of assumptions. Fortunately, with our new picture we can both explain how an implicit definition of some expression—a sentence stipulated to be true—can be rejected as false at a later date, with no change of meaning, *and* show how this does not mean that analyticity itself is illusory.

Suppose a scientist introduced the word *acid* using an implicit definition such as 'an acid is substance that turns litmus paper red.' What we all implicitly understand is that *acid* has not been introduced as shorthand for the complex expression *substance that turns litmus paper red*, but rather that the condition of *being a sample of the same underlying kind as those samples which turn litmus paper red (with respect to the context of introduction)* has been used to fix the referent of *acid*. Here our tacit knowledge scores over our language myth-corrupted theory in two respects. It knows that the implicitly defining sentence is being used to attribute a reference determiner to the expression *acid* rather than supply a synonym for it. And secondly, it knows that *acid* is being introduced as a natural kind term; what matters for membership of the extension of *acid* is not being such that you turn litmus paper red, but sharing an underlying structure with samples which do turn litmus paper red (in the context of introduction). The original reference determining condition for *acid* may well be forgotten—at any rate, it doesn't matter whether it is or not. Now suppose that the only manufacturer of litmus paper brings out a new kind which turns blue on contact with an acid, but red on contact with an alkali. The new litmus paper is slightly cheaper and soon becomes the only profitable kind, and the manufacturer eventually ceases to make the original. The old supplies are gradually used up, so that the only kind of litmus paper there is turns blue in contact with acids, but red on contact with alkalis. Then the sentence *an acid is a substance that turns litmus paper red* will be false, even though the *meaning* of *acid*—its extension and content—remains the same.[12] The reason that this is not in conflict with the account of analyticity given in Chapter 3 is that on that account *an acid is a substance that turns litmus paper red* is not analytic; its truth-value will vary with the context of introduction as the 'reverse litmus paper' example shows. Sentences of the form X $=_{def}$ YZ in empirical theories are often not analytic sentences, but merely fix a referent for the uninterpreted expression. This implies that they are *not*, pace Quine, always licenses to rewrite theories, unless rewrites may be sentences with different modal profiles, and even different temporal profiles, from the originals.[13]

5.4 CONVENTIONS OF NOTATIONAL ABBREVIATION

Quine has a further argument against truth in virtue of meaning based on the nature of definition.[14] In "Truth by Convention" he maintains that definitions are *conventions of notational abbreviation*. They come in two flavours: *simple* and *contextual*. A simple definition introduces an arbitrary shorthand for a particular expression, e.g. *kilometer* for *a thousand meters*. A contextual definition sets up indefinitely many expressions with shorthand counterparts "according to some general scheme":

$$\frac{\sin \dots}{\cos \dots} = \tan \dots$$

Thus, says Quine, definitions are merely licenses for rewriting a theory that one already has. If the first theory was true, then the rewrite will be true as well, but "considered in isolation from all doctrine, including

---

[12] And its reference determiner remains the same too—remember that the reference determiners of natural kind terms are sensitive to context of introduction. What remains true is that an acid is a substance that shared an underlying structure with samples which would turn litmus paper red *in the context of introduction.*

[13] The temporal profile of a sentence will be the profile of truth-values it takes with respect to different times. In the story above the sentence *an acid is a substance that turns litmus paper red* has a different temporal profile from the sentence *a substance that turns litmus paper red is a substance that turns litmus paper red,* since the former will be false after the change in the manufacturing process for litmus paper, whereas the latter will remain true.

[14] Devitt and Sterelny use this argument to undermine the importance of analyticity in their influential introduction to the philosophy of language. (Devitt & Sterelny 1999)

logic, a definition is incapable of grounding the most trivial statement" (1965[1935]: 78-9).

The structure of the argument is not obvious, but I think the best way to understand it is as pointing out a circularity in the appeal to definition in attempts to explain analyticity. The legislative definition 'a = b' will explain the truth of 'Fb' if 'Fa' is true. But 'Fa' might be an empirical truth about physics, justified by observation, in which case 'Fb' will be justified by observation too, and hence not be true in virtue of meaning. In order for the definition to show that 'Fb' is true in virtue of meaning then, 'Fa' must already be true in virtue of meaning. But now we have only succeeded in explaining the analyticity of 'Fb' by presupposing the analyticity of 'Fa'; the meaning of the expression introduced by definition does not *ground* the truth of the sentence, it only rests it on something else. Hence, even in identity cases, such as 'a = b', the truth of 'a = b' rests on the definition *plus* a truth of logic, namely 'a = a', and so 'a = b' will only be true in virtue of meaning if 'a = a' is. Hence in this case our appeal to definitions to defend analyticity presupposes the analyticity of such theorems of logic.

I wish to make two points concerning this argument. Quine claims that all definitions are conventions of abbreviation and hence licenses to rewrite theories, but in this he is wrong. Only a narrow class of definitions are licenses to rewrite theories. Yet Quine also has an importantly right point about the nature of analyticity. Analytic sentences express propositions that were antecedently true — it was not the introduction of the word 'bachelor,' which made it true *that* all bachelors are unmarried; that was a truth before we had words to express it.

The kind of definitions which are licenses to rewrite theories are those that attribute meaning to the definiendum by giving another expression which has the same content.

(5.18) One meter is 100 centimeters.

(5.19) Clay is Ali.

(5.20) Gorse is Furze

(5.21) Bachelors are unmarried men.

(5.22) Let *Clay* means what *Ali* means.

(5.23) Let *bachelor* mean what *unmarried man* means.

These allow the following "theories" to be rewritten:

The distance between point A and point B is 1 meter.
The distance between point A and point B is 100 centimeters.

Chris is an unmarried man. Chris is a bachelor.

Clay is 70 years' old. Ali is 70 years' old.

Gorse originates in the Mediterranean region of Western Europe.
Furze originates in the Mediterranean region of Western Europe.*

So at most, the "notational abbreviation" argument shows that a definition of a certain kind cannot ground truth. The kind of definitions which are *not* licenses to rewrite theories include merely reference-fixing descriptions, such as:

(5.24) Let *one meter* refer to the length of the meter-rule in Paris at t_0.

(5.25) I think I'm going to call this new one *Mendlow*.

(5.26) *I* refers to the agent of the context of utterance.

These definitions do not merely license rewritings in the same way:

The distance between A and B is one meter.
The distance between A and B is the length of the meter-rule

in Paris at t_0.

Mendlow   looks happy.
This new one looks happy.

I   am tired.
The agent of the context of utterance am tired.

Though the first sentence and the definition might secure the *truth* of the second sentence in the pairs above, the second sentence does not express the same proposition as the first, since the first and second sentences have different modal profiles; there are worlds of evaluation with respect to which the new sentence is true, and the old false, and so the new and old sentences must express different propositions. Hence the new sentences are not merely rewrites of the old.[15]

---

* I think it is arguable that not all of these "rewritings" preserve content, but let us grant Quine this point for now.

[15] Oddly Quine writes as if *his* examples of definitions are supposed to be of the rewriting kinds, but they do not seem to be. 'F = ma' for example, is not introducing short-hand for the expression ma. How short do we need our expressions to be? Rather it is trying to name an underlying explanatory kind.

Nonetheless, Quine is importantly right here about the relation between definition and analyticity. The fact that a sentence expresses a truth because of what its words mean does not mean that the sentence is analytic—every true sentence expresses a truth because of what its words mean. So the mere fact that a sentence expresses a truth because it is definitionally equivalent to another true sentence does not make it analytic. There is more to analyticity than this.

On Quine's picture, whatever made the old sentence true is what makes the new sentence true. And this is right—it just isn't in conflict with the correct account of analyticity. If we introduce 'b' using 'a $=_{def}$ b', then whatever makes 'Fa' true will make 'Fb' true, and in particular, whatever makes 'a $=$ a' true makes 'a $=$ b' true. But to speak of, say, the self-identity of objects as *the* cause of the truth of the sentences 'a $=$ a' (or 'a $=$ b', given how we defined 'b') is to miss the *interesting* explanation of the truth of the *sentence* for something which only redundantly determines it: the first and second occurrences of 'a' share a reference determiner (and the reference determiner for 'b' contains that of 'a'.)

6

More Arguments Against Analyticity

6.1 THE REGRESS ARGUMENT

The regress argument in Quine's "Truth By Convention" takes as its very specific but significant target the view that the primitive logical constants get their meanings through implicit definition. We begin by supposing, for reductio, that it *is* the case that the primitive logical constants get their meanings through implicit definition, that is, they get their meanings due to a stipulation that certain sentences and rules of implication containing them were true and valid, respectively. Each primitive logical constant appears in an infinite number of logical truths and logically valid rules, and the only way we could stipulate that an infinite number of sentences (rules) were true (valid) would be by stipulating that every sentence (rule) meeting a certain condition C is to be true (valid), where an infinite number of sentences (rules) meet that condition. Suppose we do this and suppose we have a sentence (rule) that meets the condition C. Then we can reason as follows:

This sentence (rule) meets condition C.

All sentences (rules) that meet condition C are true (valid).

Therefore this sentence (rule) is true (valid).

Or alternatively,

This sentence (rule) meets condition C.

If this sentence (rule) meets condition C, **then** it is true (valid).

Therefore this sentence (rule) is true (valid).

But whichever way we draw the conclusion we have to exploit antecedently understood logical constants—*all, if . . . then*, etc.—and recognise a rule of implication, either an instance of modus ponens or universal instantiation, as valid. Implicit definitions of logical constants using an infinite number of sentences and rules *presuppose* that some logical constants are already interpreted. Therefore, this is not a method by which we could have conferred meaning on the *primitive* ones. Bluntly: the method of general schemata is the only method available to the implicit definer and you have to use logic to get logic by this method (Quine 1965[1935]: 81–98).

We can think of the regress argument as having both metaphysical and epistemic points to make. The metaphysical one is that one cannot stipulate the truth of the (infinite number of) logical theorems, because without antecedent logical truths, there is nothing available to unpack the consequences of a schematic definition. The epistemic version suggests that we cannot justify or come to know logical truths by appeal to logical schemata, because any such justification must presuppose the justification or knowledge of logic.

6.1.1 A Response to the Metaphysical Regress

As I observed in Section 1.2, a sentence can be true in virtue of meaning without the proposition it expresses being true in virtue of meaning. *I am here now*, for example, has its truth guaranteed by the meanings of the expressions in the sentence, but nothing about the meanings of those expressions made it the case *that* I am here now. This fact allows for a response to the metaphysical version of the regress argument. In the case of a truth of logic, such as *snow is white* → *snow is white*, the sentence owes its truth to stipulations about '→', but the proposition it expresses—that snow is white → snow is white—is true independently of any stipulations about the meanings of the logical constants.

Thus I may stipulate that '→' is to be interpreted so as to make all instances of a schematic axiom, such as 'A → A', true, and this will make instances of that axiom, such as 'B ∨ C → B ∨ C', true.[1] Quine has pointed out, correctly, that we could not write out the argument for this (as in the argument below) without assuming that some logical constants were already interpreted (in this case, the central '→' in the first sentence):

---

[1] Schema are true just in case all their instances are true. It makes both schematic instances of that axiom, such as 'B ∨ C → B ∨ C' and also instances which are actual interpreted sentences, such as *snow is white* → *snow is white*, true.

('B ∨ C → B ∨ C' is an instance of 'A → A') → ('B ∨ C → B ∨ C'
 is true)

'B ∨ C → B ∨ C' is an instance of 'A → A'

'B ∨ C → B ∨ C' is true

However, it is one thing to point out that we cannot assume that
we have the vocabulary (→) to express the argument, and another to
say that there is something wrong with the argument. It is true *that*
'B ∨ C → B ∨ C' is an instance of 'A → A', and *that* if it is such
an instance, then it is true. Hence the sentence 'B ∨ C → B ∨ C' is
true—regardless of whether the '→' in the center of the first premise of
the argument above is interpreted or not.

After seeing this we can take the further step of noting that since
our stipulations were sufficient to make all instances of the schematic
sentence 'A → A' true, in particular they were sufficient to make
premise 1 in the argument above true—in fact '→' was interpreted
according to our plan.

This point holds for rules of implication as well as for axioms, though
to make it in the case of rules of implication, we need to get a bit clearer
on exactly what a rule of implication is, and in virtue of what such rules
are valid. Rules of implication, of the kind we normally study in logic,
are concerned with *sentences*. What is, or is not, valid is the move from
one *sentence* to the next, which is how it can be the case that a rule of
implication licenses (6.1) but not (6.2), even if we interpret *Hesperus*
and *Phosphorus* as logically proper names.

(6.1)   Hesperus = Phosphorus

        Hesperus is a planet.

        Phosphorus is a planet.

(6.2)   Hesperus = Hesperus.

        Hesperus is a planet.

        Phosphorus is a planet.

However, validity is still a semantic property of an argument. It holds of an argument in virtue of the relations between the *meanings* of the sentences (or sentence schemata) which make it up.[2] The meaning in virtue of which a sentence is true is its content. But the meaning in virtue of which an argument is valid cannot be its content because if it were, the second argument above would have to be valid if the first were. Rather, arguments are valid in virtue of their reference determiners. Though the objects of validity are not the objects of analyticity—the objects of validity are arguments, the objects of analyticity are sentences—the two properties have a lot in common.

Let us represent a rule of implication as a sequence consisting of a set of sentences (the premises) and a sentence (the conclusion), e.g. $\langle \Gamma, A \rangle$. A rule schema is then an ordered pair of a set of sentence schemata and a sentence schema. What stands to such a rule of implication as a sentence stands to a proposition? Presumably an ordered pair of a set of propositions (those expressed by the premises) and a single proposition (that expressed by the conclusion), for example, $\langle \Pi, p \rangle$. This means that the two arguments above express the same-ordered pair (at least, relative to the same context of introduction), but that is okay, since it is in fact just like the sentential case—*Hesperus is Phosphorus* and *Hesperus is Hesperus* express the same proposition, but have different logical properties too.

Quine doubts that we could introduce the primitive logical constants by stipulating, for all the rules of implication containing them, which are to be valid. He argues that since there are infinitely many valid rules,[3] this would have to be done through the stipulation that all instances of a rule of implication schema are to be valid. For instance, part of our introduction of '$\rightarrow$' might involve the stipulation that all the instances of the following schema are to be valid:

$$A \rightarrow B$$
$$A$$
$$\overline{}$$
$$B$$

---

[2] We will say that a sentence schema is valid just in case each instance of the schema is valid. Sentence schemata will thus be valid in virtue of the meanings of the sentences, which make up their instances.

[3] $p \vDash p, p \wedge q \vDash p \dots$ etc.)

Quine asks how we can get from this stipulation about the schema, to the conclusion that an instance of the schema, (say the one below) is valid.

$$(A \lor B) \to C$$

$$A \lor B$$

___

$$C$$

He notes that to use the following rule is to beg the question, since it presupposes that instances of the schema have successfully been stipulated to be valid.

(An argument is an instance of $A \to B, A \vdash B$) $\to$ (it is valid.)

$(A \lor B) \to C, A \lor B \vdash C$ is an instance of $A \to B, B \vdash B$

___

$(A \lor B) \to C, A \lor B \vdash C$ is valid.

Once again, though Quine is right that we could not assume that the linguistic form has been successfully interpreted so that it is valid, it is nevertheless the case *that* if an argument is an instance of the schema, it is valid, (this was made true by our stipulation) and true *that* $A \lor B \to C, A \lor B \vdash C$ is an instance of $A \to B, B \vdash B$ (this was true independently of our stipulation) and this is all that is required to make it the case that $A \lor B \to C, A \lor B \vdash C$ is valid. We don't actually have to be able to express the argument.

Hence the stipulation will be successfully "transmitted" to the instances of the schema, and inference rules containing the expression '$\to$' *will* be truth-preserving.

The Significance of rules of implication

The conventionally accepted definitions—the assignments of meaning in virtue of which the true sentences of logic are true—which I have in mind are not quite the ones that Quine had in mind. Quine imagines us stipulating the truth of a set of esoteric axiomatic schemata, as we can tell from his objection:

Very few persons, before the time of Carnap, had ever seen any convention that engendered the truths of elementary logic. (1965[1954]: 115)

But the meaning-fixing entities which I have in mind are not the axioms of a Frege–Hilbert style formal system, but the more intuitive rules of implication of a natural deduction system. The convention that fixes the meaning of *and* is the convention that *and* can be used (and can only be used) to conjoin any pair of true sentences. The way I like to think of this is that *and* applies correctly to the truth-value sequence ⟨T, T⟩, and from which it follows that any sentence of the form A and B, where A is true and B is true, expresses a truth. One consequence of using such rules is significant: it is that it is no longer obvious that ordinary speakers are not familiar with them.[4]

6.1.2 Response to the Epistemic Regress

I think that the epistemic version of the regress argument is much, much harder to respond to.[5] The epistemic version of the regress argument is a problem about how we can be justified in accepting sentences (or using rules of implication) expressing the truths (and rules) of logic on the basis of schematic implicit definitions. It would seem that conclusions about instances of the schemata can only be drawn if some rules of implication are taken for granted. But though, in the metaphysical case, we can take for granted that the propositional truths of logic are *true*, so that stipulation about a general case is sufficient to make an infinite number of sentences true, it is quite another matter to take for granted that the propositional truths are *known* or *justified*, so that we can take them for granted in justifying instances on the basis of schemata. I would like to be able to explain the epistemological importance of analyticity without assuming that there is any such thing as a priori knowledge. To be forced to assume that the truths of logic are known a priori or are default justified—even if we cannot express them until the primitive expressions have been defined—would be a loss to my account.

---

[4] At least to the extent that the expressions whose referents they fix are part of natural language. There's a good question about whether ordinary speakers know the rules for the material conditional, but then there's also a good question about whether they 'know logic' in any sense that would require familiarity with the material conditional.

[5] I am inclined to think it is one of the biggest unsolved problems facing philosophy today. If I were to construct a 'Hilbert List' of unsolved problems in philosophy, it would certainly make the top three—but perhaps this is just because I need to solve it and I can't.

Achilles and the tortoise

Despite much effort, I cannot claim to have formulated, or even to have learned of, a satisfactory direct response to the epistemic form of the regress argument. But I can offer an indirect reason to be optimistic about the chances of there being one. In "Carnap and Logical Truth," Quine summarises his regress argument and remarks that the difficulty is familiar from Lewis Carroll—an allusion to Carroll's brilliant paper "What the Tortoise said to Achilles" (1895). The reference to Carroll's paper ought to suggest that the regress argument is not all it seems, because, for all the similarity between Quine's argument and the one Carroll presents, Carroll clearly takes his article to be a presentation of a *paradox*. In the article, Carroll describes a meeting between Achilles and the Tortoise. The Tortoise asks Achilles to write down three sentences taken from Euclid:

(A) Things that are equal to the same, are equal to each other.

(B) The two sides of this Triangle are things that are equal to the same.

(Z) The two sides of this Triangle are equal to each other.

The Tortoise asks whether, if he accepts A and B but not Z, nor the hypothetical,

(C) If A and B are true, Z must be true.

he is under any "logical necessity" to accept Z? Achilles says he is not. The Tortoise asks Achilles to persuade him to accept Z. Achilles proceeds by asking him to accept C, which the Tortoise does willingly. Now Achilles remarks of the conclusion, Z:

"You should call it D, not Z," said Achilles. "It comes next to the other three. If you accept A and B and C, you must accept Z . . . it follows logically from them. If A and B and C are true, Z must be true."

But the Tortoise demurs:

"If A and B and C are true, Z must be true," the Tortoise thoughtfully repeated. "That's another Hypothetical, isn't it? And, if I failed to see its truth, I might accept A and B and C, and still not accept Z, mightn't I?"

Hence Achilles must ask the Tortoise to accept another conditional:

D If A and B and C are true, Z must be true

And the Tortoise does, asking Achilles to record it in his notebook along with A, B, C and Z.

"Plenty of blank leaves [in the notebook], I see!" the Tortoise cheerily remarked. "We shall need them all!"

And they will, if they are to proceed as they have so far; so long as Achilles accepts that the Tortoise, accepting sentences A and B, is under no obligation to accept Z unless he already accepts the conditional ⌜if A and B then Z⌝, then he must ask the Tortoise to accept conditional after conditional, (D: ⌜if A and B and C then Z⌝, E: ⌜if A and B and C and D then Z⌝. . . .etc.) and yet he will never persuade him of Z.

The Tortoise's epistemic point would seem to be that unless someone already accepts that a conclusion follows from a set of premises, it is impossible to teach them new premises which will justify or induce that acceptance.[6] Similarly, the epistemic regress seems to say that it is impossible to stipulate a finite set of premises which must justify or induce acceptance of derived theorems of logic.

Carroll's attitude to the Tortoise's argument is different from Quine's attitude to the regress argument. Carroll's waggish tone and references to Zeno suggest that he is not straightforwardly endorsing the Tortoise's argument, any more than he would endorse Zeno's arguments for the impossibility of change. Rather he intends the argument as a reductio ad absurdum of the Tortoise's premises. This seems like the right way to look at it. At some point Achilles has assented where he should not have and almost certainly that point is when he agrees that someone who accepts A and B, but *not* the hypothetical ⌜if A and B then Z⌝ is not "under any logical necessity" to accept Z as true. Surely, this is wrong, and what I hope is that once I understand how it is wrong, I will be able to see how the theorems of logic can be justified on the basis of a finite set. Perhaps the key lies with rules of inference. Perhaps the key lies with a better understanding of what knowledge of rules of inference involves. I regret that, for now, I cannot say.

6.2 THE INDETERMINACY OF TRANSLATION

Carnap (1955) responded to "Two Dogmas of Empiricism" by defending the claim that intension-attributing sentences and theories are

---

[6]   That is, acceptance of the fact that the conclusion follows from the premises, not acceptance of the conclusion.

testable. This would, in effect, give appropriate clarification to one of the expressions in Quine's circle, the notion of intensional meaning. Quine responded in chapter 2 of *Word and Object* with his thesis of the indeterminacy of translation, according to which two empirically adequate theories of translation—theories which state which expressions and sentences of one language mean the same as certain expressions and sentences of another—there will be no fact as to which theory is right, because there is no objective fact of the matter for the theories to be right or wrong about (Quine 1960; Harman 1999*a*: 149).

Theories of translation and the evidence for them

Quine is not explicit about the form that theories of translation should take, but he does make it clear that their theorems should match up the sentences of one language with those of another. Soames (1997: 243) suggests we take them to consist of an infinite number of sentences of the form:

> Word or phrase w in L_1 means the same as word or phrase w* in L_2.
>
> Sentence S in L_1 means the same as sentence S* in L_2.

Quine holds that the evidence for theories of translation consists of the *stimulus meanings* of sentences of the languages. The stimulus meaning of a sentence S at time t for a speaker A is an ordered pair of classes of situations, the first member of which is the class of situations in which the speaker (at t) would assent to the sentence and the second of which is the class of situations in which the speaker (at t) would dissent from the sentence. These classes are not exhaustive of the class of situations as there will be situations that will elicit neither assent nor dissent with respect to a particular sentence.

Stimulus meaning evidence constrains theories of translation in a number of ways. Quine notes that there are some sentences—*standing sentences*—for which stimulus meaning gives almost no clue as to their meaning. The stimulus meaning of (6.3) for example, will be almost indistinguishable from that for (6.4).

(6.3) There are dogs.

(6.4) Two plus two equals four.

Somewhat more useful in constraining theories of translation are *occasion sentences*. Occasion sentences are those to which a speaker will assent only after an initial prompting stimulation, for example, (6.5) and (6.6) below.

(6.5) It hurts.

(6.6) His face is dirty.

Even occasion sentences do not allow us to translate by merely matching up pairs of sentences with the same stimulus meanings, however. The reason for this is that the grounds for a speaker's assent may include background information. For example, though a speaker might only assent to *He's a bachelor* when given certain prompting stimuli, the stimulus meaning of the sentence for him is in part determined by his background beliefs about who is married. For someone else in the community the sentence may have a different stimulus meaning, even though, intuitively, the sentence means the same thing to both speakers. For this reason Quine does not make it a constraint on an adequate theory of translation that it match up occasion sentences with the same stimulus meanings. However, there is a weaker constraint. We can take advantage of the fact that the background knowledge of a speaker when he assents to one sentence is probably very similar to the background knowledge he has when he assents to another sentence—his knowledge of his friend's marital status is relatively constant and will not normally be lost suddenly only to be regained ten minutes later—and so, if two sentences have the same stimulus meaning for him, the theory should match those sentences up with a pair of sentences in the other language which also have the same stimulus meanings. This gives us the principle:

(P1) If a theory states that occasion sentence S_1 in a language L_1 means the same as a sentence S_2 in L_2, and S_1' in L_1 means the same as S_2' in L_2 then it predicts that S_1 and S_2 have the same stimulus meaning just in case S_1' and S_2' have the same stimulus meaning.

Intuitively, *observation sentences* are those for which assent or dissent depends *only* on observable facts about the current situation. An example of an observation sentence might be *that is red*. Observationality is a matter of degree, as there is usually *some* background information that could affect the speaker's disposition to respond to stimulus. The linguist can only discover which sentences are observation sentences by observing behaviour, so he needs behavioristic criteria for identifying observation sentences, and Quine says that a sentence will be more observational the more its stimulus meaning is constant for different speakers across the community. This may not be entirely successful in weeding out the effects of background information, since background information which is shared across the entire community may continue to decrease observationality in the intuitive sense, though stimulus meanings across the community are constant. Observation sentences allow for stronger constraints on theories of translation:

(P2) If a theory of translation states that two observation sentences mean the same thing, then it predicts that sentence one will have the same stimulus meaning for speakers of the language it is in, as sentence two will have for speakers of *its* language.

Theories will also make predications about the logical constants. If a theory states, for example, that a symbol of a language means the same as the English truth-functional connective *and* then it predicts that the stimulus meaning of a sentence where the symbol is applied to two other sentences should include the intersection of the affirmative stimulus meanings (class of situations in which a speaker would assent to the sentence at t) of the two sentences.

Underdetermination and indeterminacy

Theories of translation, though constrained to make only true stimulus-meaning predictions by the principles above, are underdetermined by stimulus-meaning evidence. One of Quine's most famous illustrations of this underdetermination involves the made-up native sentence *Gavagai*. The affirmative stimulus meaning of the sentence consists, all things being equal, in the class of situations where the speaker's retinae are irradiated with the kind of pattern he has when presented with a rabbit, and the class of situations where he is not. But this is consistent with theories of translation that assign *gavagai* the same meaning as *rabbit*, *undetached rabbit part* and *temporal-slice of rabbit*. These assignments of meaning may require differences elsewhere in the theory, if the theory is to remain empirically adequate. For example, a theory says that *gavagai* means the same as *temporal-slice of rabbit*, we might try to ask, at a different time, whether the same object still exists. Given the assignment of *temporal-slice of rabbit* to *gavagai*, the theory will have to assign the meaning of *the object that caused you to assent to 'Gavagai' a minute ago still exists* to a sentence from which the speaker will *dissent*. Such a theory will differ in many places from the one which assigns *gavagai* the same meaning as *rabbit*, but it need not assign the wrong stimulus meanings to any expression.

Any theory of translation which does not predict any stimulus meanings which expressions do not in fact have, will count as empirically adequate. But, since such theories will always be underdetermined by the evidence, there will be more than one such empirically adequate theory of translation. This is Quine's thesis of the *underdetermination of translation by data*.

From here there are two routes to the indeterminacy thesis.

(1) We learn what the words and sentences of languages mean by observing the behaviour of others, so whatever data is relevant to determining the meanings of the words and sentences of a language should be obtainable by observing the behaviour of its speakers. Since, by the under-determination thesis, this data does not determine a unique translation, the correct theory of translation is not determined by all the data that is admissible for determining the correct theory of translation. Quine concludes that the correct theory is not determined at all; there is no such thing as the *right* theory.

(2) The other route proceeds via a physicalist premise. All real facts are determined by the physical facts, but even if we admit all the truths of physics, the correct translation hypothesis will not be determined. But that means that which hypothesis is correct is not a real fact.

[T]heory in physics is the ultimate parameter . . . consider . . . the totality of truths of nature, known and unknown, observable and unobservable, past and future. The point about indeterminacy of translation is that it withstands even all this truth, the whole truth about nature. Quine 1975: 303

Response to the indeterminacy of translation

In my response to the argument from the indeterminacy of translation I concur with Soames' conclusions in Soames (1999*a* and 1997): neither route from the under-determination of translation by data to the indeterminacy thesis is valid. Both routes can be seen as having the following structure:

(P1) If there are facts about meaning (translation) they must be determined by other, more fundamental facts (facts about stimulus meanings/the facts of physics.)

(P2) Facts about meaning (translation) are not determined by any such facts.

(C) So there are no facts about meaning.

There is no way to construe the determination relation in this argument that makes both (P1) and (P2) true, and thus no construal on which the argument is sound. It is plausible that facts about the way the world is physically determine all the meaning facts *in the sense* that in any other metaphysically possible world in which the physical facts are the same, the meaning facts will be the same too. But the thesis that Quine actually argues for, is that from the statement of the physical facts, *we cannot tell* that some empirically adequate theory of translation is the correct one. This is *determine* in the sense in which A determines B iff B is an a priori consequence of A and it does not follow from the fact that A does not determine B in this sense, that A does not determine B in the metaphysical sense. Thus Quine's argument gives us no reason to accept the indeterminacy of translation.

6.3 TWO ARGUMENTS FROM EXTERNALISM

Externalism in the philosophies of language and mind is the view that the content of a linguistic expression or mental state can be partially determined by the environment in which the speaker or subject finds themselves—as opposed to being fully-determined by the stuff inside their own heads. For example, on the Millian view of names, the content of a name *is* the bearer of that name itself. On this view, if the name *Hesperus* is introduced using the description *the evening star* and the evening star is Venus, then the sentence *Hesperus is a planet* has as its content the proposition that Venus is a planet. But if the evening star had been *Mars*, (if the environment had been different in that respect) then the sentence would have had as its content the proposition that *Mars* is a planet instead. So, on this view, the content of the sentence *Hesperus is a planet* is partially determined by the environment.

Similarly, my twin on Twin Earth, though internally identical to me, thinks that XYZ is a liquid, whereas I think that H_2O is a liquid, because her environment contains XYZ and not H_2O, and mine contains H_2O and not XYZ (Putnam 1975). Burge's character believes falsely that he has arthritis in his thigh and not truly that he has tharthritis in his thigh because the doctors in his environment use *arthritis* to refer to a disease of the joints (Burge 1991[1979]).

So it is a standard thought for externalists that what one means can depend on what the environment is like—on whether one is in an environment where Venus is the evening star, where there is H_2O, and where there are people who use *tharthritis* for a disease of the thigh.

Two features of externalism have seemed to pose a threat to analyticity: the separation of speaker knowledge from meaning, and the separation of meaning from reference determiner. The former threatens the epistemological consequences of truth in virtue of meaning, the latter threatens the idea of truth in virtue of meaning directly.

To begin with the epistemological aspect: once it is no longer expected that in virtue of understanding an analytic sentence that the speaker know anything about the meaning in virtue of which the sentence is true, there remains no reason to think that speakers can have access to that truth through their understanding of the sentence; *the kind of meaning that is 'in their head' ain't the kind of meaning the sentence is true in virtue of.* And usually it has been assumed that the kind of meaning which makes the sentence true is its content.

On the account I gave in Part I it is reference determiner, rather than content, that is the aspect of meaning which is responsible for truth in virtue of meaning. However, the externalist's epistemological point holds for reference determiner too; reference determiner ain't always in the head either—speakers need not know the reference determiners for names and natural kind terms, and maybe not for some other expressions either if they defer to other members of their linguistic communities.

In Part III I will present a revisionary account of analytic justification in which I will concede some of the damage done to the traditional account of analyticity by externalism. I will argue that analytic justification is justification on the basis of reference determiners alone, and that to the extent that speakers do not know what those reference determiners are, they will not be able to avail themselves of analytic justifications.

But the second externalist threat is something we can deal with now. It came with the separation of content (meaning) and reference determiner and the resulting determination of content by the environment. This aspect threatens truth in virtue of meaning directly. If the meaning (content) of a sentence such as *cats are animals* varies with the environment, then in what sense can the sentence *cats are animals* be true in virtue of its meaning? It does not have a stable meaning, in virtue of which to be true, and when it *does* have a meaning, that meaning is determined by the environment. Is that not sufficient to show that the world—not just meaning—determines the eventual truth-value?

There is something right about this objection, and two things that are wrong.[7] Since the truth-value of *cats are animals* actually *varies* with context of introduction, the context of introduction does not merely redundantly determine the truth-value of *cats are animals*, but *partially determines* it. Thus the externalist is right about this: *cats are animals* is not true in virtue of meaning.

But this concession is not the whole story. The externalist's reasoning to the conclusion is faulty in two respects. He maintains that *cats are animals* is false on the grounds that a sentence whose content is determined by the environment cannot be analytic and on the grounds that a sentence whose content varies with the environment cannot be analytic. Both are false; *I am here now* contains three expressions whose contents are determined by, and vary with, the environment, but it is analytic.

The mistake at the heart of all this is thinking that it is the content of an analytic sentence which makes it analytic. The externalist supposes that to say that *cats are animals* is analytic is to say that it is true in virtue of its content, and this is why he thinks the fact that its content is determined by, and varies with, the environment is sufficient to show that it is not true in virtue of meaning in any interesting sense. In truth, analyticity is truth in virtue of reference determiner, and the reason *cats are animals* is not analytic is that its reference determiner fails to fully-determine its truth.

6.4 AN ARGUMENT FROM VAGUENESS

Philosophers sometimes say that the doctrine of analyticity is threatened by the vagueness of ordinary language. They may be alluding to a variety of issues, but one version of an argument from vagueness goes like this:

---

[7] I also note for clarity that it is true that on my conception of truth in virtue of meaning that the fact that the world contributes in some way to the determination of the truth-value of a sentence does not show conclusively that the sentence is not true in virtue of meaning. The fact that Mole is not married, for example, is part of the reason why *all bachelors are unmarried* is true, but as this state of affairs only *redundantly determines* the truth-value of the sentence, this fact is not in conflict with the claim that *all bachelors are unmarried* is analytic.

If 'all fish have gills' is analytic, then all actual *and merely possible* fish have gills. Now consider a (merely possible) ocean dwelling creature very like a fish, which can absorb oxygen through its skin, and has no gills. Is this a fish with no gills? Or it is impossible for it to be a fish, since it has no gills, and nothing counts as a fish without gills? If the former, then 'all fish have gills' is not analytic. If the latter then the sentence is analytic. Plausibly, however, *there is no right answer to the question*, because the rules governing the correct use of the word 'fish' do not legislate for this case. Hence there is no fact of the matter about whether 'all fish have gills' is analytic.

Fish is, on this story, a predicate with a partially-defined intension. There are objects (actual and possible) which are in the intension of *fish* (all halibut, and any Persian-speaking flying fish) and there are objects (actual and possible) which are in the anti-intension of *fish*, (yours and my siblings and the winged-horse Pegasus). But there are also objects which are not placed in either the intension or the anti-intension by the reference determiner for the word *fish*. Among these objects are the possible fish-like creatures who breathe through their skins. So the meaning of the word *fish*, being somewhat indeterminate, fails to determine whether or not *all fish have gills* is analytic. It is plausible that many expressions are like this, and so it is plausible that there is often no fact of the matter about whether or not a sentence is analytic. Donnellan makes this point in in his 1962 paper "Necessity and Criteria":

There is no reason, a priori, why our present usage should legislate for all hypothetical cases. Given our present circumstances, the correct thing to say is that all whales are mammals, but whether this is, as we intend it, a necessary truth or contingent is indeterminate. 1962

Carnap was also aware of the issue and it seems to have contributed to his view that the expression *analytic* was best reserved for sentences of artificial or cleaned-up scientific languages.[8]

However, the fact that an expression has an under-determined intension does not mean that it cannot support an analytic connection. Sober (2000: 245) points out that though the expressions *rich* and *poor* are

---

[8] "In the oldest books on chemistry, for example, there were a great number of statements describing the properties of a given substance, say water or sulphuric acid, including its reactions with other substances. There was no clear indication as to which of these numerous properties were to be taken as essential or definitory for the substance. Therefore, at least on the basis of the book alone, we cannot determine which of the statements made in the book were analytic, and which were synthetic for its author." Carnap 1955 "Carnap rejected the idea that the analytic/synthetic distinction marks a factual distinction among sentences in a natural language." (Sober 2000: 242–6)

vague, the sentence *rich people have more money than poor people* may still be analytic. Though it is not always clear whether someone counts as poor or rich (even when we know everything there is to know about their finances), it seems as if current usage legislates enough to tell us that whoever counts as poor will have less money than someone who counts as rich. Similarly, one might think that the intension of *male* is unclear. Perhaps is not clear, for example, whether or not it applies to some transsexuals. Nevertheless *all bachelors are male* could still be analytic.

How might this work? Sometimes people say that it will be possible to maintain an analytic connection between two expressions, even if one is vague, so long as the other is vague too, and vague in exactly the same respects. The picture they seem to have in mind is of two concepts whose intensions may be unclear in some cases, including the cases which are significant for the analytic link, but which are unclear on the same cases. For example, it might be unclear in the case of some people, whether those people are males, but if these are exactly the cases where it is unclear whether they are bachelors, we have no counterexample to the claim that *all bachelors are male* is analytic. So long as the "edges" of the concepts coincide like this, then the analytic connection is safe.

One might have two worries about this response. First, one might be concerned that this situation leaves it open that we might make the meanings of *bachelor* and *male* more determinate, and do so in such a way that some of the unclear cases become non-male bachelors. And second, one might worry about the likelihood that two expressions with indeterminate intensions should have intensions which coordinate in such a complicated, refined manner. After all, we think that the borders of such predicates are *chaotic* because we don't care about them very much. What does it matter whether a possible herring which breathes through its skin counts as a fish? Wouldn't it take an improbable coincidence for two disregarded, chaotic intension-edges to coincide in the appropriate way?

The key to understanding how vagueness and analyticity are compatible is the recognition that analyticity arises where the reference determiner of one expression is parasitic on the reference determiner of another. Whether or not, for example, *bachelor* applies to a transsexual depends on whether or not the transsexual is male. To the extent that it is unclear whether someone is male, it will be (given that they meet other conditions, such as being unmarried) unclear whether they are a bachelor. But should we decide to extend our linguistic rules, so that a particular candidate counts as male (perhaps we decide that in unclear cases the subject themselves should be allowed to decide which gender they are and this subject wants to be male), he will automatically (if also unmarried) count as a bachelor. So we need not worry that we might decide the unclear cases in ways which would make *all bachelors are male* false. Nor need we worry about the unlikely coincidence required to make the concepts of *male* and *bachelor* vague in all the same ways. It is not a coincidence; *bachelor* inherits its vagueness from *male*.

6.5 BLUE GOLD, ROBOT CATS

The sentences that are contenders for the status of analyticity are of a variety of different kinds. One kind that recurs again and again in the literature is illustrated by the sentences in the following list:

A   (a) Lead is a metal. (Locke 1993[1690]: 351)
    (b) Gold is fusible. (Locke 1993[1690]: 351)
    (c) Copper is a metal. (Harman 1999*b*: 119)
    (d) Saffron is yellow. (Locke 1993[1690]: 352)
    (e) Gold is heavy. (Locke 1993[1690]: 355)
    (f) Red is a color. (Harman 1999*b*: 128)
    (g) Blue is a color. (Katz 1997: 3)
    (h) Man is an animal. (Arnauld 1964[1662]: 320)

B   (a) Cats are animals. (Katz 1997: 3)
    (b) Whales are mammals. (Donnellan 1962: 650)
    (c) Nightmares are dreams. (Katz 1974: 288)
    (d) Dogs are animals. (Fodor & LePore 1993: 637)

C   (a) All gold is fusible. (Locke 1993[1690]: 351)
    (b) Every man is an animal. (Locke 1993[1690]: 351)
    (c) All men are animals. (White 1952: 274)
    (d) Every brother is a male. (White 1952: 274)
    (e) All men are rational animals. (White 1952: 274)
    (f) All women are female. (Harman 1999*b*)
    (g) No bachelor is married. (Quine 1965[1973])
    (h) Every triangle has three angles equal to two right angles. (Arnauld 1964[1662]: 320)
    (i) *Alle Körper sind ausgedehnt.* (all bodies are extended) (Kant 1965*b*: 14, §2)

D (a) A such and such is a so and so. (Honderich 1995)
   (b) A vixen is a female fox. (Honderich 1995)

These sentences are not, at first blush, philosophically important examples (except perhaps for (Ce and i)), which suggests that they recur in the literature for some other reason, perhaps because they are taken to be particularly *clear* or *good* examples. Locke attempted to characterise these sentences as:

propositions wherein the *genus* is predicated of the *species*, or more comprehensive of less comprehensive terms; (1993[1690]: 350)

In some cases the logical form of these sentences is clear. The sentences in (C) for example contain explicit quantifiers, so that it does seem clear that these are sentences of the form:

$$(\forall x)(Fx \rightarrow Gx)$$

But the form of the sentences in (A) is less obvious. *Red is a color* is plausibly composed of the *name red* and the predicate *is a color*, so that its form is:

$$Fa$$

But the superficially similar *Gold is fusible* does not seem importantly different from *All gold is fusible*, which is *not* of the form Fa but of the form $(\forall x)(Fx \rightarrow Gx)$. Here *gold* functions as a predicate and the sentence is true just in case *fusible* applies to everything that *gold* applies to. Similarly with *Copper is a metal*. *Red is a color* should not be understood the same way; *red is a color* is true and

$$(\forall x)((x) \text{ is red} \rightarrow (x) \text{ is a color})$$

is false; many strawberries are red, but no strawberry is a color.

6.5.1 Mistakes about Individual Sentences

A number of arguments in the literature proceed by attacking the analytic status of individual sample sentences like those above. In particular, Putnam argues that *all cats are animals* is not analytic, the computer scientists Winograd and Flores argue that *all bachelors are unmarried* is not analytic, Kripke presents examples that suggest that *gold is a yellow metal* and *tigers have four legs* are not analytic and Harman takes on, among others, *all women are female* and *red is a color.*

In some ways this is an odd strategy for critics of analyticity to pursue. A demonstration that a single sentence is not analytic—even one that has been used as an example of an analytic sentence repeatedly—might not seem significant. Even if *cats are animals* is not really an analytic sentence, for example, it might still be the case that the analytic/synthetic distinction is coherent, it might still be the case that there are many analytic sentences and it might still be the case that analyticity plays an important role in epistemology.

One popular thesis which *is* in obvious tension with the falsity of an apparently analytic sentence, however, is the thesis that whether or not a sentence is analytic or synthetic is *obvious*. However, this was never that tenable a thesis anyway. Consider the initially plausible thesis that the sentence *if x is to the east of y and y is to the east of z then x is to the east of z* is analytic. Similarly for *nothing is east of itself.* Yet Harrisburg is east of Edmonton, and Edmonton is east of Siberia, so Harrisburg is east of Siberia. Siberia is east of London and London is east of Harrisburg. So Siberia is east of Harrisburg. From which it follows that Harrisburg is east of Harrisburg. Appearances to the contrary it cannot be the case that both sentences are analytic, because it cannot be the case that they are both true.

Nonetheless, the non-analyticity of certain apparently analytic sentences, such as *all cats are animals* does have importance for the debate. It suggests that there is an alternative explanation for the appearance of analyticity. And if something other than analyticity can explain the appearance of analyticity in the case of *all cats are animals*, perhaps it can explain the appearance of analyticity in all cases.

Whatever explains speakers intuitions about *bachelors are unmarried* presumably also explains their intuitions about other allegedly analytic sentences. No reason has been given to suppose that any of these explanations involve the assumption that any of these sentences are true by virtue of meaning. (Harman 1976: 388)

In pursuing this strategy, Harman (1973, 1976) offers the sentences *all women are female* and *all bachelors are unmarried* as examples of sentences which appear to be analytic, but are in fact false. *Female* says Harman, is a more scientific term than *woman* and the Olympic committee has denied some women entry to events because they have too many Y chromosomes to count as female. The application conditions for *woman* and *female* are different and so there can be, and in fact are, women that are not female. Similarly, we sometimes call men who are awaiting divorce and living the lives of bachelors, *bachelors*. So there are married men who are also bachelors.

Winograd and Flores also take exception to the analyticity of *all bachelors are unmarried*. They question what they see as the standard account of the meaning of *bachelor* and claim that the philosopher has been working with an over-simplistic conception of the meanings of the words in that sentence. This is revealed by competent speakers willingness to use them in ways that (according to the philosopher) they ought not to be used:

> In classical discussions of semantics, the word "bachelor" has been put forth as a word that can be clearly defined in more elementary terms: "adult human male who has never been married." But when someone refers to a person as a "bachelor" in an ordinary conversational situation, much more (and less) is conveyed. "Bachelor" is inappropriate if used in describing the Pope or a member of a monogamous homosexual couple, and might well be used in describing an independent career woman. The problem is not that "bachelor" is complex and involves more terms than those accounted for in the classical definition. There is no coherent 'checklist' of any length such that objects meeting all of its conditions will consistently be called "bachelors" and those failing one or more of them will not. The question "Is X a bachelor?" cannot be answered except by considering the potential answers to "Why do you want to know?"[9]

Harman also points to Putnam's argument (Putnam 1962*b*) that *cats are animals* is not analytic. In "It Ain't Necessarily So", Putnam considers what we would say about the sentence *Cats are animals* if it turned out that cats were cleverly disguised robots sent to earth by Martians. He imagines three different cases. In the first, only some of the things we have been calling *cats* are robots. The rest are ordinary cats. Putnam thinks that in this case we would say that the robots were not cats at all, but only fake cats. *Cats are animals* would still be true. In the second scenario there were ordinary cats until 50 years ago, when the Martians "killed all of them and replaced them all overnight with robots that look exactly like cats and can't be told from cats by present-day biologists (although, let's say, biologists will be able to detect the fake in

---

[9] Winograd & Flores 1986: 112 (original quotation marks, footnotes omitted).

fifty years more)" (Putnam 1962*b*: 660). Then Putnam thinks we would say that though there were cats up until 50 years ago, the present-day things we call *cats* are not really cats, and also not really animals. In this case too, the sentence *all cats are animals* would be true. But in the last scenario Putnam asks us to consider what we should say if it turned out that there have never been any non-robot cats. Cats have always been robots.

It seems to me that in this last case, once we have discovered the fake, we should continue to call these robots that we have mistaken for animals and that we have employed as house pets "cats," but not "animals." (Putnam 1962*b*: 660)

Harman argues that this case is not a one off, and that failure to consider similar kinds of strange cases (that is, failure of imagination) has led philosophers to attribute analyticity to many other contingent sentences:

After imagining what it would be like to discover that things look red partly as the result of an extremely high-pitched sound emitted by red objects, such that, if we were to go deaf, the objects would look grey, some philosophers no longer ascribe analyticity to 'Red is a colour.' (Harman 1999*b*: 128)

Kripke (1980: 118) gives similar examples for the sentences *gold is a yellow metal* and *tigers have four legs.*[10] He asks us to imagine a situation in which it is discovered that it is only due to an optical illusion that gold appears to be yellow, 'but in fact, once the peculiar properties of the atmosphere [are] removed, we would see that it is really blue.' He predicts that rather than announcing that gold had turned out not to exist, the newspapers would run stories saying that gold had turned out to be blue.

Kripke also considers a definition of *tiger*: A tiger is a large carnivorous quadrupedal feline, tawny yellow in color with blackish transverse stripes and white belly. He claims that this does not give a definition of *tiger* in English, since it is quite possible that we could come across an injured tiger with only three legs and we would not say that it had thereby ceased to be a tiger. It presumably follows that *tigers have four legs* is not analytic.

---

[10]   It is not clear in this passage that Kripke takes his arguments to have relevance for the analytic/synthetic distinction in general. His definition of analyticity in lecture 1 is merely stipulative and he remarks at one point that *gold is a yellow metal* was never plausibly analytic in the first place.

6.5.2 Two Forms of Argument

The arguments above are of two kinds. One kind appeals to sentences to which ordinary speakers are prepared to assent to (or could reasonably be expected to assent to) in order to argue that a putative analytic sentence is false, or that the negation of an analytic sentence is true. Since analytic sentences are true, it follows that the sentence is not analytic. Examples of this strategy include Harman's arguments concerning *all women are female* and *all bachelors are unmarried* and Winograd and Flores' observations about *all bachelors are unmarried*.

The other kind of argument exploits the special modal profile that analyticity is supposed to entail. Putnam's argument concerning *cats are animals*, for example, seeks to show that *cats are animals* is not necessary and hence not analytic.

The argument from modal profile

It is strictly true that on my account of analyticity analytic sentences need not be necessary—*I am here now*, for example, is contingent and yet analytic—and that, strictly speaking, it is propositions and not sentences which are necessary anyway. But Putnam's argument is still effective. Sentences inherit modal properties from the propositions they express, and analytic sentences do have distinctive modal properties. Putnam does not really show that *cats are animals* expresses a contingent truth, but he describes a possible state of affairs in which *cats* has a different context of introduction from the one we believe it actually has. Though we don't know what the reference determiner for *cat* is (it is a natural kind term, we don't need to), we think that it was able to pick out cats (our animal familiars), because they were present in our environment, and that in an environment in which those small furry creatures were in fact robots, the reference determiner would have latched on to (non-animal) robots instead. With respect to such a context of introduction *all cats are animals* is false, and so the reference determiner of the sentence does not fully-determine its truth. Thus *cats are animals* has the wrong kind of modal profile to be analytic—Putnam is right.

Harman would conclude from this that there is an alternative explanation of the appearance of analyticity. We think that *cats are animals* is analytic, and *cats are not animals* semantically anomalous (to use Katz' terminology) because of our general, background knowledge about cats. Given what we know—and what we know that other people know—*cats are not animals* is a surprising thing for someone to say. Perhaps the best explanation of their saying it is a mistaken belief about what it means. If they have the meaning right though, of course they will assent to *all cats are animals*. This, of course, is an explanation which is available whenever a sentence appears to be analytic.

I think that Harman is right that Putnam's example shows that there must be an alternative explanation of the appearance of analyticity. But I favor a different alternative. The explanation begins by noting that native speakers who have not studied their language formally often think that they are next to omniscient about it. Native speakers, they reason, can use their language—or at the very least a large part of it—perfectly, so they must know whatever rules there are that govern correct usage. Such a belief can result in over-confident native English speakers explaining a 'rule' of English (which they have in fact just made up) to questioning non-native learners, only to be counterexampled many times over by the questioners who had to learn English via explicit rules and hard graft. (For example, proposed rule: in English one can always transform an active construction (Garfield ate the lasagne) into a passive (the lasagne was eaten) by making the object the subject and replacing the verb with 'be + past participle.' Counterexample to this rule: *to have* 'The car was had' is not a passivization of 'he had the car.') Native English speakers in this situation often find the experience very confusing.

Next we note that speakers not only think that they *must* know how their language works—how else could they use it so well?—but also that such knowledge entails knowing how the referents of expressions are determined. The language myth, remember, was not so much a philosophical theory as a pervasive folk picture of the way language works.

Finally we note that in situations where people think they *must* know the answer to a particular question (because, unless they did, they couldn't do things they can patently do), they are apt to think that the first answer that occurs to them is true. Namely, that 'change the verb to 'be+ pp'' is the rule for the English passive.

Similarly, when asked what conditions an object must meet to fall in the extension of *cat*, ordinary speakers—by which I mean to exclude many linguists and philosophers—under the belief that they *must* know what these conditions are, since they understand *cat*, give the first conditions which come to mind, often something like 'to count as a cat you have to be a small furry animal, with four legs, ears and a tail. Oh, and they torture mice and sleep during the day.' If this *were* the reference determiner for *cat*—if being a cat was a matter of being a small, furry, four-legged animal with ears, tail, and a predilection for murine suffering and sleep—then *all cats are animals* would be analytic, since the reference determiner for *animal* would be contained in that of *cat*.

This is why some sentences containing natural kind terms such as

- cats are animals

- all gold is fusible

- gold is a yellow metal

- copper is a metal

- all men are rational animals

- tigers have four legs

have appeared to be analytic. Confronted with the observation that a tiger with three legs is still a tiger, or that *cats are animals* could have been false, speakers are as uneasy as those confronted with the unpassivisability of *to have*. It's not merely that something they thought was right has been shown to be wrong; it's also that their whole picture of how language works implies that they *cannot* be wrong. They are left, not with a demonstration of the non-analyticity of, say, *tigers have four legs*, but with an outright paradox.

Thus it is not surprising that the Putnam-style counterexamples grew out of a growing appreciation for the falsity of the language myth, and in particular for the way that natural kind terms work. Speakers often don't know the conditions which an object must meet in order to count as a cat, and hence there is no need to rely on their rationalisations on the subject of the reference determiner for *cat* when considering the analyticity of the sentence.

One thing that distinguishes this explanation of the false appearance of analyticity from Harman's is that it uses a particular fact about the expressions involved in the sentence—in order to be competent with one, one does not need to know its reference determiner—to explain away the appearance of analyticity. In this, the explanation is less general than Harman's. It cannot be used to explain away apparent analyticity in cases where the speakers were right about the reference determiners of the expressions involved, or to explain away cases containing only expressions which are such that one must know the reference determiner in order to understand one. Though it is unclear quite which cases the latter will be, since, thanks to the phenomenon of deference it is unclear which expressions are like that, it seems that *bachelor* is a clear candidate. Surely those who have thought that *all bachelors are unmarried* was analytic did so because they thought that one had to be unmarried in order to count as a bachelor—and in this they were right. So my explanation cannot account for the apparent analyticity of *all bachelors are unmarried*. That sentence appears to be analytic because it *is* analytic.

The argument from what people say

Unlike Harman, Winograd and Flores, I do not believe that the fact that speakers sometimes refer to married men as *bachelors* shows that some married men are bachelors, nor that the Olympic committee's refusal to call some women *female* shows that some women are not female.

There are three reasons for this. First of all, people get things wrong, and as a result, just because people call something an X (or refuse to call something an X) does not mean that X applies to it (or does not apply to it). This is one of the things that we learned from Harman's 'witch' example: even if a linguistic community agree on the extension of a word, it does not follow that the word has the extension on which they agree. In particular, from the fact that a group of old men refused to call some women *female*, it does not follow that they are not female.[11]

Second, people use words in non-literal or technical senses. I may call someone a bachelor in the same spirit that I would call him a chicken, or a lone wolf, or a prince, and though my usage is not incorrect, it does not follow that he is a bachelor, or a chicken, or a lone wolf, or a prince. Or I may stipulate that for the purposes of what follows I take *female* to apply to all and only persons with two X chromosomes and no Y chromosome, and this may help you to understand my report, but it will not tell you much about what *female* means in ordinary English.

The final reason that relying on which sentences people will accept or utter in order to determine semantic content is dangerous is that

---

[11] Similarly, it does not follow from Microsoft's declaration that its trademark *Microsoft* has no genitive, that Microsoft's trademark has no genitive. (Pullum 2004)

people often rely on pragmatics to convey the proposition they intended to assert. Calling someone a *bachelor*, in particular, is often used to implicate that that person is an *eligible* bachelor. I may refuse to assent to the sentence *the pope is a bachelor*, not because I believe the negation of that proposition, but because I am aware that to assent to *the pope is a bachelor* would be to implicate that the pope is an eligible bachelor, which is surely false (Grice 1967[1991]).

PART III

WORK FOR EPISTEMOLOGISTS

ABSTRACT (PART III)

The apparent epistemological power of analyticity is a large part of its attraction for philosophers, but does analyticity have to allow *a priori* justification to be interesting and useful? In Chapter 7 I argue that—with respect to this debate anyway—we should stop worrying about a priority and simply consider whether analytic truths afford any *distinctive* kind of justification, whether that is genuinely a priori, or just a special kind of a posteriori justification. I consider three theories of *analytic justification*, and argue for the third. The last few pages of the book address some of the consequences of the proceeding account for some traditional theses about analyticity—including the prospects for seeing analytic justification as full-blown a priori justification.

7

Analytic Justification

One of the standard doctrines connected with analyticity—connected so intimately that some maintain that a phenomenon that did not uphold it could not properly be called *analyticity*—is that analytic sentences have special epistemological properties (Quine 1965[1954]: 110;) (Harman 1999*b*: 127). Some have maintained that these epistemic properties will provide us with *interesting and important* knowledge or methods of justification. A. J. Ayer, for example, thought that analyticity justified our beliefs in the truths of arithmetic. But other philosophers have held that epistemological import of analytic truths is meagre; Locke wrote that analytic truths "carry no knowledge with them but of the signification of words" and thought that to utter one was merely to "trifle" with words (1993[1690]).

This last part of the book is about the epistemological import of analyticity. Traditionally, analytic truths have been thought to provide access to a priori knowledge. But a priori knowledge is a philosophical Gordian knot of its own, and after explaining just why the problem of a priori knowledge is so difficult, I shall propose that we put it aside to consider whether analytic sentences provide a distinctive kind of *analytic justification*, regardless of whether that justification is strictly a priori or just a special kind of a posteriori justification. I consider three theories of analytic justification, and argue for the third. With this theory in the background, in the final section of the book, I examine some historical claims about analyticity and epistemology, in the light of what we have discovered: are analytic truths non-factual? Or trivial? Are they language or framework-relative? Does analyticity afford knowledge of language as opposed to knowledge of the world? Does someone who denies an analytic truth misunderstand it?

7.1 A PRIORI JUSTIFICATION

Whether a proposition is a posteriori or a priori is a matter of the way in which it is justified. It is a posteriori if and only if its justification depends on experience. My belief that a mouse lives in my office is an example of an a posteriori belief; its justification depends on the fact that I *saw* him last night. A belief is a priori, on the other hand, just in case it is justified independently of experience. It is controversial whether there are any a priori beliefs, but traditional candidates include the truths of logic and arithmetic, and analytic truths. Perhaps my beliefs that triangles have three sides, or that mice are self-identical, are examples of a priori beliefs. Such a conception of a priority allows that there might be a priori beliefs that require no justification (default justified beliefs) and the pair of definitions allow that there can be propositions which are neither a priori nor a posteriori—those that are unjustified. A proposition may have more than one justification, but if it has one which is a priori, then we will say that it is a priori, and not a posteriori.

If an epistemic agent possesses an a priori justification for one of their beliefs then that belief is a priori *for* that person. Only a priori beliefs can be a priori for a person, but someone might believe an a priori proposition a posteriori, if their justification for it is a posteriori—for example, someone who discovers the answer to an arithmetical sum using their calculator, or a mathematician who has proved the four-color theorem using a computer—and in that case the belief is a posteriori for them, not a priori for them.

In the interests of fashion I will also leave it open that a belief can be justified and false, and that a belief may have an a priori justification and still be false and that there are some a priori justifications that are defeasible, either empirically or by a priori means (Casullo 1988).

The standard account of the epistemological import of analytic truths holds that they are a priori. One difficulty for any attempt to defend that account is that it confuses sentences and propositions. One cannot know, as the account suggests, an analytic truth; analytic truths are sentences, and it is propositions that are the objects of knowledge. This problem looks solvable; the defender of the traditional account might select a suitably related proposition to be justified a priori on the basis of the analytic sentence. The four most obvious candidates (for an analytic sentence s expressing a proposition p) are:

(i) the proposition that s is true

(ii) the proposition that what s says is true

(iii) that p is true and

(iv) p itself

This problem will have to be solved by any adequate account of justification provided by analytic sentences, but it is a minor problem when compared to that of explaining a priori justification. Justification has to stop somewhere; I have justified beliefs, and many of those are justified by other beliefs that I have, but I hold no belief such that the following is true: it is justified by other beliefs, and those beliefs are justified by some further beliefs still and so on ad infinitum. It follows that either some of my beliefs must be justified by something other than further beliefs, such as perceptual experience, or I must be able to be justified in holding them without possessing any kind of justification at all. Either way there has to be a story about the justification of such *basic* beliefs.

Similarly with a priority. Since any a priori beliefs which I have must be either basic, or justified by other a priori beliefs, and there is no infinite regress of a priori justified beliefs, there must—if there are to be any a priori beliefs at all—be basic a priori beliefs. Perhaps every belief is justified until credibly challenged. Or perhaps there are analogues of perceptual seemings that justify basic a priori beliefs. But any serious defence of the idea that analytic truths allow us to know propositions a priori should explain how there can be any a priori justification at all and hence will need a story about the basic a priori truths (Harman 1999a: 145). This is a very difficult task and one which I intend to shirk.

Since it is so difficult to defend a priori knowledge it would be worth knowing whether an account of the epistemological import of analyticity can be given and defended independently of an account and defense of a priority. Perhaps we might maintain that there is *something* about analytic sentences, (as opposed to synthetic ones), which gives us a special kind of justification, and yet remain neutral about whether that kind of justification is a kind of a priori justification. Let us call this kind of justification, (assuming, for the moment, that it exists) *analytic justification*.

Previous theorists, our story might run, noticed analytic justification, noticed that it was special, and assumed that what was special about it was that it was a form of a priori justification. These are more cautious times and we need not concur with those earlier theorists. It is open to us to say that they were mistaken in saying that analytic justification is a form of a priori justification. Perhaps it is really just a distinctive form of a posteriori justification. It is also open to us to remain completely neutral about the connection between analytic justification and a priori justification.

This is the line that I shall pursue, but in doing so, I think I incur an obligation to show that there is a distinctive thing worthy of the name of *analytic justification*.

7.2 ANALYTIC JUSTIFICATION

Consider the proposition expressed by the following sentence:

(7.1) All bachelors are men.

There seems to be a special kind of justification available in the case of this proposition which is not available in the case of the proposition expressed by (7.2):

(7.2) All bachelors are frustrated.

In order to find out whether it is true that all bachelors are frustrated, I need to go out and examine the world, paying careful attention to the bachelors and signs of frustration. In the case of the proposition that all bachelors are men, I need only realise that *in order to count as a bachelor, you have to be a man* to justify my belief that all bachelors are men.

This thought about which things *count* as bachelors is a thought about the reference determiner for the expression *bachelor*, that is, it is a thought about the conditions for correctly applying the word *bachelor* to objects. Used in conjunction with a tacit disquotation principle (DP), (in the case of predicates it would go something like 'F(x)' only applies to Fs') and familiar logical moves allows a valid deductive argument to the conclusion that all bachelors are men. Thus the following informal argument plays an important role in the justification of the belief that all bachelors are men:

(p) The word *bachelor* only applies to something if it is a man.

(q) All and only things to which the word *bachelor* applies are bachelors.
     (DP)

(r) Everything that is a bachelor is a man.

The argument can be presented more formally to make its validity obvious. In the formalisation that follows 'B' and 'M' are predicate letters that may be interpreted by replacing them with *bachelor* and *man* respectively. 'a' is an arbitrary name for an object.

1	(1)	$(\forall x)(\text{'B' applies to } x \rightarrow Mx)$	
2	(2)	$(\forall x)(\text{'B' applies to } x \leftrightarrow Bx)$	(DP)
1	(3)	'B' applies to $a \rightarrow Ma$	(instance of (1)
2	(4)	'B' applies to $a \leftrightarrow Ba$	(instance of (2))
1,2	(5)	$Ba \rightarrow Ma$	(from 3, 4 by transitivity of $\rightarrow$)
1,2	(6)	$(\forall x)(Bx \rightarrow Mx)$	(from 5 by $\forall$ I)

This argument form will be my initial object of investigation. Perhaps the relevant argument forms for other kinds of analytic sentence, such as those containing indexicals, are different. But it would be initially interesting to see whether this kind of argument allows for a distinctive kind of justification. Here are three stories about how it might.

7.3 THEORY 1: NAIVE ANALYTIC JUSTIFICATION

It is a common thought about analyticity that analytic sentences allow speakers to gain knowledge on the basis of their semantic competence, that is, of their knowledge of the *character* of expressions in their language. In harmony with this line, our first theory holds that the propositions expressed by the premises in the informal argument above are the kind of things that anyone semantically competent with the word *bachelor* ought to know. Then if we assume the disquotation principles [J1] and [J2] below, competent speakers might come to know that all bachelors are unmarried by the reasoning in [A].

[J1] if a speaker is justified in believing the proposition expressed by some sentence that she understands, she is justified in believing that the sentence is true.[1]

---

[1] For now we will put the theory that invokes these principles on the table, and then we will discuss their plausibility (and in particular talk about failures of principle 1).

[J2] if a speaker is justified in believing that a sentence is true, and she understands that sentence, then she is justified in believing the proposition it expresses.

[A] SPEAKER (reasoning aloud): The word *bachelor* only applies to something if it is a man. (I know this in virtue of being a competent speaker.) So the sentence (p) *The word 'bachelor' only applies to something if it is a man* is true. (According to (J1) Speaker is justified in making this inference.) *Bachelor* applies to all and only bachelors (this is an instance of (DP) and one needs to know this to be competent with any sentence), so the sentence (q) *'Bachelor' applies to all and only bachelors* is true. (According to (J1) Speaker is justified in making this inference.) Now, I can see that the sentence (r) *all bachelors are men* follows from these two sentences, so that must be true as well. But if *all bachelors are unmarried* is true, then the proposition it expresses is true as well, so it is true *that* all bachelors are unmarried. (According to (J2) speaker is justified in making this inference.)

From the discussion of the analytic a posteriori sentence *Mohammed Ali is Cassius Clay* in Section 2.4 we might expect that the epistemic accessibility of analytic sentences will vary. Some sentences, those like *all bachelors are unmarried,* might be knowable by any competent speaker, whereas others, like *Mohammed Ali is Cassius Clay* are not, so that on this theory analytic sentences can be divided into two classes—those that allow competent speakers to know the propositions they express on the basis of that competence, and those that do not. Call the first class *transparent analytic,* and the second class *opaque analytic.* Theory 1 is a development of the thought that says that if a sentence is analytic, then the proposition it expresses can be known by anyone who understands it. It says:

(1a) If a sentence is transparently analytic, then it is (i) true in virtue of meaning and (ii) entailed by sentences which express propositions which must be known in order for the sentence to be understood. Anyone who understands an analytic sentence and can recognise the entailment relation between such sentences, can reason from such propositions, (given (J1) and (J2) as illustrated above) to the proposition expressed by the sentence, thus obtaining a justification for belief in that proposition.

(1b) What is epistemically interesting about transparently analytic sentences is that once they are understood, no extra *empirical* investigation is required in order to justify belief in the proposition expressed.

This naive theory does not claim that transparent analyticity is a route to a priori knowledge. The imagined Speaker has had enough experience to learn a language and can already employ logic. The claim is rather that he can come to know that an analytic sentence is true and hence the proposition it expresses, by applying standard rules of implication to sentences which express propositions that he knows in virtue of being a competent speaker. This is a method of justification not available for synthetic sentences or the propositions they express, and thus (says Theorist 1) analyticity does provide a distinctive kind of epistemological access to truths.

Two other features distinguish the inference [A] used to reach the proposition that all bachelors are unmarried. The first is that it is an inference to a conclusion about *bachelors* that apparently rests on truths about something completely different: the *word bachelor*. Second, the premise concerning the word *bachelor*, (p), has an interesting status; in some sense, it is up to the linguistic community to make that proposition true—*bachelor* could have meant anything at all and, although the community did not get together and decide what it would mean, and although there is a current meaning of the word, which may be discovered by the community, that meaning of the word is still, in some sense, up to the linguistic community. So these two features: a kind of heterogeneity between the premises and conclusion of the argument, and the odd status of the premises, further distinguish analytic justification on the naive account.

7.3.1 Problems with Naive Analytic Justification

The naive account of analytic justification, though perhaps an intuitive first stab, runs into some serious problems. It is, in general, very unclear what is required for semantic competence. In the case of Theory 1 this raises the particular worry that semantic competence might require *knowledge of the proposition expressed by the analytic sentence*. Suppose one had to know a lot in order to understand *bachelor*, including *that all bachelors are male*. Then it would be misleading to say that one can *come to know* the proposition expressed by the sentence *all bachelors are male* by deriving it from things that one knows if one understands that sentence; it *is* one of the things one has to know in order to understand the sentence.

A second problem with the naive account is similar in that it suggests that the purported new knowledge is really not new at all. Suppose that the proposition that all bachelors are men is identical with the proposition that all unmarried men are men (because the expressions *unmarried men* and *bachelors* have the same content), and thus that the analytic sentence expresses a truth of *logic*. One might not need to know that all bachelors are men in order to be a competent speaker, but instead in order to count as knowing logic. Alternatively, they might be able to come to know it on the basis of their knowledge of logic alone. Theory 1 assumes that the agent had logic at their disposal (how else were they to recognise the derivation as a valid one?) and so it may be that they only go through the reasoning suggested in Theory 1 to arrive at a proposition which they already know.

7.4 THEORY 2: NIHILISM ABOUT ANALYTIC JUSTIFICATION

These problems suggest a more skeptical theory of analytic justification, according to which the reasoning suggested in [A] is not a way of coming to know a *new* proposition about bachelors. According to this nihilist theory, it has seemed to some philosophers as if analyticity provides a distinctive justification of the proposition that all bachelors are unmarried, but this is a mistake born of ignoring the extensive knowledge required to justify belief in the premises and infer the conclusion from them.

Nevertheless there *is* a novel proposition that we can justify on the basis of our knowledge of the way that the reference of *bachelor* is fixed, and that is the belief that the sentence *all bachelors are men* is true. But, the nihilist points out, this is not as reassuring as it might seem. A proposition which predicates truth of a sentence is a proposition about language, and so it is not particularly surprising that it can be justified on the basis of other propositions about language. Is such a justification more worthy of philosophical attention than one which infers propositions about elephants from propositions about elephants? If the nihilist theory is correct, analytic justification's claim to *distinctiveness* is under threat.

The first thesis of Theory 2 ((2a) below) is shared with Theory 1, but Theory 2 replaces Theory 1's claim about the distinctiveness of analytic justification with (2b) and (2c) below.

(2a) if a sentence is transparently analytic, then it is entailed by sentences which express propositions which must be known in order for the sentence to be understood. Anyone who understands an analytic sentence can reason from such propositions, (given (J1) and (J2) as illustrated above) to the proposition expressed by the sentence, thus obtaining a justification for belief in that proposition.

(2b) **but** since the proposition expressed by the analytic sentence is required for the justification of the belief that the sentence is true, this is not a method whereby we can come by a justification of that proposition (justification must be non-circular.)

(2c) we still gain a justification of the proposition that the analytic sentence is true, but this is not a particularly interesting philosophical phenomenon.

7.5 THE PROBLEM OF SEMANTIC COMPETENCE

Unambitious nihilism notwithstanding, even our second theory has not retreated far enough to avoid problems related to semantic competence. As already noted, it is unclear what is required of a speaker in order that he be semantically competent with an expression. In the example above I assumed that a speaker is not competent with the expression *bachelor* unless he knows that the word *bachelor* only applies to something if it is a man. The dispute between Theory 1 and Theory 2 was over what extra propositions a speaker would have to know to be competent. But what is required for semantic competence is still unclear, and perhaps competence does not require even knowledge of the proposition expressed by premise (p).

What is semantic competence anyway? Intuitively, it is what one acquires when one learns a new word, and what one has when one understands an expression. But under what circumstances can a speaker be said to have learned a new word? Here are two suggestions: one might think that a speaker is competent with an expression if (i) she can use it correctly (and not incorrectly) in sentences, or alternatively, if (ii) she can have thoughts involving the expression, that is, if someone offers her a sentence containing the expression, she can thereby entertain the proposition expressed by that sentence.[2]

Both ideas are problematic. (i) is ambiguous between a reading on which this is too weak a requirement on semantic competence, and one on which it is too strong. If correct use requires only that the speaker can produce grammatical sentences containing the expression then the ten-year-old girl who comes across a new word, say *charlatan* can utter grammatically correct sentences such as *Dad, what's a charlatan?* and *Are we charlatans?, I think Fido is a charlatan!* Yet intuitively, until she's had some of these questions answered she does not understand the word, she is not yet semantically competent with it.

On a second reading (i) requires that speakers be able to produce *true* sentences containing the word (and avoid producing false ones).[3] But that is too strong. Many competent users of the expression UFO apply it incorrectly to satellites, reflections, native aircraft, and interesting meteorological phenomena. But such users understand the expression *UFO*, their error is not semantic but factual.

So perhaps we might say that semantic competence with an expression is a matter of having the ability to entertain thoughts involving that expression. It is plausible that though the ten-year-old can utter the sentence *Mum is a charlatan*, she does not really understand that sentence—she does not know what proposition it expresses until she knows what *charlatan* means. Misidentifiers of UFOs, however, *are* capable of entertaining the proposition, say, that that bright object overhead is a UFO. So it is consistent with this criterion for semantic competence that the mistake that leads to acceptance of the sentence *that bright object overhead is a UFO* is a factual one.

However the work of Burge and Putnam suggests that speakers can have attitudes to the propositions expressed by sentences, even when they have remarkably little knowledge, or even false beliefs, about the meaning of the expression (Burge 1991[1979], 1986; Putnam 1975). Burge gives examples of situations in which we would attribute propositional attitudes as a result of the utterance of sentences whose

---

[2]   It is not enough that she be able to entertain the proposition expressed by a sentence containing the expression. I can entertain the proposition that snow is white, and this is the proposition expressed by some Arabic sentence, yet I am not competent with the Arabic word for snow.

[3]   The bracketed requirement is needed to avoid making even this reading too weak a requirement on semantic competence. It does not require much to be able to produce tautologous sentences involving the expression, such as *either UFOs exist, or they do not.*

content is only incompletely understood by a speaker. He asks us to consider the case of an arthritis sufferer who comes to suspect that his arthritis has spread from his knees and ankles to his thigh. When he reports this worry to his doctor, his doctor tells him (correctly) that that cannot be so—arthritis is an inflammation of the joints. Burge's patient is surprised and no longer suspects that he has arthritis of the thigh.

Burge maintains that this is an example of a speaker to whom we are prepared to attribute beliefs involving the concept expressed by *arthritis*, even though he only incompletely understands the expression *arthritis*; his semantic competence with the expression is in doubt. Burge uses these examples to make a point about the supervenience of meaning and hence mental states on the environment outside of the brain, but my focus is slightly different and I want to use Burgian examples like this to undermine the idea that some particular piece of knowledge of meaning is required in order for speakers to be competent with an expression. Suppose we suggest that in order to understand an expression 'E', a speaker needs to know that Es are green Gs. We can imagine a speaker, like Burge's, who has had some experience with Es, yet does not know that to be an E is to be a green G. Yet he is part of a community of speakers, and there may be experts around who understand E better. Our speaker comes to believe that there are some red Gs. Perhaps he reports this belief to the experts and gets corrected. Nonetheless it seems appropriate to describe him as having believed that there are green Gs.

More particularly, we can imagine a visiting Martian who learns English by reading salacious magazines and Jane Austen. He learns that (say) Jack Nicolson is a bachelor, and that Mr. Knightly is a bachelor, and that this property often explains a commentator's speculation about their relationships with women. He comes to think that *bachelor* means something like *potential life partner for a woman*. He believes, correctly, that Mr. Darcy and his fortune are of interest to the neighbourhood because Mr. Darcy is still a bachelor. And that when the Duke of Windsor married he ceased to be a bachelor. Then the Martian notices that commentators are also interested in Whoopi Goldberg's relationships with women, and hypothesises that she, too, is a bachelor. Our alien does not have complete understanding of the word *bachelor*, but it seems right to say that he has some beliefs involving the concept *bachelor*. For example, he knows that some magazine commentators write about the personal lives of bachelors and that Austen's *Emma* contains some characters who are bachelors. He also suspects, just falsely, that Whoopi Goldberg is a bachelor.

Putnam also has examples which put pressure on the idea that a speaker is competent with an expression just in case she is able to have attitudes to the content of a sentence. In (Putnam 1975) he claims to be unable to "tell an elm from a beech tree" (presumably this is to say that presented with examples of both trees he would be unable to tell which is the elm and which the beech, not that he would be completely unable to distinguish the two trees) but suggests, plausibly, that this does not mean that the extension of *elm tree* in his idiolect differs from the extension of that expression in anyone else's (or, we might, say, from its extension in the public language.) Putnam thinks that this kind of situation is possible because of the *division of linguistic labor.*

> . . . everyone to whom gold is important for any reason has to *acquire* the word 'gold'; but he does not have to acquire the *method of recognising* if something is or is not gold. He can rely on a special subclass of speakers. The features that are generally thought to be present in connection with a general name—necessary and sufficient conditions for membership in the extension, ways of recognising if something is in the extension ('criteria') etc.—are all present in the linguistic community *considered as a collective body.* . . . (1975: 228)

Putnam suggests in the same paper that there might be some words whose use exhibits such division of labor (water, gold) and others which do not (chair). But Putnam does not tell us here how to draw the line, and someone might wonder why any word at all might not exhibit division of labor. Suppose, following new developments in interstellar travel, the circle of human acquaintance were to extend to cover intelligent, language-using centaurs. Centaurs presumably have no need for chairs, nor couches, and it is plausible that a young, English-speaking centaur in a parochial galactic backwater might be unable to tell a chair from a couch. Nevertheless he could have propositional attitudes involving the concept of a chair, simply in virtue of acquiring the word and intending to use it as it is used in his (and our) linguistic community. He could say *if that exchange student from Earth is coming to stay, perhaps we ought to get a chair* and he might believe that his family does not own any chairs.

We can think of these Burge- and Putnam-style cases as showing that semantic competence with an expression is *easy.*[4] Most people get

---

[4] But you might also think about these cases as showing that most people are not semantically competent with many of the expressions they use. I think that this is an

it simply in virtue of (i) having heard the expression, (ii) being a part of a linguistic community which uses it with a certain meaning, and (iii) intending to use it with the same meaning as it normally has in the community.[5]

Both the naive theory of analytic justification and the nihilistic one face a problem: if semantic competence is this easy, then the set of propositions that can serve as a base for analytic justification is cripplingly small. It might not include, for example, the proposition that in order to understand *bachelor*, one must know that the expression only applies to men.

The general problem of semantic competence remains one of unclarity. Because we do not know what is required for understanding, a conception of analytic justification as justification based on the knowledge required for semantic competence is beset by worries, both that we might need to know too much (e.g. that all bachelors are men, the proposition that we wish to infer on the basis of semantic competence) and also by concerns that we might need to know too little (e.g. not even that *bachelor* only applies to men, the proposition on the basis of which we wish to justify the new knowledge.)

7.6 AN ALTERNATIVE BASIS FOR ANALYTIC JUSTIFICATION

Time to change tack. What was so special about the knowledge required for one to be competent with a word anyway? Why would a justification based on that be any more interesting than one based on the knowledge required to care for elephants, or the knowledge required to be a competent astrophysicist?

One thing that one might have thought was special about the knowledge required for semantic competence, is that some of those propositions can be stipulated to be true by a speaker or by a linguistic

---

alternative way to describe the situation. But either way, it looks as if the foundation of analytic justification—the set of sentences which any competence speaker must know—is shaken. Either there are hardly any truths which a speaker would have to accept in order to count as competent, and so the foundation of analytic justification is disturbingly small. Or there are plenty of these truths, but hardly anyone knows them.

[5] As Kripke notes, if I hear the name *Napoleon* and decide that it would make a great name for my pet aardvark, I do not end up referring to the original bearer every time I talk about my pet. (1980: 96)

community. *Bachelor*, after all, could mean anything at all, and in some sense our language works because we have agreed to use it to refer to unmarried men. Another special feature might be that propositions about language can be used, in conjunction with disquotation principles, to justify non-linguistic propositions about the world. For example, we found we could use the claim that the word *bachelor* referred to things that were male and unmarried, to infer the claim that all bachelors are unmarried; we derived a claim about bachelors from a claim about the word *bachelor*.

But note that though these claims *could* plausibly be made about the claim that *bachelor* only applies to unmarried men, they are not, in general, true of the propositions which speakers need to know in order to be competent with expressions. Even if you had to know a great deal about Mediaeval Europe to understand the word *serf*, those facts about Mediaeval Europe would not be something that you could stipulate to be true and would not, for the most part, consist in propositions about language from which you could infer propositions about the world.

On the other hand, statements of the reference determiners for expressions, for example, *'bachelor' only applies to unmarried men*, can, in an important sense, be stipulated to be true[6] and from them one can infer non-linguistic facts about the world, using the form of argument that we used in the bachelor case:

1	(1)	$(\forall x)(\text{'B' applies to } x \to Mx)$	
2	(2)	$(\forall x)(\text{'B' applies to } x \leftrightarrow Bx)$	
1	(3)	$\text{'B' applies to } a \to Ma$	(instance of (1)
2	(4)	$\text{'B' applies to } a \leftrightarrow Ba$	(instance of (2))
1,2	(5)	$Ba \to Ma$	(from 3, 4 by transitivity of $\to$)
1,2	(6)	$(\forall x)(Bx \to Mx)$	(from 5 by $\forall$ I)

In the end it is not so surprising that we can get claims about the world from claims about the reference determiners for expressions in our language: such claims connect language to the world; they provide criteria which a worldly object must meet in order for the linguistic expression to apply to it. So I want to suggest that Theories 1 and 2 went wrong in supposing that analytic justification was justification

---

[6] That is not to say that I can stipulate the reference determiner for the word *bachelor* as it is used in English, but rather that the reference determiner is set, and can be set voluntarily, by the linguistic community. This is what happens in stipulative definition.

on the basis of the propositions that had to be known in order for a speaker to be semantically competent. Instead, I suggest, a justification is analytic if it proceeds from propositions about the reference determiners of expressions. These are propositions which, like the propositions used in other, non-analytic justifications, may or may not be known to competent speakers. Though we might still make the distinction between transparent and opaque analyticity, that is, between sentences which can be justified on the basis of knowledge of character and those which cannot, this distinction will no longer be central to the theory of analytic justification, since both transparent and opaque analytic truths can, in principle, be given analytic justifications.

7.7 THEORY 3: ANALYTIC JUSTIFICATION

(3a) If a sentence is analytic, then it is entailed by sentences which attribute reference determiners to expressions and disquotation principles like (DP).[7] Anyone who knows such propositions can reason from them, (given (J1) and (J2) as illustrated above) to the proposition expressed by the sentence, thus obtaining a justification for belief in that proposition.

(3b) What is epistemically interesting about analytic sentences is that anyone who knows the reference determiners for the expressions they contain is in a position to work out that the proposition expressed by the sentence is true, without undertaking further empirical investigation.

(3c) The reference determiner attribution basis of analytic justification is distinctive in two ways. The truth of such attributions is, to a large extent, up to the linguistic community to decide. They also allow the derivation of claims about the world, from claims about language.

Traditionally, analytic sentences were true in virtue of meaning and *because of this*, were supposed to be such that anyone who understood one could know that it was true. Character thus seemed crucial to whatever justification analyticity could provide. Here I am proposing a

---

[7] This is not a new definition of analyticity, but rather a claim about the wide notion of analyticity defined in §3.3, based on observation of the argument above.

break with this traditional way of thinking about analytic justification, a break which is justified by two observations: first, it is reference determiner attributions that *really* have many of the relevant properties that were attributed to the propositions that speakers were supposed to know, and second, earlier philosophers only thought that semantic competence would be sufficient for analytic justification because *they thought that being semantically competent with an expression was a matter of knowing its reference determiner.*

One of the things that seemed to be interesting about our informal argument:

(p) The word *bachelor* only applies to something if it is a man.

(q) Moreover, all only things to which the word *bachelor* applies are bachelors.

(r) So everything that is a bachelor is a man.

was that it allowed the justification of a proposition about the world, on the basis of facts about language, which, in some sense, could be stipulated by the linguistic community. This claim is admittedly vague and much more could be said about what it does and does not mean. I do not want to deny that there is a fact about the way *bachelor* is used in English, and that it may be discovered (as opposed to invented) by a learner or by future generations. Nor do I mean to claim that at some time in the past an entire linguistic community got together to stipulate the meaning of *bachelor*. Nor do I want to claim that what a speaker says when he utters a sentence is determined by his intentions (it seems to me that the speaker who claims that when he said, *the paper was all my own work* his words meant what mine would mean had I said *I was the one that downloaded it from the internet*, is just wrong about what his words meant.) Rather I wish to acknowledge that the proposition *that 'bachelor' applies to all and only unmarried men* is language relative and that which language a speaker or community of speakers will speak is up to them. The proposition that *bachelor* applies to all and only unmarried men is true relative to the (perhaps slightly idealised) version of the English language I am considering here, and false relative to an entirely imaginary version of English in which *bachelor* applies to all and only divorced bus conductors. Should we wish to make the effort, we could adopt the imaginary language tomorrow. Just as we might adopt the name *Napoleon* for our pet aardvark, without intending to use the name with the meaning it once had, so we might adopt the word *bachelor* to mean *divorced bus conductor*.

The fact that we can stipulate reference determiners has interesting implications for the justification of non-linguistic propositions on the basis of reference determiner attributions. For suppose I have come to believe, by empirical means, that, in a certain dialect of English, *bachelor* refers to all and only unmarried men and so become justified, by the now familiar reasoning, in my belief in the proposition that all bachelors are unmarried. I might be wrong in my empirically justified belief about the English dialect. Perhaps my data was misleading in some way. Yet this need not undermine my justification for believing that all bachelors are men, because I could justify my belief that all bachelors are men using any language in which *bachelor* has the reference determiner which I thought it had in the English dialect—including my own idiolect, or a language fragment which I make up. Though I might be mistaken about whether the English dialect sentence *all bachelors are men* expresses the same proposition as *all bachelors are men* in my idiolect, my justification of the proposition that all bachelors are men (the proposition expressed by *all bachelors are men* in my idiolect) need not depend on my empirical knowledge of the English dialect.[8]

7.7.1 Knowledge of Logic

Theory 3's rejection of character as the basis for analytic justification allows the theory to overcome the problems associated with semantic competence. It is not a worry for Theory 3 (as it was for Theory 1) that a speaker might already need to know that all bachelors are unmarried in order to understand the word *bachelor*. According to Theory 3, the proposition that all bachelors are unmarried is justified on a basis of reference determiner attributions, and this basis excludes the non-metalinguistic proposition that all bachelors are unmarried. Another problem for the theories that based analytic justification on the knowledge required for semantic competence was that the requirements of semantic competence could be so meagre that even competent speakers might not know that *batchelor* applies only to unmarried men. This is not a problem for Theory 3 however, since it bases analytic justification on reference determiner attributions, rather than

---

[8] See §7.8 for more about the consequences of the stipulability of claims about reference determiners.

on the knowledge required for semantic competence; whatever our final story about semantic competence, the proposition remains a reference determiner attribution.

One of our three problems remains: perhaps the sentence *all bachelors are men* expresses the same proposition as the logical truth *all unmarried men are men*. Speakers need to know some logic in order to appreciate the argument involved in an analytic justification (in our *bachelor* example, he needs to know that $\{(p), (q)\}$ entails the conclusion (r)). But in allowing our epistemic agent knowledge of logic, we might seem to be allowing him the knowledge that all unmarried men are men, and if that might be the conclusion of the analytic justification, circularity threatens once more.

The solution will come, first, from distinguishing different senses in which one might be thought to "know logic" and second from identifying the theorems of logic as analytic truths themselves. There is a sense in which an agent might be said to "know logic" which requires that they know that all unmarried men are men. Knowledge of logic in that sense is not required for an agent to be capable of appreciating an analytic justification. In another sense, knowledge of logic is required for analytic justification but knowledge of logic in that sense does not require knowledge of the proposition that all unmarried men are men.

In one sense, then, an agent might be said to know a logic L if he knows, for each of the instances of all the wffs α such that $\vdash_L \alpha$, that it is true, (or that it is a theorem.) Such an agent knows that *all unmarried men are men* is true, and so presumably he would be justified, (by J2) in believing that all unmarried men are men. But such knowledge would not be sufficient for the analytic justification we have been considering; for that the agent needs to be able to recognise that the entailment relation holds between a set of premises, and a conclusion, as in $\Gamma \vdash_L \alpha$. However, all this is all by-the-by, since no finite creature can know logic in the sense imagined here.

Perhaps we mortals could know logic in another sense: we are aware of a set of axiomatic schemata (say, for classical first-order predicate logic) and are able to apply rules of implication (say, modus ponens and uniform substitution) to these axioms in order to generate new schemata (the theorems of the logic), *and* we are disposed to believe to be true any instances of schemata so generated, on the grounds that they are instances of schemata that were so generated. A good first year logic student who has just learned about, and been impressed by, an axiomatic formulation of classical logic, probably knows logic in this sense.

Now this is not, strictly, a sense of "knowing logic" that requires that the agent know that all unmarried men are men, and so we do not have the problem that, if we require that the agent know logic in order to appreciate an analytic justification, we are already requiring that he know the conclusion of that justification. There is a different issue to be dealt with though: though such an agent's justification need not be circular, it seems that the agent can reason, using his knowledge of logic, to the conclusion that all unmarried men are men, thus reaching the conclusion of the analytic justification, but on the basis of his knowledge of logic, and not on the basis of his knowledge of reference determiners. I will return to this problem at the end of this section.

I should note here that it is not remotely plausible that someone would have to know logic in this sense in order to have analytically justified beliefs. Do we really need to know axiomatic schemata for classical logic in order to infer from the fact that someone has to be a man to count as a bachelor to the conclusion that all bachelors are men? I doubt it. So the sense in which we are required to "know logic" in order to appreciate an analytic justification must be a different one again.

Here is a third sense in which an agent might be said to "know logic" and this one better approximates what an agent would require in order to appreciate an analytic justification. In order to run through that justification one needs to be able to recognise a valid entailment relation between sets of sentences and individual sentences. From Gentzen (1964) we learned that it is possible to have a logic with no axioms, but *only* rules of implication whose theorems state entailment relations between sets of sentences (the premises) and a sentence (the conclusion): $\Gamma \vdash_{NK} \alpha$. In a Gentzen-style natural deduction system one can prove a theorem of the form $\Gamma \vdash_{NK} \alpha$ by assuming premises and applying rules of implication (such as $\wedge$-elimination and $\forall$-introduction).[9] Thus another sense in which an agent might "know logic" is this: he might know a set of rules of implication. I think it is plausible that this is the sense in which nearly everyone knows logic. To know logic in this sense, one need not know any axioms but one has to know some rules of implication, such as:

---

[9] Some of these rules allow the original premises to be discharged later on, so that we may end up with a conclusion that rests on no premises at all $\vdash_{NK} \alpha$ (this might also be written $\emptyset \vdash_{NK} \alpha$.)

$$\frac{A \quad B}{A \wedge B} \quad (\wedge E) \qquad\qquad \frac{A, A \rightarrow B}{B} \quad (\rightarrow E)$$

This is not too strong a requirement because finite creatures have to know rules of implication to know logic in any sense at all.

Though it is quite natural to talk about 'knowing rules of implication', rules of implication are not propositions, and so knowing them is not a matter of believing them. Once upon a time the natural thing for a philosopher to do at this point was to reach for Ryle's distinction between knowing *how* and knowing *that*. Knowing the rules of implication, the old-school philosopher would have said, is more a matter of *knowing how* to apply them than *knowledge that* some particular proposition is true; our epistemic agent possesses a certain *ability*. However, according to Stanley and Williamson, current linguistics suggests that knowing how to Φ is just a kind of knowledge that; an agent knows how to Φ, just in case she knows, of some way W, that W is a way for her to Φ (Stanley & Williamson 2001). If this is right then knowing a rule of implication is not a matter of believing the rule of implication, but it is a matter of believing a proposition, perhaps, in the case of the introduction rule for *and*, the proposition is that W is a way to apply *and* correctly (where W is to use it to conjoin two true sentences.)

There remains the issue that was raised several paragraphs back. Though such an agent's analytic justification would not be circular, we might still worry that he can obtain a justification which is not distinctively analytic. Suppose he begins by reasoning, using his knowledge of logic, to the conclusion that all unmarried men are men. And suppose that that is the proposition expressed by *all bachelors are men*. Then he has come to believe the proposition, but on the basis of his knowledge of logic, and not on the basis of his knowledge of reference determiners.

It is not clear that this would be a serious problem for my account of analytic justification. Many propositions can receive more than one kind of justification: the observation that my belief in Fermat's last theorem is justified by the a posteriori method of testimony does not in itself show that there is not interesting and distinctively a priori method of justifying that proposition.

However it also seems to me that using logic to reason to the logical proposition that all unmarried men are men could *itself* be a method of analytic justification. Gentzen, famously, thought that introduction rules (though not the elimination rules) for his connectives *gave the meaning of those connectives*:

The introductions represent, as it were, the "definitions" of the symbols concerned, and the eliminations are no more, in the final analysis, than the consequences of these definitions. (1964; 295)

Is there some sense in which we might think of someone who uses natural deduction rules to justify the theorems of logic as employing their knowledge of the reference determiners of the logical constants? Yes, if for example, knowing the correct inference rule for *and* is, as I have suggested, a matter of knowing *that* W is a way to apply *and* correctly (where W is to use it to conjoin two sentences which express truths.)

Thus, not only can we obtain analytic justification for the belief that all bachelors are unmarried, but we can also provide an analytic justification for the belief that all unmarried men are men, that is *for a theorem of logic*. An agent has to be able to use logic to appreciate this justification of a logical theorem, but since being able to use logic is not a matter of knowing such a theorem, his justification is not circular.

I am uncomfortably aware that these remarks on the epistemological import of analyticity sketch a very large picture, but leave many questions—both of detail and of substance—unanswered. That, I am afraid, explains the ambiguous title of this part of the book. Yet even this sketch is sufficient to allow me to evaluate some of the traditional claims that have been made about analytic truths, and that is the plan for the final section of this book.

7.8 SOME CONSEQUENCES

- are analytic truths "about language"?
- *could* analytic justification be a priori justification?
- are analytic truths non-factual?
- is analytic knowledge *real* knowledge?
- is analytic knowledge trivial?

Are analytic truths "about language"?

Locke maintained that his trifling propositions "carry no knowledge with them but of the signification of words" and there is a recognisable trend in the history of the analytic/synthetic distinction for philosophers to claim that analytic sentences are really *about* language.

This seems to me to be a manifestation of a more general tendency to claim that certain sentences or propositions are about the phenomena which justify their acceptance or assertion. Thus sense-data theorists claimed that sentences about chairs were really about sense-data, empiricists have been known to claim that scientific theories are really about observable data, and so similarly, philosophers writing about sentences like *all bachelors are unmarried* and '∀x(x = x)', which are true in virtue of meaning, have claimed that these are really claims about the meanings of words.

But on one very natural view, what a sentence or proposition is about is a matter of its semantic content, and certainly a matter of any entities it makes reference to: *snow is white*, for example, is about snow and its color, regardless of my reason for believing or asserting the proposition it expresses. *'Snow' has four letters* is about the word *snow* and the number of letters it has. This is not a matter of the way in which such claims are justified and the expressions don't magically cease to be about snow and *snow* when they occur in a logical truth, such as, *snow is white or snow is not white*. This sentence expresses a truth *about snow*, just one which may be justified on the basis of logic. Similarly, the analytic sentence *all bachelors are unmarried* expresses a truth about bachelors—the concrete, worldly objects—which may be justified on the basis of truths about language. Just as we distinguish a posteriori truths from a priori truths on the basis of their justification, and contingent truths from necessary ones depending on whether or not they could have been otherwise, so it can be useful for us to distinguish truths in another way: on the basis of their content.

Why might anyone have been tempted then to think that sentences about chairs were really about sense-data? Or that sentences about bachelors were really about the word *bachelor*? One reason might be that they have attempted to work out the content of the *sentence* by thinking about what a speaker might be trying to say when they use it. In doing this they have employed their theories about what the speaker is justified in saying, (only claims about sense-data) and what she might want to communicate (that the name *Hesperus* refers to the same planet as *Phosphorus*) in order to attribute content to her utterance, and via it to the sentence-type she uttered. But such a method assumes too naive a picture of communication, according to which a speaker says that p by uttering a sentence which expresses the proposition that p. Just as I can tell you, in the right context, that I hate you by saying *how charming of you to come by without calling*, so I can tell you that my name is *Gillian* by uttering *I am Gillian* and that the English word *bachelor* means *unmarried man* by saying *bachelors are unmarried men*. This is not to say that the literal semantic content of *I am Gillian* is that my *name* is *Gillian*, or that the literal semantic content of *bachelors are unmarried men* is a claim about the word *bachelor*.

Another ground of the thought that analytic sentences make claims about language might be an intuitive scepticism about the possibility of justifying claims about the world on the basis of claims about language. But such intuitions can be treacherous. One might also have thought that it was impossible to get necessity-style claims from contingent ones, but the counterexample:

$$\frac{\text{Hesperus exists}}{\Box(\text{Hesperus is Hesperus})}$$

shows that this is a mistake. Moreover the reference determiner attribution (p) in our informal argument, acts as a kind of bridge principle linking claims about expressions and claims about the world.

(p) The word *bachelor* only applies to something if it is a man.

(q) Moreover, all only things to which the word *bachelor* applies are bachelors. (DP)

(r) So everything that is a bachelor is a man.

Given this, it isn't so surprising that we can use claims about language to justify a claim about the world, such as the one expressed by *all bachelors are men*.

Could analytic sentences provide a priori knowledge?

Some writers have found it perplexing that anyone ever thought justification on the basis of knowledge of meaning could be a form of a priori justification. Salmon writes:

. . . the facts to which conventions give rise (meaning facts) are, by the very nature of their source, contingent rather than necessary, and knowledge of those facts is generally a posteriori (epistemically justified only by way of experience), rather than a priori. (1993: 126)

And more recently Margolis and Laurence write:

One puzzling feature of Boghossian's account is why he claims that the premises of his argument needn't be a priori. The problem is that the epistemic status of the conclusion depends crucially on the epistemic status of the premises. If the premises aren't themselves a priori, then, even if the conclusion follows, one wouldn't have the needed a priori justification in believing the conclusion just on the basis of the premises. Boghossian is surprisingly indifferent to this concern. He suggests that it's beside the point, since it is still the case that on the basis of knowing 'the meaning' of S one is thereby justified in accepting it . . . . But what if facts about meaning are themselves empirical facts? (2001)

One—fairly boring—explanation of people's calling facts justified by appeal to linguistic facts a priori might be that they had a variant, weaker notion of a priority in mind, according to which a proposition is justified a priori iff it can be justified on the basis of facts about language (and maybe logic) alone. There is also another—more interesting—possibility: perhaps they thought that *if* a belief about the world could be justified on the (admittedly a posteriori) basis of beliefs about one's natural language, it could *also* be given a strictly a priori justification. They might have thought, for example, that if you can justify a belief about the world based on facts about your natural language, you can justify it based on similar facts about your idiolect. But you don't need experience to justify your beliefs about what words mean in your own idiolect—you get to stipulate them, as you go along if needs be. So if you can justify a belief, like that in the proposition that all bachelors are male, on the basis of facts about your language, there is also a justification available from propositions your knowledge of which does not rest on experience—an a priori justification.

Are analytic truths non-factual?

Some writers have thought that analytic claims are non-factual, where this is to say that they are strictly truth-valueless. Usually this is thought to be because they fail to express a claim about the world (a fact) and writers often suggest that such non-factual claims must be accepted or rejected on the basis of their usefulness, (as opposed to their truth-value.) Perhaps surprisingly, Carnap is among their numbers:

If Quine did not treat analyticity as a theoretical term in empirical science, neither did the logical empiricist who was the main target of Quine's criticisms. Carnap thought that it is a matter of convention what sentences one regards as analytic. Claims about what is analytic are *proposals*; the question of truth and falsity does not arise. (Sober 2000: 242)

Prima facie, this is an odd idea. Analytic sentences, after all are supposed to be *true* in virtue of meaning and what they say is meant to be *knowable.* How could they also lack truth-values? Moreover, it is perfectly good English to say things like 'because of the fact that all bachelors are unmarried . . .', 'while it is true that all bachelors are unmarried . . .', 'I believe that all bachelors are unmarried' and 'I believe *that* too.' So why would anyone think that analytic sentences are non-factual?

One reason that the positivists flirted with non-factualism was their sympathy with a thought of Einstein's (Sober 2000). Einstein assumed that the speed of light reflected off a mirror was the same when returning from the mirror as it was on the way to the mirror, and this was adopted by the scientific community as a matter of convention. As he was well aware, there is no way to test this thesis, but in order to make predications using STR we need to make some assumption like this about the speed of light. Since the assumption is untestable, the positivists thought that it was strictly meaningless, and of course, meaningless things do not take truth-values and do not express facts. So for them, the assumption about the speed of light is conventional and also non-factual.

The positivists' approach to analyticity made use of the idea of convention too. They maintained analytic truths were true by convention since they are true in virtue of meaning, and the meaning of an expression is conventional. They took to thinking of analytic truths as conventional, and, like the light-ray assumption, non-factual given their theory of meaning.

One problem with this reason for thinking that analytic truths are non-factual is that verificationism is false. But there are other problems too. The sense in which an analytic truth is conventional is not the sense in which Einstein's proposal about the speed of light is conventional. Einstein held that we accepted the *proposition* that the speed of a light beam on the way to and from a reflecting surface is the same as a matter of convention. In the case of an analyticity, it is the *sentence* which has its meaning by convention. It is only a matter of convention, for example, that the sentence *snow is white* picks out the proposition that snow is white. It doesn't follow from this that it is a matter of convention that snow is white. Whether or not snow is white is not something that depends on our language, just as it does not depend on any other language. Similarly with *all bachelors are unmarried*; it is a matter of linguistic convention that this sentence expresses the proposition that all bachelors are unmarried. It does not follow that it is a matter of linguistic convention that all bachelors are men. These reasons for believing that analytic claims are non-factual—the confusion of (controversial) conventionalism about untestable scientific theses with (uncontroversial) linguistic conventionalism and the confusion of conventionalism about the meanings of sentences and with conventionalism about the truth values of propositions—are just mistakes. (Sober 2000; Boghossian 1996; Putnam 1979).

Another reason that people have thought that analytic truths were non-factual is that they think that *meaning* claims, such as *bachelor* means *unmarried man* are non-factual and they recognised that analytic claims are consequences of such meaning claims. How, they thought, could the consequences of non-factual claims be factual?

But this is not a good reason for thinking that analytic truths are non-factual. [10] Once again, though it may be a matter of convention that an analytic sentence expresses the proposition that it does, if it does express a proposition, it will inherit its truth-value from that proposition. And whether or not it is the case that all bachelors are unmarried, and whether or not snow is white, has nothing to do with the meanings of words in English or any other language. Now *all bachelors are male* just does follow from sentences about meanings, so either sentences about meanings are factual, or one can infer factual claims from non-factual ones.

Is analytic knowledge real knowledge?

Just as Locke stated that analytic truths carry no knowledge but that of the signification of words, many philosophers have thought that there was something suspect about the kind of knowledge afforded by analytic truth:

It is to be noticed that "Either some ants are parasitic or none are" provides no information whatsoever about the behaviour of ants, or indeed, about any matter of fact. And this applies to all analytic propositions. They none of them provide any information about any matter of fact . . . We see then, that there is a sense in which analytic propositions do give us new knowledge. They call attention to linguistic useages . . . but we can also see that there is a sense in which they may be said to add nothing to our knowledge. For they tell us what we may be said to know already. (Ayer 1990[1936]: 79–80)

[10] One possibility is that acts of definition (however formal or tacit), rather than being proposals, are a kind of speech act which (all being well) makes it the case that the definition expresses a truth (rather like sentences of the form *I hereby promise. . ., I hereby pronounce . . ., I hereby name this ship. . .'.).

There seem to be three sceptical positions with respect to analytic knowledge, and a number of writers on analyticity slide between two or more of these:

(i) An analytically justified belief is not knowledge at all.

(ii) An analytically justified belief can only be knowledge of the meanings of words.

(iii) Analytic justification is not a method of justifying any proposition which the epistemic agent does not know already, that is, analytic justification does not *extend* our knowledge.

I think that the main reason for thinking that analytic justification does not provide knowledge is the belief that analytic truths are non-factual. Since that belief was a mistake, there seems to be no reason to accept so extreme a skeptical view.

The second skeptical position, according to which analytic truths afford only knowledge of the meaning of words, clearly owes some of its support to the false view that analytic truths are *about* the meanings of words. One might also believe it because one believes that one cannot justify the proposition expressed by *all bachelors are male* without already knowing that all bachelors are male. Someone who believed this would hold, like our earlier nihilist about justification, that our informal argument merely allowed us a justification for the metalinguistic proposition that the sentence *all bachelors are male* is true. But as I showed in Sections 7.7 and 7.7.1, there is no need to be so nihilistic about analytic justification.

Finally, someone might believe that analytic justification is not a way of coming to know a *new* proposition. On my view of analytic justification this cannot be quite right; if nothing else, claims about reference determiners allow the justification of claims about the truth-values of analytic sentences. But someone might still think that analytic justification does not allow us to come to know new claims about the world. This would be a natural position for someone who identifies analyticity with Fregean-analyticity (sentences which can be demonstrated on the basis of logic and definitions) and who believes that definitions do not allow us to express new truths, but merely to rewrite old ones. Such a person might believe that analytic sentences are just rewritten theorems of logic, and that logic is justified on the basis of intuition, or a priori reasoning which does not involve analyticity. But according to the account outlined here the *propositions* of logic receive analytic justification and hence that 'old' knowledge was known on the basis of analyticity anyway, and so analytic justification *is* still a way of coming to know something new.

Is analytic knowledge trivial?

Yet maybe there is something to the thought that analytic knowledge is restricted, or shallow in some way. Imagine you are an amnesiac agent, waking up in your context at a certain time in a certain possible world. Your senses are dulled. What can you learn through analytic justification alone? Well you can learn that all bachelors are unmarried, that grass is green or that it is not, that you are here now and that if he exists, the shortest spy is the shortest spy. All well and good perhaps, but if you were presented with pictures of 20 different contexts with their agents, times and locations (and your eyesight improved enough for you to see them), you would be unable to pick your context from the others on the basis of that knowledge. It is not quite true to say that analyticity allows you to learn nothing distinctive of your context—after all, in context A I would learn the proposition expressed by *I am here now* in context A but in context B I do not learn that, rather I learn the proposition expressed by *I am here now* in context B. So, thanks to the indexicals, I do learn something distinctive about my context via analytic justification. But it doesn't help me in distinguishing that context from any other. If this is right, then there would indeed be a use to which analytic justification cannot be put. But it would be perverse to think that analytic justification was use-*less* on the grounds that it can be used by anyone, at anytime, anywhere.

Bibliography

Arnauld, A. (1964/1662), *The Art of Thinking: Port Royal Logic*, trans. by James Dickoff and Patricia James (New York: The Bobbs-Merrill Company).

Ayer, A. J. (1990[1936]), *Language, Truth and Logic*, Harmondsworth: Penguin Books.

Beaney, M. (Summer 2003), 'Analysis', in E. N. Zalta, (ed.), *The Stanford Encyclopedia of Philosophy* (The Met. Res. Lab.), (Stanford, Calif.: Stanford University Press). *http://plato.stanford.edu/archives/sum2003/entries/analysis/*

Benacerraf, P. (1981), 'Frege : The last logicist', *Midwest Studies In Philosophy*, 6, 17–35.

Boghossian, P. A. (1996), 'Analyticity reconsidered', *Noûs* 30/3, 360–91.

——— (1997), 'Analyticity', in C. Wright & B. Hale, (eds.), *A Companion to the Philosophy of Language* (Oxford: Blackwell), 331–68.

Braun, D. (Fall 2001), 'Indexicals', in E. N. Zalta (ed.), *The Stanford Encyclopedia of Philosophy* (The Met. Res. Lab.), (Stanford: Stanford University Press). *http://plato.stanford.edu/archives/fall2001/entries/indexicals/*

Burge, T. (1986), 'Individualism and psychology', *Philosophical Review* 95, 3–45.

——— (1991/1979), 'Individualism and the mental', in D. Rosenthal (ed.), '*The Nature of the Mind*' (London: Oxford University Press), 536–67.

Burgess, J. (2005), 'Tarski's tort'. Unpublished lecture. *http://www.princeton.edu/~jburgess/anecdota.htm*

Carnap, R. (1955), 'Meaning and synonymy in natural languages', *Philosophical Studies* 6(3), 33–47. Reprinted in (Carnap, 1958).

——— (1958a), *Empiricism, Semantics and Ontology*, 2nd edn., (Chicago and London: University of Chicago Press), 205–21.

——— (1958b), *Meaning and Necessity: A Study in Semantics and Modal Logic*, 2nd edn., (Chicago and London: University of Chicago Press).

——— (1958c), *Meaning Postulates*, 2nd edn., (Chicago and London: University of Chicago Press), 222–9.

Carroll, L. (1895), 'What the tortoise said to Achilles', *Mind* 4/14, 278–80.

Cartwright, R. (1962), 'Propositions', in R. Butler (ed.), *Analytical Philosophy* (Oxford: Blackwell), 81–103.

Casullo, A. (1988), 'Revisability, Reliabilism, and A Priori Knowledge', *Philosophy and Phenomenological Research*, 49. Repr. in Albert Casullo, (ed.), 'A Priori Knowledge' (Aldershot: Ashgate/Dartmouth), (1999).

——— (1992), 'Analyticity and the A Priori', in P. Hanson & B. Hunter (eds.), *Return of the A Priori*. Canadian Journal of Philosophy, suppl. vol. 18', (Calgary: University of Calgary Press).

Chalmers, D. J. (2004), 'The foundations of two-dimensional semantics', in M. Garcia-Caprintero & J. Macia, (eds.), *Two-Dimensional Semantics: Foundations and Applications* (Oxford: Oxford University Press), also available at http://consc.net/papers/foundations.html.

Chomsky, N. (1975), 'Quine's empirical assumptions', in D. Davidson & J. Hintikka (eds.), '*Words and Objections*', rev. edn., (Dordrecht: D. Reidel).

Coffa, A. J. (1991), *The Semantic Tradition from Kant to Carnap: to the Vienna Station* (Cambridge: Cambridge University Press).

Creath, R. (2004), 'Quine on the intelligibility and relevance of analyticity', *in* R. F. Gibson, ed., *The Cambridge Companion to Quine* (Cambridge: Cambridge University Press), 47–64.

Devitt, M. & Sterelny, K. (1999), *Language and Reality: An introduction to the philosophy of language*, 2nd edn., Cambridge, Mass.: MIT Press.

Dickoff, J., & James, P. (1964), *The Art of Thinking: Port Royal Logic*, chap. intro. (New York: Bobbs-Merrill Company).

Donnellan, K. S. (1962), 'Necessity and criteria', *The Journal of Philosophy* 59/22, 647–58.

Evans, G. (1973), 'The Causal Theory of Names', *Aristotelian Society, suppl. vol.* xlvii, 197–200.

_____ (1982), *The Varieties of Reference*, ed. John McDowell (Oxford: Oxford University Press).

Feferman, A. B., and Feferman, S. (2004), *Alfred Tarski: Life and Logic* (Cambridge: Cambridge University Press).

Fine, K. (1994), 'Essence and modality', *Philosophers' Annual* 17, 151–66.

_____ (1995), 'Senses of essence', in W. Sinnott-Armstrong (ed.), *Modality, Morality and Belief*, (Cambridge: Cambridge University Press), ch. 5, 53–73.

Fodor, J., and LePore, E. (1993), 'Précis of *Holism: A Shopper's Guide*', *Philosophy and Phenomenological Research* 55/3.

Frege, G. (1964), 'The concept of number' (excerpt from the *Foundations of Arithmetic*), in P. Benacerraf and H. Putnam (eds.), *Philosophy of Mathematics: Selected Readings* (Englewood Cliffs, NJ: Prentice-Hall Inc), 85–112.

_____ (1980[1884]), *The Foundations of Arithmetic*, 2nd edn., (Evanston, Ill.: Northwestern University Press).

Gentzen, G. (1964), 'Investigations into logical deduction', *American Philosophical Quarterly* 1/4, 288–306.

Glanzberg, M. (2006), 'Quantifiers', in E. Lepore & B. Smith. (eds.), *Handbook of Philosophy of Language*, (Oxford: Oxford University Press).

Grice, H. P., and Strawson, P. F. (1956), 'In Defense of a Dogma', *The Philosophical Review* 65.

_____ (1967[1991]), *Studies in the Ways of Words*, (Cambridge, Mass.: Harvard University Press).

Harman, G. (1967), 'Quine on meaning and existence', *The Review of Metaphysics* 21, 124–51.

_____ (1973), *Thought* (Princeton, NJ: Princeton University Press).

_____ (1976), 'Katz' credo', *Synthese* 32, 387–94.

_____ (1986), *Change in View* (Cambridge, Mass.: MIT Press).

_____ (1999*a*), Analyticity Regained?, in 'Reasoning, Meaning and Mind', (Oxford: Oxford University Press), ch. 7.

_____ (1999*b*), 'The death of meaning', in *Reasoning, Meaning and Mind* (Oxford: Oxford University Press).

_____ & Kulkarni, S. (2006), 'The problem of induction', *Philosophy and Phenomenological Research*. Papers from the Rutgers Epistemology Conference 2005.

Hempel, C. (1965), 'Studies in the logic of confirmation', *in Aspects of Scientific Explanation and other essays in the Philosophy of Science* (Oxford: The Free Press).

_____ (1985[1950])'Empiricist criteria of cognitive significance: Problems and changes', in A. P. Martinich (ed.), *The Philosophy of Language*, 4th edn., (Oxford: Oxford University Press), 34–46.

Honderich, T. (1995), *The Oxford Companion to Philosophy*, (Oxford: Oxford University Press).

Horwich (1992), 'Chomsky versus Quine on the analytic-synthetic distinction', *Proceedings of the Aristotelian Society* 92, 95–108.

Jackson, F. (1998), *From Metaphysics to Ethics: A Defence of Conceptual Analysis* (Oxford and New York: Clarendon Press).

Kant, I. (1911/1787), *Kant's gesammelte Schriften, herausgaben von der königlich Preußlichen Akademie der Wissenschaften, Erste Antheilung (Werke), Dritte Band: Der Kritik der reinen Vernunft, Zweite Auflage 1787* (Berlin: Druck und Verlag von Georg Reimer).

_____ (1965*a*), *Critique of Pure Reason*, trans. Norman Kemp-Smith. (New York: St. Martin's Press).

_____ (1965*b*), *Prolegomena zu einer jeden kuenftigen Metaphysik, die als Wissenschaft wird auftreten koennen sections 266–267* (Hamburg: Verlag von Felix Meiner), 13–22.

_____ (1992), 'Jäsche logic', in J. M. Young (ed.), *Lectures on Logic* (Cambridge: Cambridge University Press) 520–640.

_____ (2004), *Prolegomena to Any Future Metaphysics*. (Cambridge Texts in the History of Philosophy) rev. edn., (ed.) Gary Hatfield (Cambridge: Cambridge University Press).

Kaplan, D. (1989*a*), 'Afterthoughts' in J. Almog, J. Perry and H. Wettstein (eds.), *Themes from Kaplan* (New York: Oxford University Press).

_____ (1989*b*), 'Demonstratives: An essay on the semantics, logic, metaphysics, and epistemology of demonstratives', in J. Almog, J. Perry and H. Wettstein (eds.), *Themes from Kaplan*, (New York: Oxford University Press).

Katz, J. (1967), 'Some Remarks on Quine on Analyticity', *Journal of Philosophy* 64, 36–52.

Katz, J. (1974), 'Where things now stand with the analytic-synthetic distinction', *Proceedings of the Aristotelian Society* 28, 387–94.

––––– (1992), 'Analyticity', in E. S. Jonathan Dancy (ed.), *A Companion to Epistemology* (Oxford: Blackwell), 11–17.

––––– (1997), 'Analyticity, necessity and the epistemology of semantics', *Philosophy and Phenomenological Research* 57/1, 1–28.

King, J. C. (Summer 2005), 'Structured propositions', in E. N. Zalta (ed.), *The Stanford Encyclopedia of Philosophy* (Met. Res. Lab.) (Stanford, Calif.: Stanford University Press). *http://plato.stanford.edu/archives/sum2005/entries/propositions-structured/*

Kripke, S. A. (1980), *Naming and Necessity* (Oxford: Blackwell).

Leibniz, G. W. von (1968/1714), *Monadology*, (La Salle, Il: Open Court), 251–72.

Lewis, D. (1973), *Counterfactuals* (Oxford: Blackwell).

––––– (1976), General semantics, in B. Partee (ed.), 'Montague Grammar', (New York: Academic Press), 1–50.

Locke, J. (1993/1690), *An Essay Concerning Human Understanding* (London: Everyman).

MacFarlane, J. (2002), 'Frege, Kant and the logic in logicism', *The Philosophical Review* 111/1.

––––– (2005), 'Making sense of relativism about truth', *Proceedings of the Aristotelian Society* 105, 321–39.

Margolis, E., and Laurence, S. (2001), 'Boghossian on Analyticity', *Analysis* 61(4), 293–302.

––––– , ––––– (2003), 'Should we trust our intuitions? deflationary accounts of the analytic data', *Proceedings of the Aristotelian Society* 103/3, 299–323.

McDermott, M. (2001), 'Quine's holism and functionalist holism', *Mind* 110, 977–1025.

McDowell, J. (1977), 'On the Sense and Reference of a Proper Name', *Mind* 86/342, 159–185.

Miller, A. (1998), *Philosophy of Language*, Fundementals of Philosophy (Montreal and Kingston: McGill-Queen's University Press).

Montague, R. (1974), *Formal Philosophy: Selected Papers of Richard Montague*, in Richmond H. Thomason. (ed.) (New Haven, Conn. Yale University Press).

Murzi, M. (May 2004), 'Rudolf Carnap', in J. Fieser (ed.), '*The Internet Encyclopedia of Philosophy*', IEP. http://www.iep.utm.edu/c/carnap.htm.

Naess, A. (1966), *Cognition and Argument: Elements of Applied Semantics*, (London: Allen and Unwin Ltd.).

Orenstein, A. (2002), '*W. V. Quine*, Philosophy Now,' (Chesham: Acumen).

Pullum, G. K. (2004), '*Microsoft presriptivism*', in *Language Log*, (Movable Type). http://itre.cis.upenn.edu/~myl/languagelog/archives/000933.html#more.

Putnam, H. (1962*a*), 'The analytic and the synthetic', *in Mind, Language and Reality* (Cambridge: Cambridge University Press), ch. 2, 33–69.

―――― (1962*b*), 'It ain't necessarily so', *Journal of Philosophy* 53, 658–71.

―――― (1975), 'The meaning of "meaning"', in *Mind, Language and Reality: Philosophical Papers*, vol. 2', (Cambridge: Cambridge University Press).

―――― (1979), 'Analyticity and a priority: Beyond Wittgenstein and Quine', *Midwest Studies in Philosophy* 4, 423–41.

―――― (1985[1973)]), 'Meaning and reference', in A. P. Martinich (ed.), *The Philosophy of Language,* 4th edn., (Oxford: Oxford University Press), 288–95.

Quine, V. W. O. (1960), 'Translation and meaning', in *'Word and Object'*, Cambridge, Mass.: MIT Press, ch. 2.

―――― (1951), 'Two Dogmas of Empiricism', *Philosophical Review* 60, 20–43.

―――― (1965/1935), 'Truth by convention', *in The Ways of Paradox and other essays* (New York: Random House), cha. 9, 70–99.

―――― (1965/1954), 'Carnap and Logical Truth', in *The Ways of Paradox and other essays* (New York: Random House) ch. 10, 100–25.

―――― (1965/1973), 'Vagaries of definition', in *The Ways of Paradox and other essays* (New York: Random House), ch. 7, 50–5.

―――― (1975), 'Reply to Chomsky', in D. Davidson & J. Hintikka (eds.), *Words and Objections*, rev. edn., (Dordrecht: D. Reidel).

Rey, G. (Fall 2003), 'The analytic/synthetic distinction', in E. N. Zalta (ed.), *The Stanford Encyclopedia of Philosophy* (Meta. Res. Lab.), (Stanford, Calif.: Stanford University Press). http://plato.stanford.edu/archives/fall2003/entries/analytic-synthetic/.

Salmon, N. (1982), *Reference and Essence*, (Oxford: Blackwell).

―――― (1993), 'Analyticity and a priority', *Philosophical Perspectives* 7, 125–33.

―――― and Soames, S. (eds.) (1988), *Propositions and Attitudes*, in *Oxford Readings in Philosophy*, (Oxford: Oxford University Press).

Schlick, M. (1932), 'Positivism and realism', in A. Ayer (ed.), *Logical Positivism* (The Free Press of Glencoe), 82–107.

Soames, S. (1987), 'Direct reference, propositional attitudes, and semantic content', *Philosophical Topics* 15/1.

―――― (1997), 'Skepticism about meaning: Indeterminacy, normativity, and the rule-following paradox', supp. vol. 23. *Canadian Journal of Philosophy*, 211–49.

―――― (1998), 'Facts, truth conditions and the skeptical solution to the rule-following paradox', *Language, Mind and Ontology* 12, 313–48.

―――― (1999*a*), 'The indeterminacy of translation and the inscrutability of reference', *The Canadian Journal of Philosophy* 29/3, 321–70.

―――― (1999*b*), *Understanding Truth*, (New York: Oxford University Press).

―――― (2001), *Beyond Rigidity*, (Oxford: Oxford University Press) chs. 9–11.

―――― (2003), *Philosophical Analysis in the Twentieth Century: the dawn of analysis,* vol. 1, (Princeton, NJ: Princeton University Press).

Sober, E. (2000), 'Quine', Suppl. 74. *Aristotelian Society*.

Stalnaker, R. (1999), *Context and Content*, (Oxford: Oxford University Press).

Stanley, J., and Williamson, T. (2001), 'Knowing how, knowing that', *Journal of Philosophy* 98/8, 411–44.

Thomason, R. (1974)(ed.), R. Thomason, intro., 'Formal Philosophy: Selected Papers of Richard Montague', (New Haven, Conn.: Yale University Press), 1–69.

White, M. G. (1952), 'The analytic and the synthetic: An untenable dualism', in L. Linsky, ed., *'Semantics and the Philosophy of Languag'* (Urbana: University of Illinois Press), 272–86.

Winograd, T., and Flores, F. (1986), *Understanding Computers and Cognition: A New Foundation for Design* (Norwood, NJ: Ablex Publishing Corporation).

Wittgenstein, L. (1953), *Philosophical Investigations* (Oxford: Basil Blackwell).

Index

Lightning Source UK Ltd.
Milton Keynes UK
176943UK00004B/4/P